BROWN EGGS  JAM JARS

Aimée Wimbush-Bourque

BROWN EGGS & JAM JARS

Family Recipes from the Kitchen of
SIMPLE BITES

Photography by Tim and Angela Chin
Illustrations by John Wimbush

PENGUIN

an imprint of Penguin Canada Books Inc., a Penguin Random House Company

Published by the Penguin Group

Penguin Canada Books Inc., 90 Eglinton Avenue East, Suite 700,
Toronto, Ontario, Canada M4P 2Y3

Penguin Group (USA) Inc., 375 Hudson Street, New York, New York 10014, U.S.A.

Penguin Books Ltd, 80 Strand, London WC2R 0RL, England

Penguin Ireland, 25 St Stephen's Green, Dublin 2, Ireland (a division of Penguin Books Ltd)

Penguin Group (Australia), 707 Collins Street, Melbourne, Victoria 3008, Australia
(a division of Pearson Australia Group Pty Ltd)

Penguin Books India Pvt Ltd, 11 Community Centre, Panchsheel Park,
New Delhi – 110 017, India

Penguin Group (NZ), 67 Apollo Drive, Rosedale, Auckland 0632, New Zealand
(a division of Pearson New Zealand Ltd)

Penguin Books (South Africa) (Pty) Ltd, 24 Sturdee Avenue, Rosebank,
Johannesburg 2196, South Africa

Penguin Books Ltd, Registered Offices: 80 Strand, London WC2R 0RL, England

First published 2015

1 2 3 4 5 6 7 8 9 10

Copyright © Aimée Wimbush-Bourque, 2015

Photography by Tim and Angela Chin
Illustrations by John Wimbush

Manufactured in the U.S.A.

LIBRARY AND ARCHIVES CANADA CATALOGUING IN PUBLICATION

Wimbush-Bourque, Aimée, author
     Brown eggs and jam jars : family recipes from the kitchen of simple bites / Aimée Wimbush-Bourque.

Includes index.
ISBN 978-0-14-319050-9 (pbk.)

     1. Cooking. 2. Cookbooks. I. Title.

TX715.6.W543 2015   641.5   C2014-907252-X

eBook ISBN 978-0-14-319438-5

Visit the Penguin Canada website at www.penguin.ca

Special and corporate bulk purchase rates available; please see www.penguin.ca/corporatesales or call 1-800-810-3104.

To Danny, with gratitude for his lasting love, support—
and all the extra-hot, maple-sweetened cups of coffee

CONTENTS

Introduction   viii

Useful Ingredients   xvi

Helpful Tools and Equipment   xxii

Spring

1   Sugaring Off   3

2   Brown Eggs   25

3   Picnics   45

Summer

4   Backyard Grilling   69

5   Daytrips   93

6   Harvest Dinner   113

Autumn

7   Jam Jars   139

8   Orchard Outings   165

9   Comfort Foods   187

Winter

10   Holiday Gatherings   211

11   Sunday Dinners   239

12   Batch Cooking   259

13   Pantry Staples   281

With Gratitude   303

Index   305

INTRODUCTION

I always imagined I would raise a family just as I had been brought up, in the countryside with hay fields to run through at sunset and a lake to wade in on blistering July afternoons. We'd have an orchard, or a sprawling raspberry patch, and we'd grow our own vegetables in tidy rows on this homestead.

It wasn't until I was pregnant with my second child, living in a Montreal suburb, that I realized the rural move was an impractical dream. As most young families do, we had settled where there was good, steady work. We had bought our first house near family, understanding the value of those relationships, and we had surrounded ourselves with a close group of friends. Who is to say that escaping to the country—and that coveted berry patch—would have brought us more fulfillment than our current community?

But true happiness comes from within, no matter the exterior circumstances, and eventually I realized that many of the simple joys I had experienced as a child in the country could be reproduced in an urban home. What was stopping me from introducing the country girl to city life?

Our journey as urban homesteaders

My husband, Danny, and I began with small steps. We dug up a portion of lawn and planted a garden. A few prickly raspberry canes in the corner, two mounds of soil with rhubarb crowns, a row of oregano along the stone path—these were the first plants to go into the soil, and always the first to show signs of life in the spring. As they thrived, so did I, and my garden corner of the yard brought much contentment.

Next, I dusted off a relic I had managed to abscond with when I left home: my mother's handwritten cookbook. Working my way through it, I experimented with my grandmother's canning recipes, preserved on faded yellow paper, marked up with notes in the margins. From pickles to tomatoes, most recipes were for large batches—Baba was a Ukrainian farmer's wife on the Canadian Prairies—and so I always ended up with far more than our little family of four could use. I started an annual preserves swap, both to share my bounty and to encourage my friends to take up the old custom of preserving. It helped that canning was making a sweeping comeback, both on food blogs and in magazines.

More preserving occurred thanks to acquaintances who gave me free access to their backyard brambles after they had harvested their fill. I brought home armfuls of rhubarb and buckets of red currants and filled the backseat of my car with grapes and crab apples, with a basket full of mint and oregano spears on the front seat. Back in my kitchen, while my babies slept, I turned the rhubarb into jam and the currants into luscious syrup. I gently stewed the grapes and hung them overnight in cheesecloth to extract their sweet, dark juice. The crab apples went into a quart jar along with a real splurge—a bottle of vodka and a cup of sugar. I wrapped it up and set it in a dark place until Christmas, when I portioned a translucent crab

apple liquor into small jars and gave them out as gifts. It took a few seasons, but eventually I was heading into each winter with an ample selection of jams, jellies and preserves. I was homesteading in my own way, and it felt wonderful.

Over the next few years, we took more steps toward embracing the traditional-foods movement. We visited orchards in spring and again in the fall, both glorious times of the year to escape suburbia. We sought out local growers for our insatiable appetite for berries and braved the U-picks with a toddler and a baby. We dropped in on a beef farm to show our boys where beef came from and left with half a grass-fed cow in frozen, vacuum-sealed packages. I can't remember when we started composting, but it was all part of the seemingly natural progression into urban homesteading. Somewhere along the way we started talking about getting chickens, and rain barrels, and a real fire pit ... right about when we started looking for our next home—still within city limits, but with a sliver more of land.

From the moment I set foot onto our future property, I knew it was something magical. From the lane, where we were parked next to the leaning realtor's sign, the house didn't look like much: a two-story white house with tired green shutters and no shrubbery befriending the wraparound porch. The backyard, however, took my breath away. A long, emerald lawn sloped down to the edge of a maple forest, luminous with color in the autumn sunshine. Immense cedar hedges and one massive weeping willow lined the sides of the yard, giving the space a secluded feeling. Although the yard itself was exceptionally bare, I could already envision a wooden swing set and a row of raised vegetable beds. If I squinted hard enough, I could even picture a small chicken coop off to the side, and beyond, a clearing in the trees with a fire pit. Oh, the *potential*! We moved in shortly before the first snow, five years ago, and put down our first roots.

In a thoroughly modern world filled with every grocery convenience imaginable, I've chosen to invest time in age-old traditions that center around the kitchen. On that third of an acre where we settled just outside Montreal, I preserve produce in season, maintain a kitchen garden, keep a small flock of hens and tap maple trees in spring.

Along with my husband, Danny, I am passing on to my children—nine-year-old Noah, seven-year-old Mateo and little Clara, three—values about food culture based on my own childhood memories.

My history of homemade

When I tell people I was a goatherd girl, they look dubious. Yet this simple remark, accurately reflecting my primitive past, is often the hardest for people to wrap their heads around. It's not the fact that my family lived rurally with no running water, telephone or electricity; nor that my mother homeschooled me, my brother and two sisters; nor that we raised all of our own produce on our tiny lakeside property. But the eyebrows inevitably shoot up when I mention the goats. "It's true," Danny usually chimes in. "And she'd milk them and make cheese with her mother in their rustic country kitchen." Eventually, after a story or two about my goat-herding past, my friends admit that they now better understand my current romance with urban homesteading.

When I was a child, each day began with collecting eggs from the nests in the henhouse and snipping herbs from the garden for our omelets. There was homemade bread to toast and spread with homemade wild strawberry jam, and our own yogurt to spoon over bowls of fragrant stone fruits we'd preserved in honey syrup. My family of six gathered around the thick oak table set with my parents' Royal Doulton wedding china, and thus began our day, sharing a wholesome breakfast almost entirely produced on our tiny quarter acre in Northern Canada.

Equipped with two kerosene lamps and a jar of pencils for our homeschool work, that table was the crux of our home. It sustained egg sorting, bread kneading, vegetable chopping and home canning. My sister Haidi and I spent many an eve around that table, dusted in flour, baking for the farmers' market in town. We stayed up until the Yukon's midnight sun streaked golden colors across Lake Laberge and the kitchen counters were lined with loaves of buttermilk oat sandwich bread and glistening egg-glazed challah. Our family's famous butter tarts would be carefully packed between tea towels, and trays of molasses cookies sat awaiting transportation.

Mine was a simple and unspoiled childhood, one that shaped me forever and instilled in me a lifelong love of nature and living off the land, of cooking and baking from scratch.

Our family food life

Although I love where we live today, I am the first to admit that our small property is no backyard oasis. The squirrels flit in and out of the garden, stealing cherry tomatoes in their cheeks, or worse—taking a single bite and then leaving them on the vine. On swelteringly hot July days, when the air is devoid of a breeze, smells from the chicken coop waft by our picnic table. Our grass is often overgrown and there are endless weeds to pull. Somehow there is always one sly chicken in the flock that doesn't produce daily, and oh, look—the cats have left another headless shrew on the stoop. But it's our slice of paradise, where we learn about where food comes from and the effort that goes into growing it. Our children are alongside to learn. We're doing life together the best we know how, and it's all part of our ever-evolving family food culture.

If I were to be graded on our garden production, amount of canned preserves or even chicken-to-egg yield, my homesteading efforts would certainly never earn me a blue ribbon from the fall fair. Still, I don't define my success by the rows of jam jars in the pantry or bags of frozen vegetables in the freezer. It is our day-to-day quality of life that yields contentment. Since we've slowed down and focused our attention more on nature and the simpler things in life, we've grown closer as a family. Self-sufficiency, no matter on what scale, is enormously rewarding, as much for the feeling of independence it brings as for its powerful connection to the past—to culture, family and heritage—and families have a lot to glean from practicing it.

Do you inhale the smell of earth that clings to the roots of the just-picked vegetables at your farmers' market? Do you gravitate toward fields of flowers in the summer and picnic on the first sunny day of spring? Have you daydreamed about moving to a farm? If so, it sounds like you may identify with gardening, raising chickens and cooking the way I do. I want to inspire you to connect your family with its food right where you are. It may begin with a tomato pot on the patio or a batch of homemade pizza dough on your countertop—but every small visceral experience counts toward stepping off the beaten path on your own terms. I believe you'll find creating your own family's food culture to be a vibrant and reviving journey.

From blogger to cookbook author

Food has ever been my preoccupation, and by the time I was seventeen, it was my occupation, too. My first restaurant job in the tiny ski town of Smithers, B.C., confirmed my passion for cooking and set me on the path that led me to writing this cookbook. Before the children came along, I went to culinary school, which led to several years of cooking in fine-dining establishments, dabbling in catering and some personal chef work. Then I traded my tongs and chef whites for a laptop and a camera, and married my two passions—mothering and cooking—by becoming a food blogger with an emphasis on whole foods for the family table.

I soon met Tsh Oxenreider of *The Art of Simple* website, who invited me to become the editor of a new food blog she had been thinking about. We launched *Simple Bites* (www.simplebites.net) in 2010 to an audience hungry for simple family recipes, DIY tutorials and getting away from processed foods. With the goal of making every post insanely useful, I dedicated myself to a newfound career in food writing, recipe developing and social media.

It felt like my entire life had led up to the most rewarding job I had ever had. Readers wrote to announce they had made jam for the first time and felt completely liberated. They rediscovered the holiday spirit while following my gingerbread house tutorial. They were brutally honest about their own picky children and converted to baby-led feeding, ditching the puréed foods. I'll never forget one email I received late one Thanksgiving night from a single father. He had just followed my roast turkey tutorial (page 220) for his first time cooking Thanksgiving dinner for his two girls, and dinner had turned out perfectly. I sensed his letter was about more than roasting a bird; if he could get through the most family-centric holiday of them all, with a perfect roast turkey to boot, he was going to be just fine as a single dad. I openly wept when I read his email.

My articles on bringing kids into the kitchen and the garden were always well received, so I continued to expand in that area. In 2013, the highly esteemed food magazine *Saveur* named *Simple Bites* the Best Kids' Cooking Blog in its Best Food Blog Awards. Shortly afterward, I signed a deal to write *Brown Eggs and Jam Jars*. Just as I had felt ready to take blogging from hobby to business, I now knew going from blog to book was the next natural step in my path. I still had plenty of stories to tell and plenty of recipes to share.

About the recipes

Just like on my blog, the recipes in this book embrace year-round simple food with fresh flavors for the family-minded home cook. As often as possible, I choose organic produce, freshly ground spices, free-range eggs and grass-fed meats.

Here you'll find over 100 recipes, simple tutorials and tested tips for cooking with kids. I've included several features about urban homesteading as well. My rural homestead upbringing, my years of restaurant experience and my everyday life as Mama all contributed to these recipes. I've updated recipes that painted my beloved childhood landscape, so they continue to splash color throughout my daily repertoire: my mother's melt-on-your-tongue Maple Pecan Butter Tarts (page 19), the spiced hot cocoa we'd drink after an afternoon of sledding (page 207) and, of course, a tutorial for homemade yogurt (page 301). You'll also find a few favorite recipes from *Simple Bites*, such as Lemon Oregano Roast Chicken (page 126) and One-Bowl Carrot-Spice Oatmeal Muffins (page 197).

The recipes are inspired by the seasons and the joyous events they bring. After surviving the cold winter, we treat ourselves during the sweet sugaring-off season. Wear your winter boots and bring a good appetite for the hearty dishes such as Maple Cider Baked Beans (page 12) and Maple Pepper Glazed Pork Chops (page 17).

Let's plan a picnic amidst the first spring wildflowers. We'll spread a quilt and nibble gougères stuffed with smoked salmon and baby arugula from the garden (page 55).

Join us for a late-summer harvest dinner and feel free to bring the children. They will keep busy with a scavenger hunt in the forest and gunnysack races while you relax with a glass of Stone Fruit Sangria (page 133) and a triangle of Summer Squash and Parmesan Galette (page 119).

When the weather cools, meet us in the orchard for a family outing. I'll bring Clara's favorite Sour Cream Pear Pie (page 180) and a thermos of hot soup. Eat as many crisp apples as you wish!

If you like to swap homemade goodies, join in for either my jam swap or holiday cookie exchange—the door is open! We'll sip tea or bourbon-spiked eggnog (page 236) and catch up over Currant Scones (page 160) and Cinnamon Shortbread Bars (page 229).

Sunday dinner is a tradition in our home. I'll smooth the tablecloth, set out wine glasses and serve you a slow-cooked cider ham (page 247). A little civility helps to pass the long winter. Getting together over seafood chowder (page 242) with friends like you makes the day special.

Although the recipes are arranged by season, you can of course enjoy most of them at any time of the year, like my boys' absolute favorite, Tender Baked Meatballs (page 273) with Mild Marinara (page 270), the ever-adaptable Citrus Cheesecake (page 252) or our breakfast staple, Maple Walnut Granola (page 11).

My hope is that between the covers of this cookbook you will find delicious recipes, captivating stories and an encouraging perspective to help you provide healthful food for your family. It is my desire as well that this book encourages you to take your first steps into homesteading, no matter where you live. Few of us give up everything we've worked

for to buy a piece of land and move to the wild, but urban homesteading offers myriad ways to embrace our modern domesticity and find contentment in it, right where we are. This book will help get you started.

I sincerely hope this cookbook speaks to your heart and mind, as well as your soul and body. Please let me know if it has inspired you in any way. Email me at aimee@simplebites.net.

USEFUL INGREDIENTS

Whenever I got stuck writing this book, I reorganized my pantry. There was something simultaneously soothing and fulfilling about wiping down the jars of beans and lentils, tidying the tins of whole spices and scrubbing that inevitable sticky patch under the molasses carton. The upside of these therapeutic kitchen sessions was that my pantry stayed orderly and I maintained a tidy list of items for my next shopping trip.

The benefits of a well-stocked pantry run much deeper than simply being organized. A well-rounded assortment of ingredients encourages scratch cooking, aids and abets a commitment to whole foods and helps you save money if you stock up when the sales are on.

If you are setting up a pantry, it's good to know how to best store items for maximum shelf life. Heat, cold, air, light, moisture, odors, critters—any one of these can ruin our food, and all can be prevented. Plastic bags or cardboard boxes are not effective for long-term food storage. Dry ingredients need to live in a hard container such as glass, hard plastic or metal. These containers not only help keep ingredients airtight but also combat the sprawl that tends to happen behind closed doors—and in drawers.

A handful of foods should be kept in the freezer, again in airtight containers, to extend their storage life:

- Flours
- Nuts
- Spices—especially ground spices
- Grains—wheat germ, hemp hearts, ground flax, etc.
- Seeds—sunflower, sesame, etc.

I use glass jars and tins of all sizes to display our foods. Most of my dry pantry items are stored in glass jars, which are absolutely my storage container of choice. Why?

- They are airtight.
- They're reusable and recyclable.
- They display their contents so I can find what I need at a glance.
- They have a rustic look to them that suits my country kitchen.

Stackable tins and reusable plastic containers are excellent for controlling pantry sprawl of smaller items such as crackers, noodles, tea bags and baking supplies.

Be sure to rotate the items in your pantry, to ensure ingredients stay fresh. If you've transferred items into containers, mark the date with a piece of masking tape and a pen on the lid or the bottom of the containers so you remember when you bought them.

Don't stock prepackaged and processed foods in your pantry; you'll only eat them if you do. If you're serious about maintaining a diet of nourishing foods, one of the best things you can do is stock your pantry with quality wholesome ingredients. You'll be inspired to try new recipes—and have the resources to follow through with making them. Challenge yourself to learn to cook or bake with one new ingredient each month.

Perhaps you already know which pastas and quick-cooking grains you grab for harried weeknight meals, which variety of beans you eat the most, and the selection of oils and vinegars you gravitate toward for your salads. You have your favorites and I have mine, which I am sharing in this section.

The list below includes most of the ingredients found in this cookbook. I've omitted a few basics, such as baking powder, as I assume you already have them on hand. All these ingredients can be found in more progressive grocery stores and in well-rounded health food stores.

As often as possible, choose ingredients that are organic or produced without herbicides or pesticides and that are non-GMO and free-trade.

From the pantry

FLOURS
- unbleached all-purpose flour
- whole wheat bread flour
- buckwheat flour

OATMEAL
- steel-cut oats
- old-fashioned rolled oats
- quick oats

SWEETENERS
- raw cane sugar
- maple syrup
- honey
- molasses
- dark turbinado sugar

DRIED FRUITS
- prunes
- dates
- currants
- cranberries

BEANS
- canned or dried kidney
- pinto
- navy
- black

GRAINS
- brown rice
- puffed brown rice
- farro
- millet
- pearl barley
- whole wheat couscous
- fine cornmeal

CANNED ITEMS

- tomato paste
- crushed and diced tomatoes
- tomato sauce
- coconut milk
- tuna in olive oil
- clams
- clam juice
- pumpkin purée

PASTAS

- whole wheat penne
- pappardelle
- spaghetti
- orzo

VINEGARS

- apple cider
- balsamic
- rice
- red wine
- white wine
- sherry
- white

OILS

- extra-virgin olive
- sunflower
- coconut
- peanut
- grapeseed

SALT

- fine sea salt
- Maldon salt
- pickling salt

NUTS AND SEEDS

- walnuts
- almonds
- cashews
- hazelnuts
- pine nuts
- pecans
- pistachios
- sunflower seeds
- black and white chia seeds
- hemp hearts
- poppy seeds
- sesame seeds

SPREADS

- sunflower seed butter
- peanut butter
- almond butter

CHOCOLATE

- good-quality dark
- dark cocoa powder
- white chocolate chips

MISCELLANEOUS

- pure vanilla extract
- panko crumbs
- unsweetened shredded coconut
- popping corn
- pectin
- active dry yeast
- powdered gelatin
- coffee beans
- sparkling water

From the spice shelf

It is my firm belief that using good-quality dried herbs and spices can elevate the flavor of a dish with little effort and minimal cost. Having worked for a top-quality spice purveyor in the past, I've learned a few things about buying and storing spices; here are a few tips.

Shop for herbs and spices at ethnic markets, at spice shops or through reliable online retailers. Avoid generic grocery store brands, as their quality may be compromised if they have sat in a warehouse for months before being shelved.

Purchase whole spices and grind them yourself to retain maximum potency and the fullest flavor. Whole spices stay fresher for longer than ground. To grind spices, I use either a microplane, a mortar and pestle, or a small electric coffee grinder. Store ground spices in an airtight container in the freezer to maximize their shelf life.

Don't buy spices in bulk for your home kitchen because they do go stale. Remember, if you're buying good-quality spices, you won't need to use as much in cooking, as they will be much more potent than standard grocery-store fare. A little goes a long way.

When you can, grow your own herbs or buy from a friend or family member who has a garden. To dry them, hang bundles of fresh herbs upside down until they are completely dry, then fill mason jars with their fragrant leaves.

Herbs and spices used in this book include:

- allspice
- basil
- bay leaves
- cardamom
- celery seeds
- chipotle chili powder
- cinnamon
- cloves
- coriander seeds
- cumin seeds
- garam masala
- granulated garlic
- ground ginger
- dry mustard
- yellow mustard seeds
- nutmeg
- onion powder
- oregano
- black peppercorns
- white peppercorns
- pumpkin pie spice
- red pepper flakes
- saffron savory
- star anise
- vanilla beans

From the refrigerator

When my siblings and I were teens, the running joke was that one could never find anything to eat in the refrigerator, but by golly, there were no fewer than seven varieties of gourmet mustard. We groaned about it, but when it came time to pack a picnic, we sure had a nice selection of condiments. Nowadays, the contents of my refrigerator are more varied, although I still have several jars of mustard on hand. Here's what keeps them company:

- Free-range eggs
- Thick-cut bacon; bacon grease
- Fresh-pressed apple cider (unfiltered nonalcoholic raw apple juice that can be found in the refrigerated section of your whole foods store)

CONDIMENTS

- Dijon mustard
- grainy mustard
- tamari soy sauce
- sesame oil
- Sriracha
- mayonnaise (page 35)
- salsa

DAIRY

- unsalted and salted butter (I keep salted butter around for popcorn, topping vegetables and sandwiches. Unsalted is for everything else.)
- buttermilk
- 2% milk
- half-and-half (10%) cream
- table (18%) cream
- heavy (35%) cream
- yogurt (page 301)
- sour cream
- ricotta cheese
- Parmesan cheese
- cream cheese

From the freezer

- berries—all kinds, but especially blueberries and cranberries
- corn kernels
- green peas
- stocks—chicken, vegetable, fish and beef

From the liquor cabinet

- red, white and rosé wine
- Grand Marnier, triple sec or other orange-flavored liqueur
- bourbon
- gin
- dark rum
- Sortilège
- ice cider

HELPFUL TOOLS AND EQUIPMENT

When we moved into our current house, my empty kitchen looked enormous compared to the cramped space I had just vacated. I remember my father-in-law, Brian, exclaiming that I would never be able to fill all the cupboards. But I knew myself better.

Despite my best organizing, the kitchen space filled up to capacity, and I eventually set up industrial shelving for small appliances and other bulkier items. I named them my "homesteading shelves," as everything from canning pots to maple sap buckets, egg cartons and aprons took up residence there. Since everything is easily within reach, I use my tools and equipment much more frequently than when everything was buried three feet deep in a corner cupboard.

It's important to me to keep around only the tools and equipment I use a lot. Twice a year I cull my kitchen, giving away items that I no longer use or that need to be replaced. I also do a seasonal rotation—out with the holiday cookie cutters and in with the popsicle molds, for example. I store out-of-season items in a closet out of the way, while frequently used items, such as picnic plates in July, are stored within arm's reach.

SMALL APPLIANCES

This category should make your life easier instead of complicate it further. There's a small appliance for practically everything now, and frankly, I think most are a waste of space and money. Here are four I consider extensions of my own hands.

- Blender
- Magimix food processor and juicer attachments
- KitchenAid stand mixer, with grain mill, ice cream maker and pasta roller and cutter attachments
- Slow cooker

POTS AND PANS

I've never owned a full set of pots and pans, preferring to mix and match my own according to my needs.

- Cast-iron skillets, large and small
- Saucepans with lids, large and small. I use Scanpan. Not only is it environmentally friendly but it has a toxic-free coating that is highly durable.
- Sauté pans, large and small. I use All-Clad.
- Enameled cast-iron oval or circular French (Dutch) oven. I use Le Creuset.

- Small copper pots for sauces, melting butter, etc.

- Stainless steel stock pot

- Enameled metal canning pot with rack. I use Granite Ware.

BAKEWARE

My collection of bakeware seemed to amass from every source other than an actual store. I inherited battered cake pans, was given more pie tins than I can count, and I salvaged the rest from garage sales. Once a Bake King, always a Bake King.

I couldn't get by without a few rimmed baking sheets, a muffin pan and a trusty springform pan.

I prefer glass pie plates (such as Pyrex) because they produce a golden-brown, crisp bottom crust.

I love the oven-to-table appeal of enamelware and use my 13- × 9-inch (3 L) cake pan for everything under the sun.

I constantly use two Le Creuset enameled cast-iron baking dishes, one small, one large. They are able to go from stovetop to oven, and are attractive enough to go straight to the table.

Lastly, everyone should own a pretty Bundt pan, and of course cooling racks are a must.

KNIVES

Using the correct knife for the task can markedly improve your cooking by giving your food the appropriate size and texture, accomplishing the job safely and efficiently, and treating the food product with respect.

My knives are an assortment that I have collected over the years. They don't match, but they are always razor sharp.

- Paring knife

- Utility knife

- Large chef's knife

- Serrated knife

- Santoku (Japanese) vegetable knife

- Boning knife

- A folding pocketknife with a case that comes to the garden with me daily, as well as on the occasional picnic or daytrip

- Sharpening steel

GADGETS, UTENSILS AND OTHER SMALLER ITEMS

Back when I worked in restaurant kitchens, I was so strongly against gadgets that I could hardly look you in the eye if I knew you used a garlic press. As far as I was concerned, 99 percent of cooking tasks could be completed with a knife, and the rest required a can opener.

Nowadays, I've made my peace with everyday kitchen tools, but I still keep mine to a minimum. If I don't reach for it at least once a week, it's gone.

- Can opener

- Digital scale

- Tongs

- Heat-resistant silicone spatulas

- Bamboo mixing spoons

- Whisks

- Cutting boards. I use a large wood one, but there are many eco-friendly options.

- Microplane grater

- Vegetable peeler

- Nesting mixing bowls. Look for ones with a nonslip base. I use Eco Smart, which are made from recycled materials.

- Liquid measuring cups. I prefer heat-resistant glass such as Pyrex.

- Nesting dry measuring cups

- Measuring spoons

- Silicone pastry/basting brush

- Rolling pin

- Colander and sieve. These don't need to be fancy, just durable. Choose enamel or stainless steel over plastic.

- Pancake lifter

- An assortment of ladles and serving spoons

- Salad spinner

I always have aluminum foil, parchment paper and plastic wrap on hand. For a complete list of canning equipment, see page 146.

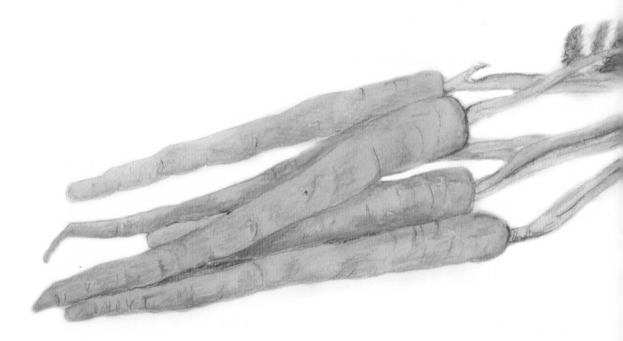

HOMESTEADING

Building a Greener Kitchen

On our urban homestead, we recycle constantly, compost enthusiastically and choose seasonal produce most of the time. Nevertheless, there is always so much more we can do to be environmentally aware, and we continue to challenge ourselves to do better.

Here is a list to get you started on your kitchen "greenover" and inspire you to be a conscientious cook. Remember, do what you can, when you can; take small steps, and don't stop.

1. MAKE SUSTAINABLE FOOD CHOICES.
This may be the most important decision you make for feeding your family, and it is an excellent place to start on the road to a greener kitchen.

- Eat in-season and local foods as much as possible.
- Learn to cook meals from scratch.
- Preserve your own foods as much as possible.
- Grow something, anything.

2. SHOP SMART.
While buying local is an excellent start, there is more to smart shopping than considering how far food travels to your table.

- Make a menu plan and stick to your grocery list. Successful menu planning can help shrink gas and grocery bills, cut back on waste and help you cut out convenience foods.
- Bring reusable shopping and produce bags.
- Buy in bulk. Fewer trips to the store means less fuel emissions and saves time, energy and money.
- Buy organic. Supporting crop rotation and pesticide-free food is a win-win situation for both the farmers and you.
- Buy fair-trade. Help to support safe work conditions and fair wages for farmers and producers.

3. BE AN ENERGY-WISE COOK.
Learn about low-carbon cooking and progressive techniques such as hypercooking (forgoing preheating the oven for baking things like casseroles, and turning off an oven or pot early and allowing the food to finish cooking with residual heat).

When possible, use small appliances (toaster oven or microwave, for example) instead of heating an oven.

Keep refrigerator doors open for as short a time as possible. Follow good freezer maintenance (page 276).

4. EAT MORE PLANTS.

It's what my mother has been telling me for years, and it's vital to our long-term health. Now it's trendy too! Ultimately, eating more plants can help reduce the strain on our environment, as the meat industry is responsible for a notable amount of water and air pollution.

Two simple ways to get started on your part-time vegetarianism are:

- Turn your side dishes into main dishes. Instead of making meat the centerpiece of your meal, serve smaller portions of it and add an extra vegetable to the menu.

- Embrace the Meatless Monday movement. Pledge to serve one meatless meal a week in your home. For more information, visit www.meatlessmonday.com.

5. IMPLEMENT THE FOUR R'S OF DAILY COOKING.

- Reduce. Buy only what you need. Minimize food waste.

- Reuse. Love those leftovers and kitchen scraps! Give that lettuce-washing water to plants, turn the chicken carcass into a soup and toss lemon rind into the dishwater for an instant deodorizer.

- Repurpose. Save your glass jars, plastic containers and tin cans (for seedlings) for a reincarnation.

- Recycle. Stay up to date with what's recyclable in your area, and then max out your bin! Recycle vegetable scraps and lawn trimmings into compost (page 89).

Environmentally friendly practices are a dime a dozen, but implementing them in the home doesn't happen overnight. Like any lifestyle change, they are best put into practice gradually—start with little actions that can be realistically maintained.

SPRING

1
SUGARING OFF

*Buttermilk Buckwheat Pancakes • Maple Walnut Granola • Maple Cider Baked Beans •
Cabbage, Carrot and Cashew Slaw with Maple Soy Vinaigrette • Maple Pepper Glazed Pork
Chops • Maple Pecan Butter Tarts • Sticky Maple Blueberry Pudding*

"Listen, Mama, there's music in the forest," announced my six-year-old, Mateo. With the return of chirping birds to our back woods comes the lyrical "ping-ping-ping" of the dripping maple water hitting the bottom of the aluminum bucket. This sugaring season is the sweet antidote to that torturous time when winter has long outstayed her welcome and spring is still weeks away. It is known in these parts as Canada's fifth season, and we welcome it with outstretched pots, ready to harvest the precious liquid and reduce it to maple syrup.

We know the sap is running when the sunlight coaxes the thermometer above freezing during the day but at night the mercury slumps back into the frigid zone. These temperature swings cause the sap to travel up the trunk of the Canadian sugar maple, bringing life to the limbs. Along the journey, we respectfully take a portion to bring to our table.

The very first time we drilled into a sugar maple at the back of our homestead, the water spurted out, misting our astonished faces, tasting sweet and earthy. Danny tapped a spout into the hole and my eldest, Noah, moved in for a taste. As our boys took turns slurping the sugary nectar straight from the tree, my eyes met my husband's over their bent heads. *This.* This was in our backyard. We only need to vigilantly collect it, slowly reduce it and carefully remove the spouts when the season is over. How enormously wonderful.

That first spring, I felt as though I was on a permanent sugar high, but it was the elation derived from producing this national treasure, perhaps Eastern Canada's most prized resource, on our own land. I made everything imaginable with both the straight maple water and the syrup that I had reduced. I filled a traditional stoneware bean pot with filtered sap and tipped small white beans into it, along with a slab of double-smoked bacon and half an onion. An afternoon in a slow oven was all it took to transform that assemblage into a dinner fit for hungry, red-cheeked brothers tumbling in from the cold.

Like true Canadian boys, my sons embrace the snowdrifts without tiring. Night falls early, even at the beginning of spring, and most afternoons I must press my nose against the window to spot them playing amidst their snow tunnels and ice towers to beckon them in for dinner. They are downhearted to see the snow melt, but one thing convinces them that the approaching spring is a good change, and that is sugaring-off season.

Maple syrup is our all-round preferred sweetener. We drizzle it over our oatmeal by the pitcher and stir it into our coffee by the spoonful. It flavors salad dressings, chocolate cake (page 204) and our favorite chili (page 262). I bake it with nuts and dried currants in a flaky dough for a twist on a butter tart, and reduce it into a thick sauce to coat roasted pork chops. With Canada producing nearly 80 percent of the world's maple syrup, it's the sweetest way to eat local.

A DAY IN THE SUGAR BUSH

Changing weather conditions mean that each spring yields varying amounts of our own maple syrup, although we average two gallons of precious gold. Danny's aunt and uncle, however, operate on a much larger scale. Once every spring—easily one of the most anticipated events of the year—they invite the extended family to go sugaring off on their forty-acre maple bush. We dress in layers and tote a contribution to the family potluck dinner. One year I took five pounds of thick-cut bacon, each slice lovingly brushed with maple syrup and baked until caramelized. That made for a tantalizing ride, as the incredible smell filled the car.

When we arrive at Marc and Lynn's and spill out of the car in our rubbers and mud pants, the smell of wood smoke greets us, followed by the faintly sweet maple syrup vapors escaping through the tree branches toward the blue sky beyond. We spot the puffs of smoke, and immediately the children are off down the slushy trail, following the sounds of barking dogs. On each side of the path, saplings are interspersed with strong, mature maples, and a lidded tin bucket hangs from nearly every tree. Not only is Uncle Marc one of the few remaining maple syrup artisans who still collects sap by hand, but he also reduces it in the open air over a roaring wood fire.

We gather around a massive steel box with a boiler on top and a raging furnace below and connect with family. Enamel mugs of venison chili, harvested and made by Marc, are handed to us when we arrive. Some years there is a deep-fried turkey, served in thick slices of meltingly tender breast and drizzled with warm maple syrup. It's hard to remember eating anything so good.

The college kids find the stash of whole cream and a bottle of vodka in a nearby snowbank and mix equal parts in a paper cup. They finish the mix with a generous pour of fresh maple syrup and stir it with a snapped twig for an authentic Canadian cocktail. I sample a sip, but knowing I have three little ones to keep up with, I defer to the maple tea, a mug of boiling maple water with a tea bag dunked into it. It warms my hands and my belly, and no additional sweetener is required.

The day passes with sap collecting, sleigh riding and listless fireside gazing. The youngest succumb to the combination of fresh air and warm sun and doze in our arms, while the school-age children flit through the trees, inventing games and chasing dogs. All of them are no doubt strung up on copious amounts of maple taffy (page 23).

By the time the sun slants behind the tall maples, my sugar rush has left me, taking my energy stores with it. I need coffee, and set off to hunt some down. Stepping into Lynn's spacious homestead kitchen, I'm pleased to see it is a bustle of activity and there are signs of a promising feast to come. Baked beans with maple and apple cider (page 12) bubble on the stove, six dozen eggs are stacked on the counter awaiting a hot skillet, and pork in its many delectable forms is warming, including the maple-glazed bacon that so tempted

us during the car ride. My sister looks up from her post behind the griddle, where she's turning out buttermilk buckwheat pancakes (page 9) with skill. She doesn't object as I snitch one.

Whether lured by the smells from the kitchen or driven by the need for dry feet, a steady stream of people pile into the house. Soon muddy rubber boots and various other footwear grow on the back porch like wild mushrooms multiplying on a rotten log. To my relief, my brother-in-law and resident coffee geek, Kevin, pumps out expertly prepared pots of French press coffee. We stir in maple syrup (what else?) and sigh with pleasure at the first sip. Then it is time to eat, again.

There's nothing like a day of fresh air to work up an appetite, and this is apparent as we devour the baked beans, bacon and pancakes plus scrambled eggs, bison sausages, coffee cake, bagels and hash browns. Everything is topped with maple syrup; a tribute to our day in the sugar bush.

My hands wrapped around one last cup of coffee, I watch the sun set over the valley that stretches out below the farmhouse. I savor a maple pecan tart, but more so, I savor the moment. The love in the room enfolds me and clings as tight as the wood smoke on my clothes. It saturates, and lingers, leaving me warm from head to toe.

BUTTERMILK BUCKWHEAT PANCAKES

On weekend mornings I can't flip these pancakes fast enough for my children, especially when served with our own maple syrup. Fortunately, they are substantial enough to keep all of us going until lunchtime. I stock a bag of organic buckwheat flour exclusively for this recipe in my freezer, where it stays fresh. It provides a nutty flavor, but doesn't weigh down the pancakes.

MAKES 10 (6-INCH/15 CM) PANCAKES

1. Preheat oven to its lowest setting.

2. In a medium bowl, whisk together buckwheat flour, whole wheat flour, baking powder, baking soda, cinnamon and salt.

3. In a large bowl, whisk together melted butter, maple syrup and eggs, then stir in buttermilk. Dump dry ingredients into wet ingredients and beat just until combined. Do not overmix.

4. Heat a griddle or large cast-iron skillet over medium heat. Grease with cooking oil. Spoon batter onto griddle 1/3 cup (75 mL) at a time. Cook for 1 1/2 minutes, or until small bubbles form around the edges. Flip and cook until golden brown on the bottom, about 1 more minute.

5. Place pancakes on a baking sheet or in a pie plate lined with a clean tea towel. Cover pancakes and keep warm in oven while you cook the remainder of the pancakes. Serve pancakes hot with softened butter and pure maple syrup.

1 cup (250 mL) buckwheat flour

1 cup (250 mL) whole wheat flour

1 teaspoon (5 mL) baking powder

1/2 teaspoon (2 mL) baking soda

1/2 teaspoon (2 mL) cinnamon

1/2 teaspoon (2 mL) salt

1/4 cup (60 mL) unsalted butter, melted

1 tablespoon (15 mL) pure maple syrup

2 large eggs

2 1/4 cups (550 mL) buttermilk

1/2 teaspoon (2 mL) cooking oil

KITCHEN TIP

When cooking pancakes, the right pan makes all the difference. I prefer to cook my pancakes in a large cast-iron skillet, which evenly distributes the heat, making for evenly cooked pancakes. A generous splash of oil in the pan before the batter goes in ensures those desirable crispy edges.

MAPLE WALNUT GRANOLA

Homemade granola is a household staple that tastes better than anything you can buy and is much cheaper to make yourself. Ours is sweetened with maple syrup, while applesauce aids in forming those delicious clusters.

Noah and Mateo like their breakfast version plain, no raisins or other dried fruit, *merci*, although I shake in a few sunflower seeds and walnuts for texture. For an extra-special version of this granola, I add ¼ cup (60 mL) organic maple flakes for a burst of sweetness. They're available from online retailers and some Canadian grocers.

MAKES 6 CUPS (1.5 L)

1. Position oven racks in middle and top third of oven and preheat oven to 300°F (150°C). Line two rimmed baking sheets with parchment paper.

2. In a large bowl, stir together applesauce, maple syrup, oil, salt and cinnamon. Add oats, walnuts, sunflower seeds and maple flakes, if using. Stir well to combine everything, taking care that the oats are fully coated.

3. Divide the oat mixture between the baking sheets and spread to an even layer. Bake for 25 to 30 minutes, until golden brown, rotating the baking sheets and giving the granola a stir halfway through the baking time.

4. Turn off oven. Dry granola for 15 minutes in the oven with the door slightly ajar, then cool completely on the counter.

⅔ cup (150 mL) applesauce (page 155)

½ cup (125 mL) pure maple syrup

3 tablespoons (45 mL) extra-virgin olive oil

¾ teaspoon (4 mL) salt

½ teaspoon (2 mL) cinnamon

4 cups (1 L) old-fashioned rolled oats

1 cup (250 mL) walnut pieces

½ cup (125 mL) unsalted sunflower seeds

¼ cup (60 mL) organic maple flakes (optional)

STORAGE

This granola will keep in an airtight container for up to 1 week or in the freezer for up to 3 months.

MAPLE CIDER BAKED BEANS

These delicious beans can simmer on the back of a woodstove or over a fire for hours and get better and better each time you dip into the pot for a serving. When we are sugaring off, I use maple water—the clear tree sap—as the primary liquid, but for the rest of the year, I love the fruitiness that the fresh apple juice contributes.

The levels of flavor in this bean dish are more pronounced on the second day, so you may want to make them in advance. If you make the recipe without the bacon, add a teaspoon or so of salt at the end of the cooking time. If you have a traditional bean pot, this recipe will put it to good use. A Dutch oven also works well. Alternatively, stew the beans on low in a slow cooker overnight and wake up to a hearty breakfast.

SERVES 8

2 cups (500 mL) dried white navy beans

1 medium onion, chopped

4 slices thick-cut bacon, chopped

½ cup (125 mL) pure maple syrup

¼ cup (60 mL) molasses

2 tablespoons (30 mL) tomato paste

1 tablespoon (15 mL) Dijon mustard

4 cups (1 L) fresh-pressed apple cider (unfiltered, raw apple juice)

1 tablespoon (15 mL) cider vinegar

½ teaspoon (2 mL) freshly ground black pepper

1. Place beans in a large bowl, cover with water and let soak overnight. The next day, drain well and place in a large pot. Cover with water again, place over high heat and bring to a simmer, then reduce heat to medium and simmer for 45 minutes.

2. Preheat oven to 300°F (150°C).

3. Drain beans, rinse and place in a 4-quart (4 L) Dutch oven or baking dish with a lid. Add onion, bacon, maple syrup, molasses, tomato paste and Dijon. Pour in apple cider; stir to combine.

4. Cover and bake for 3 hours. Remove the lid and bake for an additional hour; the juices will reduce.

5. Remove from the oven and stir in cider vinegar and pepper. Add more salt if desired. The beans will still have some liquid, but they will absorb much of it as they cool.

VARIATION

If you're not serving young children and want to really transform these baked beans, stir ¼ cup (60 mL) bourbon into the pot in the last 30 minutes of cooking.

STORAGE

These baked beans will keep in an airtight container in the refrigerator for up to 5 days or in the freezer for up to 6 months.

CABBAGE, CARROT AND CASHEW SLAW WITH MAPLE SOY VINAIGRETTE

Seasons mingle in this salad. Our staunch winter staples of cabbage and carrots are enlivened by the appearance of the first spring asparagus, so tender that I like to enjoy it raw. We're sugaring off on our homestead in the early spring, so even salad dressings get a touch of maple syrup. The colors of this salad are pale and soft, so reminiscent of an Easter palette. I often serve this dish on the holiday, doubled or tripled and accompanied by a cider-braised ham (page 247).

SERVES 6

1. MAKE THE DRESSING   In a small jar, combine rice vinegar, maple syrup, tamari, lemon juice and garlic. Cover and shake well. Add olive oil and sesame oil. Cover and shake again until creamy. (Dressing may be made up to 3 days ahead and refrigerated. Bring to room temperature before using.)

2. MAKE THE SALAD   Rinse asparagus and pat dry. Snap off and discard the woody bottoms, then peel asparagus. Using a vegetable peeler, shave asparagus and carrots into ribbons. Thinly slice radishes.

3. In a large bowl, combine asparagus and carrot ribbons, radishes, cabbage and the maple soy dressing. Toss well to coat salad. Sprinkle with chopped cashews and finish the salad with a pinch of sea salt. Serve at once.

For the dressing

1 tablespoon (15 mL) rice vinegar

1 tablespoon (15 mL) pure maple syrup

2 teaspoons (10 mL) tamari soy sauce

2 teaspoons (10 mL) lemon juice

1 garlic clove, minced

3 tablespoons (45 mL) olive oil

1 tablespoon (15 mL) sesame oil

For the salad

8 large asparagus spears

3 large carrots, peeled

6 spring radishes

6 cups (1.5 L) chopped napa cabbage (about 1 small head)

1 cup (250 mL) unsalted toasted cashews, coarsely chopped

Pinch of fine sea salt

MAPLE PEPPER GLAZED PORK CHOPS

My children would prefer to drench nearly all their food in maple syrup, and come sugaring-off season, it almost feels natural to let them. This recipe lets us meet halfway, with crispy seared pork chops and a simple sauce featuring the local specialty.

I use bone-in pork chops because I find them to be more flavorful and less inclined to dry out during cooking. If you're not making this for young children, increase the pepper by ½ teaspoon (2 mL) or so and enjoy the sweet heat. If you are feeding hungry folks who have been hauling sap, serve these chops with Maple Cider Baked Beans (page 12); for a lighter meal, they pair beautifully with my Cabbage, Carrot and Cashew Slaw (page 15).

SERVES 4

1. PREPARE THE PORK CHOPS   Pat pork chops dry with paper towel and season lightly with sea salt. Heat olive oil in a large skillet over medium-high heat. Add pork chops and brown on both sides, about 2 minutes per side. Reduce heat to medium and cook for another 3 minutes.

2. Remove pork chops from pan and place on a plate. Tent loosely with foil.

3. MAKE THE GLAZE WHILE PORK CHOPS REST   Return the pan to medium heat and add cider vinegar, scraping any browned bits off the bottom. Allow vinegar to come to a boil. Add maple syrup and pepper; bring to a boil again, stirring constantly. Boil hard for 1 minute, stirring constantly. Remove from heat. The sauce should be quite thick and syrupy, but still pourable.

4. Place rested pork chops on a platter and drizzle extravagantly with maple pepper glaze. Serve at once.

4 bone-in pork chops, about ¾ inch (2 cm) thick
½ teaspoon (2 mL) fine sea salt
1 tablespoon (15 mL) olive oil

For the glaze
2 tablespoons (30 mL) cider vinegar
⅓ cup (75 mL) pure dark maple syrup
1½ teaspoons (7 mL) freshly ground black pepper

MAPLE PECAN BUTTER TARTS

Not only is the butter tart deeply rooted in Canadian culture, but it is one of the few sweet treats I remember enjoying from my whole-foods upbringing. The recipe in my mother's tattered handwritten cookbook showed equations for ten times the amount given here, as my sister and I routinely made these tarts to sell at the weekend farmers' market. During the long ride into town, I made it my duty to eat all the broken ones that were deemed unfit to sell. Thus a lifelong love for butter tarts was firmly established.

I've tweaked my mother's recipe over the years to make it my own. Swapping maple syrup for the usual corn syrup came when I moved to Quebec, and pecans always seemed a better match than the traditional walnuts. Alongside the maple and nuts, these tarts are full of dried currants and toasted coconut; they are chewy and yes, a little bit gooey. They are a three-bite delight, encased in a thin, flaky crust and delivering just the right amount of sweetness.

MAKES 12 TARTS

1. Preheat oven to 350°F (180°C).

2. MAKE THE TART SHELLS   On a lightly floured counter, roll pie dough to 1/8-inch (3 mm) thickness. Use the ring of a large mason jar lid or a 3 1/2-inch (9 cm) round cookie cutter to cut out 12 circles of dough. You may need to gather the scraps and roll again to get a full dozen.

3. Gently press the rounds into the cups of a standard muffin pan. Place in the refrigerator to chill while you make the filling. This allows the dough to rest, resulting in a flakier crust.

4. MAKE THE FILLING WHILE TART SHELLS CHILL   Sprinkle pecans and coconut onto a small rimmed baking sheet or pie plate and toast in the oven for 4 to 5 minutes, shaking the pan occasionally to ensure even toasting. Remove pan from oven when the coconut is light brown. Let cool.

5. In a medium bowl, whisk together egg, sugar and butter until creamy. Add currants, maple syrup, cream, vanilla and salt; mix well. Toss in toasted pecans and coconut and stir to combine.

6. TO ASSEMBLE   Stir filling and divide among chilled tart shells, stirring again before each scoop to ensure ingredients are evenly distributed.

7. Bake for 20 minutes or until tarts puff slightly and tops are golden. Let cool slightly before enjoying.

1/2 recipe Basic All-Butter Pie Crust (page 293)

For the filling

1/4 cup (60 mL) chopped pecans

2 tablespoons (30 mL) unsweetened shredded coconut

1 medium egg

1/4 cup (60 mL) raw cane sugar

2 tablespoons (30 mL) unsalted butter, softened

1/4 cup (60 mL) dried currants

1/4 cup (60 mL) pure maple syrup

2 teaspoons (10 mL) half-and-half (10%) cream

1/2 teaspoon (2 mL) pure vanilla extract

Pinch of salt

STORAGE

These tarts will keep in an airtight container for up to 4 days or in the freezer for up to 8 weeks.

STICKY MAPLE BLUEBERRY PUDDING

Years ago, before its worldwide fame, I worked one Saturday at my neighborhood restaurant, Au Pied du Cochon, filling in for a friend who was sick. It was a night of fantastic spectacle and thrilling cooking. Across from customers seated at the open bar, I produced plate after plate of venison tartare, poutine, pig ear salad and *soupe à l'oignon*—all delivered at dizzying speeds. Halfway through dinner service, chef Martin Picard clanged on a dinner bell and the barman poured a round of ice-cold hard cider for the kitchen staff. I gratefully gulped mine back as I stood next to a hissing deep-fryer and a salamander belching out heat. Then, even before the last appetizer went out, the dessert orders were pouring in. I scooped white cake batter into bowls and drowned it in maple syrup and cream before sending it to the oven. When it came out, blistering hot and angrily bubbling over the sides, it was *pouding chômeur*, a sticky "poor man's" pudding.

My version of this popular provincial dessert has a little more sauce and features blueberries, the small wild ones hailing straight from my freezer, preserved in their prime months earlier. Fresh berries may be used, as well as cultivated, because this dessert should be in rotation all year round. This recipe can easily be doubled or tripled. Note that the cake batter must chill for 24 hours, so begin this recipe the day before you plan to serve it.

SERVES 6

For the cake

3 tablespoons (45 mL) salted butter, softened

¼ cup (60 mL) raw cane sugar

1 large egg

½ cup (125 mL) all-purpose flour

½ teaspoon (2 mL) baking powder

For the sauce

¾ cup (175 mL) pure maple syrup

¾ cup (175 mL) heavy (35%) cream

¾ cup (175 mL) fresh or frozen blueberries

STORAGE

These puddings will keep, covered and refrigerated, for up to 2 days. Reheat in the oven or microwave before enjoying.

1. MAKE THE CAKE BATTER AHEAD OF TIME   In a small bowl and using a sturdy wooden spoon, cream together butter and sugar until smooth. Beat in egg until creamy, about 1 minute. Add flour and baking powder; stir to combine. Batter will be stiff. Cover surface with plastic wrap and refrigerate for 24 hours.

2. Preheat oven to 450°F (230°C). Place six 1-cup (250 mL) ramekins or half-pint (250 mL) wide-mouth jars on a baking sheet.

3. MAKE THE SAUCE   Combine maple syrup and cream in a small pot and bring to a boil, stirring occasionally.

4. Pour 2 tablespoons (30 mL) of hot sauce into each ramekin. Spoon 2 tablespoons (30 mL) of blueberries on top. Divide chilled cake batter into 6 portions (about 2 tablespoons/30 mL each) and crumble over blueberries. Drizzle remaining sauce over batter, about 2 tablespoons (30 mL) per dish.

5. Bake for 17 to 19 minutes, until cake is lightly golden and sauce is bubbly around the edges. Let puddings cool for 5 minutes before serving.

HOMESTEADING

Harvesting Maple Syrup in Your Backyard

Making maple syrup in your backyard is the sweetest thing going, so here are my quick tips for small-scale, DIY production.

Sugaring off begins about a month before the last snow. Ideal conditions are when the temperature drops below freezing at night, but reaches at least 40°F (4°C) during the day.

Select a sugar maple with a trunk at least 9 inches (23 cm) thick. Tapping anything smaller is harmful to the longevity of the tree.

Most spouts require a 7/16-inch (approximately 11 mm) drill bit, which you'll use to tap the side of the tree that receives the most sun. Drill into your tree on a slight upward slant—17 degrees is optimal. This allows the sap to drip down with gravity and flow through the spout.

Gently tap a spout into the hole, hang a bucket on the hook and cover the bucket with a lid to prevent too much "nature," such as leaves, bark and twigs, from falling into the bucket. Depending on the temperature and how fast the sap flows, a 1.5-gallon (5.6 L) bucket can fill in about three hours or overnight.

If you're collecting from more than one tree, collect the sap by pouring it into a larger bucket; we use a 5-gallon (19 L) bucket.

Back in the kitchen, strain the maple sap through a clean tea towel, and then, if you have space, let it sit in the refrigerator overnight or on the back porch to allow any remaining sediment to settle out. This will give you a clearer product. The next day, slowly pour the sap into a large pot, being careful to leave the sediment at the bottom of the bucket.

Turn on your stove's exhaust fan (this is important, because there's a lot of steam!) and bring your sap to a boil over high heat. Reduce the sap until it "aprons"—the syrup comes off a spatula in a slow curtain or sheet. This will happen at 7°F (4°C) above the boiling temperature in your area, or around 219°F (104°C) if you live at sea level. Time will vary depending on the amount of sap you have. Depending on your heat source, 5 gallons (19 L) of sap will reduce to maple syrup in about 4 hours, and will yield about 1 pint (500 mL) of pure organic maple syrup.

KIDS CAN
make maple taffy

At the tender ages of three and one, Noah and Mateo developed an affection for maple taffy on snow or, as it is called here in Quebec, *tire d'érable*, and that remains the highlight of their sugaring-off season. They kneel in the snow, mittens tossed aside, popsicle sticks in hand, eyes squinting in the brilliant sunshine, and wait for the pour. They roll their own taffy pops, then settle back into a snowbank to attend to the business at hand. It is sticky business, during which all is silent, save for the sounds of small forest creatures and snow dripping from branches high above. After a long winter, spring makes a sweet entrance.

MAKES 10 MAPLE LOLLIPOPS

Have a shallow 13- × 9-inch (3 L) pan of packed snow ready or a clean, packed snowbank nearby.

Boil 1 cup (250 mL) of pure maple syrup over medium-high heat until it reaches the soft-ball stage (238°F/115°C), about 5 to 7 minutes.

Carefully pour the hot syrup over the packed snow, making rows about the width and length of a butter knife.

Hand a popsicle stick to each child.

Have the children place a popsicle stick perpendicular to one end of the maple row and roll it up into a maple taffy lollipop.

Roll a lollipop for yourself and enjoy this ultimate sweet treat together.

HAVE READY:
- Packed snow
- Pure maple syrup
- Medium pot
- Candy thermometer
- Popsicle sticks

2
BROWN EGGS

Coconut Cream Baked Oatmeal • Chocolate Croissant Bread Pudding • Roasted Asparagus and Eggs with Crispy Bacon • Niçoise Salad with Asparagus • Mayonnaise • Spinach and Ricotta Pappardelle • Shrimp and Egg Fried Rice with Green Garlic • Roasted Rhubarb Eton Mess

It was the poultry barn at our local fall fair that sparked our initial interest in owning chickens. As our family strolled along the rows of beribboned birds, we identified wild turkeys, doves, Muscovy ducks and chickens of all breeds. We laughed as two ornery roosters conducted a spat through the bars of the cages, and exclaimed over the fluffy feet of fancier hens. A large incubator at the end of one of the rows stopped us in our tracks, however. Little wet beaks were chipping away at shells in one corner, while in another, tiny tufts of fluff were toppling over each other. Out of the soft yellow down, the bright eyes of the newly hatched chicks peered up at us in classic "Are you my mother?" fashion. We were smitten. Then and there we vowed to raise a flock of poultry on our homestead the following spring.

Our ambitions for backyard chickens were by no means founded solely on the cute chicks and handsome cocks we saw that day, although they gave us the nudge we needed to begin. I grew up with a henhouse in the backyard, so I was fully aware of the commitment, although my only memories of owning hens are despicable ones: Mucking out the henhouse on sticky summer afternoons. Whitewashing the coop. Breaking the ice every morning on the water bucket. And the inevitable butchering day each fall. No, there was nothing romantic about my notion of owning chickens.

Still, I wanted hens for two reasons: fresh eggs and little farmers.

The difference between supermarket specimens from caged birds and eggs from a hen that has had access to earth, greens, fresh water and exercise is noticeable even before you see the yolk. The shell gives it away. Hens that have enough calcium in their diets and access to sunlight (vitamin D) lay eggs with harder shells. As the hens age, the shells will thin slightly, but will still be harder than those of store-bought eggs.

The yolk of a fresh farm egg is shockingly different from that of an older, commercial egg. The yolk is bright orange and stands up tall instead of slumping into the white. As a whole, the egg is rich and satisfying to eat and leaves you understanding why many people consider the egg to be a near-perfect food. It contains almost all the nutrients essential for life—just vitamin C is missing, so enjoy yours with a slice of orange on the side.

Farm-fresh eggs, then, are a good reason to get out of bed every morning. But more than that, they provide a daily reminder to my children of where their food really comes from. Where was the egg before it was stacked in cartons in the supermarket cooler? They can tell you that, and they can also discuss where the egg was before it landed in the nesting box.

Each smooth, brown egg discovered by my children is a small gift, held carefully in hand as they cross the grass to the kitchen and delivered safely to my kitchen. Eggs are their favorite breakfast—and lunch and dinner, for that matter—and we eat as many as our hens produce.

Owning six hens generates just enough chores to keep our munchkins busy but not overwhelm them. The lessons to be learned, however, are many and have lifelong value. For example, they've learned how to consider others before themselves—the chickens get their bucket of kitchen scraps before they eat their own breakfast. They are responsible for collecting the eggs, as well as keeping track of production. Discipline has been a lesson learned, as they must remember to draw the latch that lifts the ramp and shuts the birds in safely for the night. They've learned of loss—one morning Noah went skipping out in his dressing gown and rubber boots to discover that a fox had broken in and—well, let's just say the fox caused a ruckus.

We "harvest" our chickens every fall, and the children are further educated about where food comes from. (See "How to talk to your kids honestly about meat" on page 42. And if you are interested in reading more, on my blog I've detailed our small-production butchering system.) Our hens are layers, which means they don't have much meat on their bones, since their energy has been focused on laying eggs. They are also semi-free range, and being active toughens the meat. They give us terrific eggs, but they are not suitable for roasting, so on harvest day, we make chicken stock in bulk (page 286). It feels really, really good to be raising even a smidgen of our own food.

So far the children have opted out of butchering, and that is fine. They understand what is happening and are okay with it; they just don't wish to participate and we won't insist … yet! I think when they are older it will be a fascinating science lesson.

Eggs are synonymous with spring on our homestead, not because of anything foil-wrapped or dyed and arranged in a basket, but because we pick up six young hens from a local farm around Easter, and they are laying by Mother's Day. As the buds start to open, grasses thicken and microbial bugs and earthworms proliferate, our pastured chickens stretch their legs and get down to the business of scratching and eating. With this buffet comes a host of vitamins and nutrients that enhance our free-range eggs; springtime is when eggs are at their nutritional peak.

If owning a small flock of hens isn't in the works for you now, consider sourcing fresh eggs from a local farm. Look for organic free-range or cage-free eggs. In Canada, eggs labeled "organic" must be free range as well, and how many hens you can have in a given space is clearly defined and audited. However, strict labeling is not the case further abroad, so ensure that your eggs are coming from hens with access to fresh air and field.

COCONUT CREAM BAKED OATMEAL

A coconut crème brûlée from my catering days inspired this dish—that and my family's undying love of all things oatmeal in the morning. Always an enthusiast of the do-ahead breakfast, I developed this recipe to be mixed together the evening before and chilled overnight to absorb the liquid. The results are creamy, delicious and well received by the little critics.

In this recipe, the eggs add a little extra protein as well as a custard-like richness to the dish. A sprinkling of toasted coconut and a drizzle of additional honey are our preferred toppings to finish off this nourishing breakfast.

SERVES 4

1. MAKE AHEAD   Generously grease a 3-quart (3 L) casserole or 9-inch (2 L) square baking dish with coconut oil. In a medium bowl, beat eggs, coconut milk, honey and vanilla until smooth. Add water, oats, 1/4 cup (60 mL) of the coconut and salt. Mix well.

2. Pour mixture into the prepared casserole and cover with plastic wrap. Refrigerate overnight.

3. In the morning, preheat oven to 350°F (180°C).

4. Remove plastic wrap and bake oatmeal for 35 to 40 minutes or until set in the middle. Meanwhile, toast the remaining 1/4 cup (60 mL) coconut in the oven on the side, stirring once or twice, for 4 to 6 minutes or until light golden.

5. Drizzle oatmeal with a little extra honey and sprinkle with toasted coconut. Serve hot.

1 teaspoon (5 mL) coconut oil

2 medium eggs

1 small can (5½ ounces/160 mL) coconut milk

1/3 cup (75 mL) liquid honey, warmed

1/2 teaspoon (2 mL) pure vanilla extract

2 cups (500 mL) water

1 cup (250 mL) steel-cut oats

1/2 cup (125 mL) shredded unsweetened coconut, divided

1/4 teaspoon (1 mL) salt

CHOCOLATE CROISSANT BREAD PUDDING

After being served one too many Mother's Day breakfasts in bed consisting of cold toast and gray eggs, I decided to concoct a decadent breakfast dish that could be prepared in advance with minimal fuss. This bread pudding fit the bill, pairing croissants with a rich chocolate custard for a refined take on a brunch favorite. My loving family need only place it in the oven to bake and whip a little cream to garnish. Serve this bread pudding with a piping-hot coffee, and I am one happy mama.

You can whip the leftover egg whites into a fluffy omelet to serve on the side to round out the brunch, if you like.

SERVES 6 TO 8

2 cups (500 mL) 2% milk

4 ounces (125 g) bittersweet chocolate

6 egg yolks

⅓ cup (75 mL) raw cane sugar

½ teaspoon (2 mL) pure vanilla extract

Pinch of salt

6 day-old croissants

KITCHEN TIP

For an overnight option, prepare the bread pudding in advance but do not bake. Cover with plastic wrap and refrigerate up to 12 hours. Remove plastic wrap and bake as directed, but add 5 to 7 minutes to the cooking time.

1. Preheat oven to 350°F (180°C). Butter a 12- × 4-inch (2 L) loaf pan or a 9-inch (2 L) square baking dish.

2. In a medium saucepan, heat milk over medium heat while you coarsely chop the chocolate. When the milk is very hot and the surface begins to quiver, remove from heat and add the chocolate. Slowly whisk until the chocolate is melted and the mixture is smooth.

3. In a medium bowl, whisk egg yolks and sugar together until light and creamy. Beat in vanilla and salt. Pour in a cup or so (about 250 mL) of the warm chocolate milk and whisk to combine. Add the remaining chocolate milk and stir well.

4. Slice open the croissants as if you were going to make a sandwich, then cut each half in half again. Dunk all the croissant quarters into the custard and let soak for 10 minutes.

5. With a fork, lift out the soaked croissants and arrange them in the prepared baking dish, assembling them back into a croissant shape, with their rounded tops facing up. Drizzle any remaining custard over the top.

6. Bake for 20 to 25 minutes or until the custard has set. Allow the bread pudding to cool for a few minutes and then serve warm.

ROASTED ASPARAGUS AND EGGS WITH CRISPY BACON

I used to hesitate every time my boys asked for a bacon-and-egg breakfast. Maybe it was the grease I'd have to deal with, or the prospect of juggling two pans plus a toaster, when really I just wanted to relax on a Sunday morning. This recipe is my solution to their requests. Everything is roasted in one pan, where the flavors meld perfectly, enhanced with fresh thyme and a little lemon zest. It is always a welcome brunch item, and for a short while, there is quiet around the table.

SERVES 4

15 asparagus spears
  (about ⅔ pound/350 g)
8 slices bacon
½ teaspoon (2 mL) lemon zest
Leaves from 2 sprigs fresh thyme
½ teaspoon (2 mL) freshly ground
  black pepper
4 large eggs

1. Preheat oven to 450°F (230°C).

2. Wash asparagus thoroughly, and snap off the tough ends. Use a vegetable peeler to remove the bottom two-thirds of peel.

3. Lay the bacon slices side by side in a roasting pan. Roast for about 8 minutes or until crispy. Transfer the bacon to a paper towel. Drain off most of the fat, leaving about a tablespoon (15 mL) in the pan.

4. Add asparagus to the pan and shake it around gently to coat in the fat. Arrange the asparagus in a single layer and sprinkle with lemon zest, thyme leaves and pepper. Roast asparagus for 8 minutes or until it begins to soften.

5. Line up the asparagus spears next to each other so they're touching. Gently crack the eggs in a row on top of the asparagus. Roast for another 3 to 4 minutes or until the eggs have reached the desired doneness. Return bacon to the pan, bring the finished dish to the table and serve at once.

NIÇOISE SALAD WITH ASPARAGUS

With tender new asparagus and salty olives nestled in among spring greens and tiny boiled potatoes, this salad is a well-rounded meal on a plate. It is as fresh as the spring eggs from our own chicken coop that inspired it. A traditional niçoise calls for green beans and tomatoes, so feel free to keep making this salad straight through the summer even when asparagus season is finished.

My method in step 2 guarantees a perfect hard-boiled egg every time.

SERVES 2 AS A MAIN, 6 AS A SIDE

1. MAKE THE DRESSING   Mash garlic with sea salt, using the flat side of your knife blade on a cutting board. When it is a fine paste, transfer it to a small bowl. Whisk in vinegar, tarragon, Dijon and pepper. Drizzle in olive oil while whisking; the dressing should look creamy. Set aside.

2. MAKE THE SALAD   Place eggs in a small pot and fill with water to cover by 2 inches (5 cm). Bring to a boil over high heat. Boil rapidly for 1 minute. Remove from heat, cover, and let stand for 10 minutes. Meanwhile, fill a large bowl with ice and cold water. When the timer rings, transfer the boiled eggs to the ice bath to cool. Once cooled, peel eggs and slice in half; reserve. Keep the ice bath for the vegetables.

3. Place potatoes in a medium pot and fill with water to cover by 2 inches (5 cm). Bring to a boil over high heat. Reduce heat to medium and boil for 10 minutes or until the potatoes are still firm but can be easily pierced with a fork. Meanwhile, trim ends from asparagus spears so each spear is 4 inches (10 cm) long; reserve the ends for another purpose.

4. When the potatoes are fork-tender, add asparagus to the pot and boil for 90 seconds. Drain the pot and transfer the potatoes and asparagus to the ice bath. Once cooled, drain them well and lay them on a clean tea towel to dry.

5. Remove the outer leaves of the Boston lettuce and reserve them for sandwiches or for lettuce wraps (page 52). Gently tear apart the middle leaves and the hearts of the lettuce and distribute them around a large serving platter. Arrange the potatoes and asparagus on top, followed by the boiled eggs. Drain the can of tuna and break the fish into 5 or 6 large chunks; arrange them over the salad. Finally, sprinkle the olives around the salad.

6. Just before serving, give the dressing one final whisk and drizzle generously all over the salad. Top with additional tarragon leaves and finish with a sprinkling of sea salt.

For the dressing

1 large garlic clove, peeled
½ teaspoon (2 mL) sea salt
2 tablespoons (30 mL) red wine vinegar
1 tablespoon (15 mL) chopped fresh tarragon
½ teaspoon (2 mL) Dijon mustard
Pinch of black pepper
3 tablespoons (45 mL) olive oil

For the salad

3 large eggs
8 ounces (250 g) small red potatoes (about 8), scrubbed
1 pound (500 g) medium-thick asparagus
2 heads Boston lettuce
1 can (6 ounces/170 g) solid tuna
½ cup (125 mL) pitted niçoise or Kalamata olives

MAYONNAISE

One of North America's favorite condiments, mayonnaise is a staple that can be used as a base for dips and salad dressings (see Creamy Ranch Dressing, page 56), not to mention slathered on burgers and sliced tomato sandwiches. If you go through as much as we do, it's a good idea to master making it from scratch. I also like to make my own to avoid the additives and preservatives found in most store-bought versions.

I use a whole egg, straight from our henhouse, because I find the mayonnaise tastes less eggy than when made with only yolks. I like to taste olive oil too, but not an overpowering amount, so I replace half with peanut or grapeseed oil. A squeeze of lemon and a splash of vinegar added at the end bring a bit of tang to the spread, making it irresistible come mealtime.

MAKES 1¼ CUPS (300 ML)

STARTING TIP: Have all ingredients at room temperature. You can cheat by setting the egg in a bowl of warm water for 5 minutes.

1. In a small (3-cup/750 mL) food processor, blend egg and Dijon until smooth.

2. Measure the oils into one liquid measuring cup. With the food processor running, drizzle in the oil very, very slowly in a thin stream. It should take at least 4 minutes to add all the oil. When you are finished, the emulsion will have yielded pale yellow, creamy mayonnaise.

3. With the processor running, slowly pour in the lemon juice and vinegar. Add the salt. Turn off the machine and taste the mayonnaise. Add more salt if needed. Transfer mayonnaise to a jar and refrigerate.

1 large egg

½ teaspoon (2 mL) Dijon mustard

½ cup (125 mL) olive oil

½ cup (125 mL) peanut or grapeseed oil

1 tablespoon (15 mL) freshly squeezed lemon juice

1 teaspoon (5 mL) white wine vinegar

½ teaspoon (2 mL) salt

STORAGE
This condiment will keep in an airtight container in the refrigerator for up to 4 days.

SPINACH AND RICOTTA PAPPARDELLE

In the spring, when I need inspiration for a quick dinner, I slip on rain boots and head outdoors. Spinach is one of the first crops up in the garden, and when I see the young leaves waving at me, I immediately know what I'll make. I gather a bowl of leaves, as well as a few eggs from the chicken coop. Together they will be the base for an easy pasta sauce, and we will be eating within twenty minutes. If having two superfoods in one dish doesn't persuade you to make this dish, then perhaps the simplicity of the recipe will. This is a fast and easy vegetarian dinner that even my kids can whip up from scratch.

SERVES 4 TO 6

2 tablespoons (30 mL) salted butter

5 cups (1.25 L) packed fresh baby spinach

Salt

1 pound (500 g) pappardelle

2 egg yolks

½ cup (125 mL) ricotta cheese

2 tablespoons (30 mL) table (18%) cream

¼ cup (60 mL) grated Parmesan cheese

Freshly ground black pepper

1. Bring a large pot of salted water to a boil. Meanwhile, melt butter in a large skillet over medium heat. Add all the spinach to the pan and salt lightly. Using a pair of tongs, turn spinach in the pan until it is wilted but not completely cooked, about 2 minutes. Remove from heat.

2. Boil pasta for 5 to 7 minutes or according to the package's recommended cooking time.

3. Meanwhile, in a large serving bowl, whisk together the egg yolks, ricotta and cream.

4. Drain pasta and add it to the ricotta mixture. Toss well to coat. Add wilted spinach and Parmesan and mix well. Season with salt and freshly ground pepper as needed and serve at once.

SHRIMP AND EGG FRIED RICE WITH GREEN GARLIC

My travels in Malaysia gave me a lifelong affection for fried rice, piled high, steaming hot and studded with tender shrimp and sweet peas. As it turns out, Southeast Asian home cooking translates into a family-friendly dinner, especially when prepared with our own eggs and garden peas. This version is mild enough for the kids to enthusiastically tuck into, yet still provides plenty of flavor for more mature palates.

Green garlic, or spring garlic as it is sometimes called, is the new, immature garlic that makes an early appearance at local markets and in my garden. Use green garlic in recipes that call for onions, green onions or leeks and enjoy the mild yet fresh flavor. Garlic scapes and wild ramps are also delicious in this dish.

SERVES 4

2 tablespoons (30 mL) tamari soy sauce

1 tablespoon (15 mL) sesame oil

1 tablespoon (15 mL) freshly squeezed lime juice

1 teaspoon (5 mL) raw cane sugar

½ teaspoon (2 mL) Sriracha

4 sprigs fresh green garlic, washed

1-inch (2.5 cm) knob fresh ginger, peeled

3 teaspoons (15 mL) peanut or grapeseed oil

4 eggs, lightly beaten

8 ounces (250 g) medium shrimp (31–40), peeled and deveined

3 cups (750 mL) cold cooked brown rice (leftover is best)

1 cup (250 mL) cooked peas

Fresh cilantro leaves and additional fresh garlic, for garnish

1. In a small bowl, whisk together soy sauce, sesame oil, lime juice, sugar and Sriracha; set aside.

2. Remove and discard roots from garlic; chop garlic into ¼-inch (5 mm) rounds. Grate ginger on a microplane or finely mince. Set garlic and ginger aside.

3. Heat a large nonstick skillet over medium heat. Pour in 1 teaspoon (5 mL) of the peanut oil. Add the eggs and quickly scramble them. Transfer the eggs to a plate and set aside.

4. Pour the remaining 2 teaspoons (10 mL) oil into the pan and increase heat to high. Add the chopped green garlic; stir-fry for 30 seconds. Add the grated ginger and the shrimp. Stir-fry for 2 minutes or until shrimp are light pink and just cooked through.

5. Add rice and peas. Toss the mixture together. Pour the soy-lime sauce over dish and cook, stirring, for 1 minute. Add the scrambled egg; toss ingredients together again. Serve at once with additional Sriracha and garnished with fresh cilantro leaves and fresh garlic.

HOMESTEADING

Raising Urban Chickens

The simple act of raising your own chickens brings you to the very essence of the miracle of food and helps you understand the importance of raising livestock sustainably. Here are a few suggestions to get you started raising your own chickens.

Make sure there are no local ordinances against keeping chickens. If there aren't, let your neighbors know about your plans. If they have any concerns, offer to share a dozen eggs once in a while.

Learn as much as you can on the subject from books, blogs and websites. One of the best online chicken-raising websites and forums is www.backyardchickens.com.

One hen per family member plus one is a good number to plan for. One chicken will lay an average five to six eggs a week, so even two hens will ensure you get about a dozen eggs a week. Family and friends will always be eager to take any extras off your hands.

Before you purchase your chickens, make sure the breed is suitable for your climate. Some breeds are more heat-hardy or cold-hardy.

Build a chicken coop. Again, consider your climate. Housing doesn't have to be fancy; an unused garden shed can easily be converted into a coop. Plan for about three or four square feet (0.3 to 0.4 square meters) per chicken inside the henhouse and ensure that it is secure against predators.

Invest in an automatic waterer. Access to plentiful fresh water is essential to keep up egg production.

Chickens eat more than you think. Save kitchen scraps, give them access to a free-range run and offer a grain feed specifically for layers.

ROASTED RHUBARB ETON MESS

Looking for a truly delicious and fun spring dessert? Start by roasting the season's freshest fruit into syrupy submission. Whip egg whites sky-high and bake them into meringue clouds. Finally, beat cream until it holds its shape but slides off a spoon. Then place fruit, meringues and cream in the middle of the table, pass around bowls or jam jars and instruct everyone to build their own Eton Mess. I guarantee bowls will be licked clean.

With something titled "Mess," there is no wrong way to assemble this dessert, but I suggest you first crumble meringues into your bowl, top with cream and finish with a generous spoonful of roasted fruit.

SERVES 6

4 cups (1 L) rhubarb cut in 1-inch (2.5 cm) pieces

4 tablespoons (60 mL) pure maple syrup, divided

2 large egg whites, at room temperature

½ cup (125 mL) granulated sugar

1 teaspoon (5 mL) pure vanilla extract, divided

1½ cups (375 mL) heavy (35%) cream

VARIATIONS

There's no need to reserve this dessert exclusively for spring. Try it later in the summer with roasted strawberries or stone fruit such as plums or cherries, or even in winter with a pan of caramelized oranges or apples.

STORAGE

The rhubarb will keep, covered and refrigerated, for up to 2 days. The meringues will keep in an airtight container at room temperature for up to 2 days.

1. Preheat oven to 400°F (200°C). Lightly butter a 13- × 9-inch (3 L) roasting pan or glass baking dish.

2. Spread rhubarb in the pan in a single layer and drizzle with 3 tablespoons (45 mL) of the maple syrup. Roast for 20 minutes. Remove from the oven and cool. (Rhubarb may be prepared up to 2 days ahead.)

3. Reduce oven to 200°F (100°C). Line a rimmed baking sheet with parchment paper. Place egg whites in the clean bowl of a stand mixer and beat on low until frothy. Increase speed slightly and beat until egg whites are thick but not glossy, about 5 minutes. Sprinkle in the sugar, 1 tablespoon (15 mL) at a time, beating for about a minute between additions. The best meringues are not rushed. When all the sugar is added, meringue will be thick and shiny. Beat in ½ teaspoon (2 mL) of the vanilla.

4. Using a soup spoon, drop meringues in 12 mounds on the prepared baking sheet. Flatten slightly with the back of the spoon. Don't worry about making them look pretty or even.

5. Bake meringues for 3 hours, then turn off the oven and let them dry in the closed oven for an additional hour. Store in an airtight container until ready to serve. (Meringues may be made up to 1 day ahead.)

6. Whip cream to soft peaks. Add remaining ½ teaspoon (2 mL) vanilla and remaining tablespoon (15 mL) maple syrup. Divide meringues among 6 bowls, crushing them slightly. Top with whipped cream. Divide roasted rhubarb and accompanying juices among the bowls. Serve at once.

HOW TO TALK TO YOUR KIDS HONESTLY ABOUT MEAT

A friend recently emailed me about her three-year-old, saying, "Help! My son has just found out that we eat animals. He's sworn off meat until I promise 'they' won't kill any more animals. Maybe I should tell him about how we raised rabbits for meat when I was a kid!"

I had to chuckle, but it's a common quandary. At a certain age, children tend to clue in to the reality that their bacon and burgers once had tails and ears. Because I believe that (grass-fed, pasture-finished) meat is part of a healthy diet, Danny and I have talked honestly with our kids about meat since they were two years old.

"Why?" is usually the first question from concerned (or just curious) little people. "Why do we kill animals?" or "Why do we eat meat?" As with any sensitive topic, it's best to be straightforward and honest in your answers. Tell them the truth, and then let them decide. And decide they will!

I suggest beginning with a conversation about "food as fuel," because it's an easy concept for children to grasp. "Everybody eats" is another good approach, starting with the robin and the worm and moving up the food chain.

Children conjure up storybook settings for farm animals, and I have found these are the best images to encourage. Cows grazing on pasture, hens scratching in the field—this is the kind of agriculture we should be supporting anyway. If you can assure your children that the locally raised animals you choose to eat have led happy lives, that is a step toward earning their trust. Animals are not suffering for us while they live, but when their time is up, well, such is the cycle of life.

One of the reasons my family won't eat at fast-food chains is because the animals used to supply their meat and eggs are often kept in inhumane conditions. As our children grow older, we will tell them more about feedlots and factory farms and will continue to introduce them to the farms and conditions we support instead.

Take time to convey your respect and appreciation for the animals we eat. We've done so by explaining why we eat meat only three or four times a week and balance out our diets with legumes, eggs and other proteins. We also use as much of the animal as possible. My boys see me making stock from bones, and as soon as they were old enough to understand, I explained that this was to ensure that no part of an animal that was harvested for our needs was wasted.

Read together about others who raised food for basic survival, such as the Ingalls family in the *Little House on the Prairie* series. Explain that we just go about it in a different way now. Learn about the ways many people in other parts of the world hunt or fish for their basic needs. It doesn't have to be such a foreign concept.

Don't leave out the middleman, the butcher. (When they are a little older you can explain about the abattoir.) To my kids, this is the person who really turns the pig into bacon.

Children are naturally drawn to animals, especially the cute ones, so for some it may be a mindbender to find out we do indeed eat them. I've always explained that God made some animals as pets to love (cats and dogs, for instance), some as wildlife to observe and marvel at (polar bears, elephants) and some for our food needs. It helps to an extent, but kids will still put their own spin on things.

I still laugh about the time when we were expecting some very important company from out of town and I wondered aloud what to cook for dinner. Mateo practically leapt from his chair at the dinner table, waving his arms in the air and saying, "I know! I know! We could harvest a chicken for them!" Laughter rippled around the table. I thanked him for his suggestion, but advised him that we needed to keep all of our hens around for egg production. His sentiment was not overlooked, however.

For my son, killing a chicken was an act of honor, for both the guest and the bird. Isn't that a noble way to approach eating meat?

3

PICNICS

Cumin Olive Oil Crostini • Radish Chive Butter • Gingery Pickled Asparagus • Shrimp and Spring Pea Lettuce Cups • Smoked Salmon and Arugula Gougères • Creamy Ranch Dressing • Strawberry Lemonade • Chia Pudding with Roasted Strawberries and Pistachio Crumbs • Crispy Cocoa Date Bites

When spring finally comes to our homestead, we have an insatiable desire to vacate the house and feel the sun on our faces. So down the back steps, across the sloping lawn and into the forest we go, a picnic basket bumping alongside us, searching for the first trilliums and ramps of the year. Any day that has a picnic in the plans always holds a tinge of excitement and mystery. Will we find the perfect spot, not too sunny, not too windy? Will the food survive the journey, however short?

The last patches of snow are gone and the forest is a carpet of wildflowers, stretching out between fallen logs like a bride's train. We spread a quilt and nibble Shrimp and Spring Pea Lettuce Cups (page 52) while we watch the birds flit through the trees. My boys are happy enough with two slabs of homemade bread slapped together with apple butter, a lunch they devour in enormous bites while swinging from branches. The opportunity to escape the dining room table is a freeing one for them. After we eat, I'll stretch out on the quilt for a few minutes and read to Clara while the boys romp through the trees, hunting for toads. It is a soul-rejuvenating change from the long winter.

Anytime we bring food outdoors, it's a picnic. Sometimes it's just a glass of strawberry lemonade (page 57) and a plate of crostini on the back stoop, with freshly picked radishes from the garden (page 47). Other afternoons it's a full Mother's Day picnic, transported lakeside or to a sprawling park and laid out on a cloth-covered picnic table. For fancier occasions, I'll bake puffy gougères and stuff them with smoked salmon and fresh baby arugula (page 55). I'll layer roasted strawberries and creamy chia pudding in a jar and pack silver teaspoons for serving. A chilled bottle of bubbly is nice, but not necessary, as lemonade is everyone's favorite anyway.

I have an unabashedly romantic opinion of picnics, with the food and the setting both playing important roles. I love to pack bites that take time to assemble and enjoy. Picnicking is different from daytripping; it's more about the company and the experience than the journey or the destination. In fact, a short journey is best for picnics. I want to be sprawled on the grass or playing Frisbee as soon as possible.

I've been planning picnics forever, it seems. I celebrated my nineteenth birthday with a picnic. Instead of crashing the local pub with my older siblings, we raided the greenhouse for cherry tomatoes and baby cucumbers, tucked a load of homemade bread and a pocketknife into a basket, recruited a few friends and set off on a hike. After an hour or so of trekking, our party reached a lookout, where we threw ourselves on the mossy rocks, ravenous. My sister Haidi produced a dark chocolate torte and a few pounds of Montreal smoked meat, a nod to a certain young man back in Quebec who was missing the occasion. It was the sweetest gesture, and not lost on my sentimental nineteen-year-old self. That was a picnic to remember, absent boyfriend and all.

These days, our family are picnic fanatics in all four seasons. In early spring, we begin in the sugar bush with a thermos of maple tea, a mug of baked beans (page 12) and maple taffy on the snow (page 23). Later we're surrounded by wildflowers and ramps (also known as wild leeks) and we munch sandwiches with radish butter (page 50) and sip strawberry lemonade. Summer brings urban picnics, where we spread thick slices of zucchini cornbread (page 163) with jam and eat them on our laps at the Montreal Jazz Festival. In autumn, we frequent orchards or farms and I pack a tin of carrot spice muffins (page 197) to accompany the local cider and apples. I even have a popular post on *Simple Bites* for a winter picnic. With proper planning and an adventurous spirit, a snow picnic can be as much fun as a summer picnic! Brilliant sunlight, crisp cool air and a peaceful blanket of white snow—now that is the mix for an invigorating outing.

Whatever the month, tips for packing a picnic remain the same:

- Garbage in, garbage out.
- Eat seasonally.
- Remember napkins or wet wipes.
- Pack a pocketknife for portioning.
- Have fun!

A wedge of cheese, a fresh baguette, a pint of berries and a bar of chocolate are all you really need to picnic, but I'm sharing a handful of my favorite recipes in this chapter for a truly memorable picnic. They are designed to be lingered over and shared with friends. Should you prefer entertaining indoors, they also work well as tidy little appetizers for an evening of fun with friends.

CUMIN OLIVE OIL CROSTINI

When I first moved to Quebec, it never ceased to amaze me that I could slip off down the street three minutes before dinner and return with an impeccable baguette to accompany our meal. And when the fresh loaf is so readily available, who wants leftovers? Well, if they are turned into crostini, I do.

With this recipe, you can revive a day-old baguette with a cumin-infused olive oil and then toast it into spiced, crispy bites. For easy entertaining, keep a tin of these crostini in the freezer and warm them in the oven minutes before serving. Pair the crostini with Radish Chive Butter (page 48) for a spring bite that is as delightful as the season.

MAKES 30 CROSTINI

1. Preheat oven to 350°F (180°C).

2. In a small saucepan, heat olive oil gently over medium heat for 1 minute, until fragrant. Partially crush cumin seeds using a mortar and pestle, then add to olive oil. Remove from heat and let infuse for 5 minutes.

3. Slice baguette into 1/4-inch (5 mm) rounds and arrange in a single layer on a baking sheet. Brush each slice with the cumin olive oil. Bake for 13 to 15 minutes, until golden and crisp. Let cool on the baking sheet.

1/4 cup (60 mL) olive oil
1 1/2 teaspoons (7 mL) cumin seeds
1 day-old baguette

STORAGE
These crostini will keep in an airtight container at room temperature for up to 5 days or in the freezer for up to 3 weeks. Recrisp on a baking sheet in a 375°F (190°C) oven for 5 to 8 minutes.

RADISH CHIVE BUTTER

Radish butter is the gateway to a lifelong love of this underappreciated spring vegetable—just ask a handful of my closest friends who have had their palates opened to its delights. It takes only a few minutes to make, and once you set out a bowl of this butter with accompanying crostini or thinly sliced baguette, you'll want to spend the rest of the afternoon nibbling. As far as perfect picnic fare goes, it's hard to improve upon. We can thank the French for the pairing of radishes and butter—and for the accompanying baguette, for that matter.

Use unsalted butter, as the salt will cause the radishes to weep, but serve the butter with a small dish of flaky salt for garnish.

MAKES ½ CUP (125 ML)

¼ cup (60 mL) unsalted butter,
    at room temperature

4 radishes

1 tablespoon (15 mL) chopped
    young chives

Flaky sea salt, for garnish

STORAGE
This butter will keep, covered and refrigerated, for up to 2 days.

1. Place butter in a small bowl. Using a microplane, grate radishes into the butter. Add chopped chives. Cream the mixture together with a sturdy spatula until it is a unified paste.

2. Transfer radish butter to a small serving dish and serve at room temperature with the sea salt for garnish. Pair with Cumin Olive Oil Crostini (page 47) or use as a spread on cucumber sandwiches.

GINGERY PICKLED ASPARAGUS

I won Danny over to the side of pickled asparagus lovers on a cold winter night when our power was out. The kids were tucked into their warm beds, having dined on peanut butter and banana sandwiches, and we moved about a candle-lit kitchen, preparing our supper. I popped the lid off of a jar of asparagus I had pickled seven months earlier and rummaged in the dark refrigerator for a wedge of cheese. He opened a bottle of Riesling and tore into a bag of kettle chips. We stretched out on the living room floor, and so began one of the most perfect meals I can remember. The crunchy and tangy pickled asparagus spears contrasted sharply with the crisp saltiness of chips on our tongues. A wedge of mild Brie and a sip of sweet wine rounded out our little feast. We polished off the entire jar of pickles; some things are not meant for hoarding.

Asparagus is abundant in the spring, yet has a short growing season. Pickling helps to extend that period. Choose the freshest asparagus you can find and be sure to wash it properly.

MAKES 3 (12-OUNCE/375 ML) JARS

1. Review canning basics on page 146 and prepare a hot water bath with three 12-ounce (375 mL) jelly jars and lids according to step 2 on page 147. Bring a medium pot of water to a boil for blanching the asparagus.

2. In a small pot, combine vinegar and pickling salt; bring to a boil, then reduce heat and keep hot.

3. Rinse asparagus thoroughly under cool running water. Trim asparagus so the spears fit into the jars with 1/2 inch (1 cm) of headspace; they will be about 3 inches (8 cm) long. Working in batches, drop 3 asparagus at a time into the boiling water and blanch for 1 minute. Remove them with a slotted spoon and drain on a clean tea towel.

4. Pack the blanched asparagus into the jars. Add 1 garlic clove, 1 slice of fresh ginger and 1/2 teaspoon (2 mL) of mustard seeds to each jar. Carefully pour the hot vinegar over the asparagus spears and fill to within 1/2 inch (1 cm) of the top. Wipe the jar rims with a clean cloth and seal the jars.

5. Process for 10 minutes in hot water bath according to steps 4 and 5 on page 147. Wait at least 1 week before opening.

2 1/2 cups (625 mL) rice vinegar

3 tablespoons (45 mL) pickling salt

2 large bundles of medium-sized, firm-headed asparagus (about 2 1/2 pounds/1.125 kg)

3 small garlic cloves

3 slices (1/4 inch/5 mm) fresh ginger (unpeeled)

1 1/2 teaspoons (7 mL) yellow mustard seeds

STORAGE

These pickles will keep on a pantry shelf for up to 1 year. Remove rings and label the jars with the date.

SHRIMP AND SPRING PEA LETTUCE CUPS

Tiny wild-caught shrimp have their moment in the spotlight in one of the most refreshing bites of the season. Before heading out on a picnic, whip up this simple salad and pack it to go along with a head of washed lettuce. Upon arrival, fill lettuce leaves with a spoonful of this crunchy salad and enjoy them like wraps.

Feel free to adapt this dish to suit your tastes. Add a minced jalapeño if you like spicy foods, or double up on the fresh cilantro, or use other fresh herbs from your garden. It is an easily customizable lunch that never fails to please. If fresh peas are out of season, replace with diced cucumber. If your shrimp is salted, don't be tempted to add additional salt to the salad. The shrimp contribute all the saltiness you need.

SERVES 4

8 ounces (250 g) fresh or frozen baby Nordic shrimp

½ avocado

Juice of 1 lime

1 cup (250 mL) shelled fresh green peas

½ orange bell pepper

½ mango, peeled

2 green onions

5 or 6 sprigs fresh cilantro

2 tablespoons (30 mL) olive oil

1 head Boston lettuce

1. If shrimp are frozen, place in a colander under cold running water until they thaw. This takes just a few minutes. Lay shrimp out in a single layer on paper towel to drain.

2. Use a spoon to remove avocado flesh from its peel. Dice it and place in a medium bowl. Sprinkle with a teaspoon (5 mL) of the lime juice and toss gently to coat. Add shrimp and green peas.

3. Dice bell pepper and mango; toss them on top of the peas. Slice green onions into rings and add those as well.

4. Remove cilantro leaves from the stems and give them a rough chop. Sprinkle them over the salad along with the remaining lime juice and the olive oil. Mix everything together gently. If you are planning a picnic, transfer salad to a container with a tight-fitting lid and refrigerate until departure. Don't forget to pack a spoon.

5. To serve: Remove 8 leaves from the Boston lettuce and arrange on a platter. Peel off 8 more lettuce leaves and tuck a second layer into the larger ones. Divide shrimp salad among the 8 lettuce cups. Enjoy immediately.

VARIATION
Wrap salad in rice paper wrappers for refreshing summer rolls. Also, a minced jalapeño pepper brings the perfect component of heat to the dish.

SMOKED SALMON AND ARUGULA GOUGÈRES

These golden, cheesy puffs just happen to be beloved by everyone in our house—children included—and can be made weeks in advance or an hour before you need them. They are transformed easily by using different cheeses, herbs and spices, and are delicious stuffed for a light picnic lunch.

MAKES ABOUT 30 GOUGÈRES, SERVING 8 AS A SNACK

1. MAKE THE GOUGÈRES   Position oven racks in the middle and lower levels of oven and preheat oven to 425°F (220°C). Line two rimmed baking sheets with parchment paper.

2. Combine water, milk, butter, salt and pepper in a medium saucepan. Cook over medium heat, stirring occasionally, until the butter melts and the milk is hot, about 2 minutes.

3. Add flour and stir vigorously until a ball of dough forms and pulls away from the sides of the pot. Continue stirring vigorously until the dough is no longer sticky, about a minute. Stir enthusiastically for another minute or so, until the dough is smooth and glossy.

4. Remove from heat and cool dough for 1 or 2 minutes. Crack in the eggs, one at a time, stirring to fully incorporate each one before adding another. When all the eggs are added, the dough should be stiff enough to stand, but soft enough to spread. Add cheddar and chives; stir to combine.

5. Using a 1½-tablespoon (20 mL) ice cream scoop or two soup spoons, drop about 30 tablespoon-sized dollops of the dough about 2 inches (5 cm) apart onto prepared baking sheets. Alternatively, use a piping bag to drop small mounds of dough onto the sheets.

6. Bake for 10 minutes. Rotate baking sheets from front to back and top to bottom, then reduce oven to 375°F (190°C) and cook for another 10 minutes or until the puffs are golden and crisp (ovens vary, so begin checking them after about 7 minutes). Turn off oven and leave the puffs in the closed oven for 15 to 20 minutes so the insides can thoroughly dry out. Remove from oven and cool completely on the baking sheets.

7. TO ASSEMBLE   Make a slit in the side of the gougères and stuff each with smoked salmon and arugula. Add a dab of cream cheese if desired.

For the gougères

½ cup (125 mL) water
½ cup (125 mL) milk
⅓ cup (75 mL) unsalted butter
½ teaspoon (2 mL) salt
½ teaspoon (2 mL) black pepper
1 cup (250 mL) all-purpose flour
4 large eggs
1¼ cups (300 mL) grated cheddar cheese
2 tablespoons (30 mL) chopped fresh chives

For the sandwiches

4 ounces (125 g) sliced smoked salmon
1 cup (250 mL) fresh baby arugula
Cream cheese (optional)

VARIATION

Replace the smoked salmon with a slice of Montreal smoked meat.

STORAGE

Baked puffs will keep in an airtight container in the freezer for up to 4 weeks. Reheat at 350°F (180°C) until hot. Gougère dough can be portioned and frozen on baking sheets. Transfer to freezer bags and store for up to 2 months. Bake directly from frozen, adding 4 or 5 minutes to the baking time.

CREAMY RANCH DRESSING

I gravitate toward creamy salad dressings in the spring, and this ranch dressing is my mainstay. Simple to whisk together, this dressing is more than a dip for carrots. It pairs exceptionally well with most fresh spring produce, including radishes, snap peas, new cucumbers, asparagus and ramps. Toss it with a chopped salad and crumble bacon on top. Serve it alongside grilled shrimp garnished with a squirt of fresh lemon. Add a dab to gougères stuffed with smoked salmon (page 55). For picnics, pack a small jar of dressing as well as a bag of seasonal crudités and enjoy a crunchy dip al fresco.

MAKES 2 CUPS (500 ML)

1 cup (250 mL) sour cream

½ cup (125 mL) yogurt (page 301) or buttermilk

½ cup (125 mL) mayonnaise (page 35)

1 large garlic clove, minced

2 tablespoons (30 mL) chopped fresh dill

1 tablespoon (15 mL) lemon juice

1 teaspoon (5 mL) sea salt, or to taste

½ teaspoon (2 mL) black pepper

½ teaspoon (2 mL) onion powder

¼ teaspoon (1 mL) ground celery seeds

1. Whisk all ingredients together in a bowl until lump-free and well combined. Transfer to a jar with a lid and chill for at least 2 hours, ideally overnight, for the flavors to blend.

2. To serve: Shake well and toss desired amount with salad.

VARIATION
3 tablespoons (45 mL) chopped fresh parsley may be substituted for the dill.

STORAGE
This dressing will keep, refrigerated, for up to 4 days.

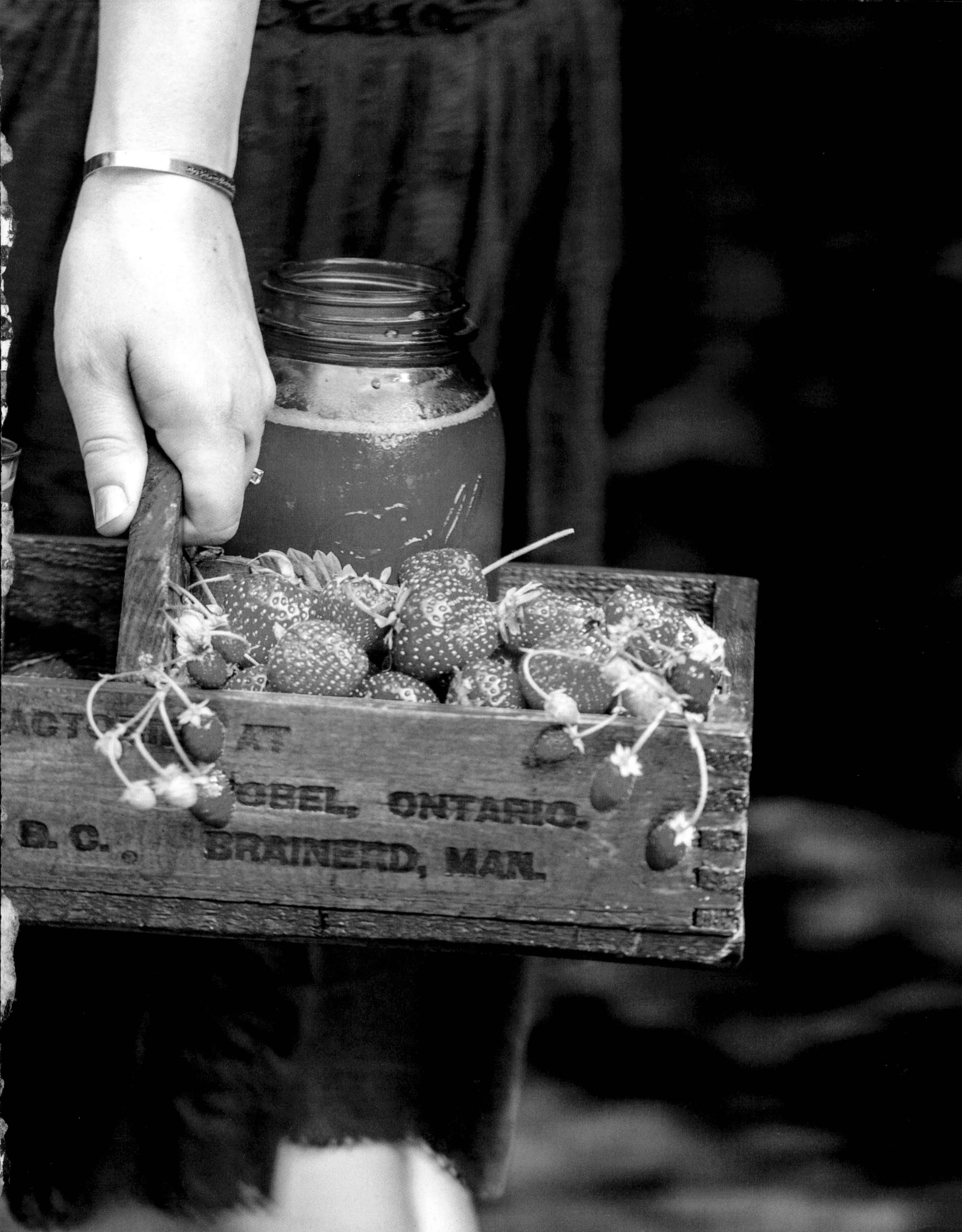
AT
OBEL, ONTARIO.
B. C.
BRAINERD, MAN.

STRAWBERRY LEMONADE

This version of lemonade is both delicious and thirst-quenching. In late spring, when flats of sun-ripened strawberries are at their lowest price, I buy several at a time and turn them all into a lemonade concentrate. It keeps in the freezer until Mateo's February birthday, when I shake it up with ice and pour strawberry lemonade around the table. It is his absolute favorite beverage, and what are birthdays for if not favorites?

MAKES 12 CUPS (2.8 L) LEMONADE

1. In a large bowl, toss sliced strawberries with sugar and let sit at room temperature while you juice the lemons. Juice the lemons and strain the juice into a measuring cup; you should have 1 cup (250 mL).

2. In a blender, whiz together macerated berries and their juice with lemon juice. This is your lemonade concentrate.

3. To serve: Combine 1 part lemonade concentrate with 2 parts water. Mix well, add several ice cubes and serve at once.

4 cups (1 L) sliced ripe strawberries
½ cup (125 mL) raw cane sugar
4 lemons

VARIATION

Lime juice is a fantastic substitute for the lemon, and Strawberry Limeade is every bit as tasty.

STORAGE

The lemonade concentrate will keep, refrigerated, for up to 3 days or in the freezer for up to 1 year.

CHIA PUDDING WITH ROASTED STRAWBERRIES AND PISTACHIO CRUMBS

A pint of sun-ripened local strawberries can perish in a matter of hours, especially those that are organic and pesticide-free. Roasting the strawberries is my standard method for saving the fruit and creating a delectable dish out of blemished berries. Slow-roasting enhances their natural sweetness and draws out the juices to yield a pungent syrup that self-sauces the roasted berries. They are sublime spooned into yogurt (page 301) or poured over pancakes, but I love them best layered in a simple chia pudding. It's a healthy finish to a picnic and won't weigh you down for the walk home. The dessert can be made a day ahead of time.

SERVES 4

1. In a wide-mouth jar or a plastic container with a lid, whisk together milk, chia seeds, vanilla and 1 tablespoon (15 mL) of the maple syrup. Set aside while you prepare your berries.

2. Preheat oven to 250°F (120°C). Line a baking sheet with parchment paper.

3. Rinse the strawberries under cool water and spread on a paper towel to dry. Remove the stems with a small knife and spread the berries on the baking sheet.

4. Drizzle berries with remaining tablespoon (15 mL) maple syrup and sprinkle with a pinch of salt. Place in the oven. Give your chia pudding another whisk and place in the refrigerator to chill for at least 6 hours or up to 1 day.

5. Roast the strawberries for 45 to 60 minutes, until they have darkened, softened and released their pungent juices. Let cool completely on the baking sheet. They will release more juice as they cool. Transfer to a bowl or jar, using a spatula to scrape all the sauce from the pan. Refrigerate until ready to use.

6. Finely chop the pistachios or grind them to medium fine. Place 1/4 cup (60 mL) roasted berries in the bottom of each of 4 half-pint (250 mL) jars. Cover berries in each jar with 1/3 cup (75 mL) chia pudding. Top with 2 tablespoons (30 mL) pistachio crumbs. Seal jars and chill until ready to serve. Tuck jars into a small cooler for transporting to the picnic site.

1 cup (250 mL) whole milk

3 tablespoons (45 mL) chia seeds (preferably white)

1/4 teaspoon (1 mL) pure vanilla extract

2 tablespoons (30 mL) pure maple syrup, divided

3 cups (750 mL) strawberries, quartered if large

Pinch of salt

1/2 cup (125 mL) toasted pistachios

VARIATION

Spice up the pudding by adding a pinch of ground cardamom and freshly ground black pepper to the berries before roasting.

STORAGE

Assembled, the pudding will keep in the refrigerator for up to 2 days.

CRISPY COCOA DATE BITES

These have become one of our favorite nut-free nutritious treats for school lunches and everyday snacking. I developed them for the kids, but more often than not I'm the one who eats them all, with an accompanying cup of tea. The combination of dates, honey and cocoa makes a wholly satisfying nibble that satiates the sweet tooth. As a bonus, the bites pack and travel well, making them good candidates for a picnic.

Your health food store or the organics section of your grocery store will have the sunflower seed butter, hemp hearts and puffed brown rice needed for this recipe.

MAKES 24 BITES

1 cup (250 mL) sunflower seed butter

11 Medjool dates, pitted

2 tablespoons (30 mL) cocoa powder

2 tablespoons (30 mL) liquid honey

Pinch of salt

2 cups (500 mL) puffed brown rice

2 tablespoons (30 mL) hemp hearts

1. In a food processor, pulse together sunflower seed butter, dates, cocoa powder, honey and salt until smooth. The mixture will be quite thick.

2. Transfer mixture to a medium bowl. Stir in puffed rice and hemp hearts until well combined. I find it easier to use my hands for this part. The mixture will resemble a stiff cookie dough.

3. Scoop out by the tablespoonful and roll into balls, pressing the mixture firmly together.

STORAGE
These bites will keep in an airtight container for up to 7 days or in the freezer for up to 3 months.

HOMESTEADING

How to Build Raised Garden Beds

As a child, I remember watching my mother coax our garden to flourish in raised garden beds on our rocky, windswept property. It's a practical way to garden, as the beds help to prevent soil erosion and keep out weeds. The soil warms earlier in the season, meaning you can plant sooner. Raised beds also aid good drainage and look nice and tidy in rows.

When Danny and I began developing our urban homestead, I was adamant about putting in four large raised beds as one of our early projects. Raised beds can be supported with boards or rocks, raked into hills or built as sturdy wood boxes dug into the ground. The latter is how we built ours. Raised beds can also be tucked in along a fence or next to a patio, which looks lovely; just be sure they receive at least six hours of sunshine a day. Space them with enough room to pass a lawn mower down the pathways in between. Here are a few more tips on building raised beds.

- Four feet (1.2 m) is the widest you want to build your boxes, so you can comfortably reach the middle of the garden from either side. You can make the boxes as long as you want. We built ours with a 6-inch (15 cm) ledge all around, where I can perch to work the soil and plant without straining my back. It's also a delightful place to set a cup of coffee and begin the day with the sun on my face.

- You are essentially building a bottomless box. Measure twice, cut once! We used 4- × 6-inch rough-cut hemlock beams, as we wanted a sturdy garden that would stand the test of time. We also put drainage holes in the bottom tier to make sure the beds didn't become bathtubs when it rained. Your local lumber yard or home renovation store will have a selection of plank sizes to choose from.

- Before adding soil, place a layer of heavy cardboard down in the bottom of the bed. It will keep the weeds from coming up in full force (don't worry, it will compost eventually). Buy the best organic soil you can afford. Good soil will supply you with the best produce and is well worth the investment.

KIDS CAN
learn life lessons
from the garden

Our boys were naturally curious about gardening when we built our raised beds. They helped to hammer the spikes into the wood, and rode on the neighbor's small backhoe when he moved our load of dirt for us. I think they envisioned a cornucopia from the garden—rows of perfectly straight corn, Bugs Bunny carrots by the bushel and green beans reaching to the sky—but reality provided a few lessons along the way.

One spring, five-year-old Mateo planted peas, pushing dozens and dozens of hard, shriveled seeds into the earth and patting to cover. He watered the patch enthusiastically, and we had so much warm sunshine that their bright green shoots soon popped up. Before long, they were three inches high and we talked about how they would flower and then produce a pod that matures.

He was primed for the picking when a routine morning watering showed that groundhogs had ravaged the shoots. Every single little plant had been nibbled down to a stub, barely visible in the earth. It took him only a few seconds to process what had happened. His eyes filled with tears, but as I moved in to console him, he turned, slowly walked toward our garden shed and disappeared inside. Incredibly, he reappeared clutching the remaining seeds.

What a lesson in tenacity! He may have muttered a few angry words against the pesky animals, but he replanted the entire patch. Luckily, it was early enough in the spring to get a second crop in the ground. I helped him plant a ring of marigold plants around the plot, which worked wonders to keep the critters at bay. We talked about prevention, faith and perseverance for both gardening and life.

His eight-year-old brother, Noah, was not without tests that season, either. His vegetable of choice was the green bean. We had planted them in a rectangular shape around stakes and he watered them faithfully. We marveled daily at their rapid growth. By mid-July, they were six feet high and flowers were beginning to bloom at the tips, waving toward the sky. I told him it wouldn't be much longer before he could enjoy fresh green beans. That was a few days before the storm hit.

We heard the tornado before we saw it. I rushed to the window just in time to see a wave of ferocious wind and rain pulling branches and bushes almost sideways and bending trees into unnatural lows. One second, the massive willow edging the yard was waving wildly, the next it was lying across thirty feet of our lawn—with the raised-bed gardens completely flattened underneath. As I frantically gathered three children in my arms to huddle away from the windows, I thought of Noah's beans. I thought of my tomatoes and cucumbers too, and all other life in my carefully tended garden. I couldn't help but feel a pang for what was sure to be a total loss.

Sure enough, the bean patch was damaged beyond repair. Plants were uprooted and ground into the soil. With a growing season as short as ours, we could not replant at the beginning of August. There would be no harvest that year, save for the root crops.

Afterward, Noah and I talked about planning for the unexpected and how gardening was about something so much bigger than what we could control. It was a lesson in thankfulness (better the garden flattened than our home) and an opportunity for us all to examine the silver lining. It's not always easy to see the hidden blessings in life's hardships, but this one was literally staring us in the face on the morning after the storm. Danny and a neighbor were busy clearing the tree and repairing the fence, and they did so in *full sunlight*. Where the towering willow had formerly shaded the garden substantially, warm light now fell full on the soil. Although we had lost much that July, the accident dramatically increased our chances for growing bigger and better crops in seasons to come.

I knew my boys would be ready to plant alongside me.

SUMMER

4
BACKYARD GRILLING

Grilled Green Bean and Portobello Salad with Feta • Peach-Glazed Grilled Salmon Fillets •
Roasted Peach Barbecue Sauce • Tim's Asian Fusion Wings • Cheeseburgers with Smoky Onions •
Cucumber and Bell Pepper Relish • Grilled Stone Fruit Salad • Cucumber Honeydew Agua Fresca

Open-fire cooking was the grilling method in my childhood, and dinner often took place just a few steps beyond our kitchen garden and down the path to the rocky beach, where my parents had a makeshift outdoor kitchen. It was my job to collect the driftwood along the lakeshore for the fire, which my father laid in a ring of bedrock, while my mother tossed a salad of our own garden lettuce and sweet green peas.

The lake was the calmest in the evening. Loons caused the only ripples as they cut through the surface with their telltale black-and-white-speckled coats before diving deep again, fishing for their supper. Across the bay, my older brother and sister cast lines in the still water from their canoe, fishing for our own dinner. Lingcod, pike and lake trout all lived in Lake Laberge, and we feasted on them all summer long.

My brother Josh cleaned the fish then and there on the shore, and we rinsed their cavities in the ice-cold lake until the water ran clear through their gills. We laid a grate over the coals, stuffed the fish with fresh herbs and set them to grill on the grate. The catch of the day never took long to cook, and soon we peeled back the blackened skin and lifted generous fillets of flaky white fish off the backbone. I piled my plate high with salad and grilled fish, kicked off my flip-flops and stepped into the canoe. I liked to perch on the bow while I ate, trailing my feet in the water and lazily drifting a few feet from shore. The conversation of my family floated across the water toward me, along with the last puffs of smoke from the fire.

It was in restaurant kitchens where I expanded my grilling repertoire, striving for flawless marks on a stack of New York strip loin steaks or the perfect char on a platter of calamari. I blackened poblano peppers and onions for a fire-roasted salsa, discovering how heat brings out the sweetness in the peppers and caramelizes the onions to perfection. I learned the art of seasoning, developing a crust, and how to rest meats before serving. I got many burns in along the way, and shed a lot of tears from the smoke, but there is no better way to pick up grilling tips (page 73) than from practicing night after night for dozens, sometimes hundreds, of customers.

Nowadays, I couldn't imagine cooking at home without a grill. In spring, I load it up with asparagus and spring onions, to be finished with merely a drizzle of olive oil and a sprinkling of salt. All summer produce gets a turn on the grill, from nectarines and peaches in a lazy summer dessert (page 88) to tender green beans and mushrooms in a warm salad (page 76). Between the fruit and the vegetables are mounds of sticky chicken wings (page 82) and generous hamburgers (page 85), hanging out together in their smoky habitat and driving everyone wild with their smells. Occasionally I'll grill a whole fish, like we did when I was a child, but most often I'll brush salmon fillets with a homemade roasted peach barbecue sauce (page 78) and serve it to some very happy customers I like to call my family.

Open-fire cooking is still my favorite way to barbecue. Nothing else provides that intense smoky flavor, so utterly typical of the outdoors. I like the way it requires all of my attention— maintaining the fire, rotating the ingredients, staying out of the smoke, and checking for cooking temperature. I must stay by the fire and tend to the cooking, and yet it is always a relaxing task.

The art of the summer potluck barbecue

The ketchup-spitting, relish-slopping activities that occur pool-side from June through August bring a bad name to grilling. Gray, prefrozen hamburger patties from the superstore contain goodness knows what and taste like cardboard even when slathered with condiments. With hot dogs now linked to cancer, it's a wonder they are still handed out to children every weekend at practically every social event. This isn't grilling, it's a cooking cop-out.

Still, gathering with friends is my favorite part of summertime, so I embrace the potluck barbecue: it's a stress-free way to entertain. A simple sharing of tasks keeps the gathering under budget and the workload manageable.

When it comes to potlucks, you, as the host, must take on the main dish. Friends from out of town and sleep-deprived new parents can contribute the drinks or a sliced melon, others can provide a salad or dessert, but you should always prepare the protein. But don't do as I did once, and prepare grass-fed beef kebabs for twenty guests. It seemed like a good idea on paper, but during the party I found myself standing alone outside in the rain, grilling some sixty skewers. I didn't trust anyone else to grill the meat (all that money!). Some birthday that was.

To guarantee a successful—and manageable—spread, here are a few suggestions:

- **Planning a casual gathering with another couple?** Prepare Peach-Glazed Grilled Salmon Fillets (page 78) and Grilled Green Bean and Portobello Salad with Feta (page 76). Set a nice table and have your guests bring the wine and dessert.

- **Entertaining 6 to 8 people?** Make a big batch of Tim's Asian Fusion Wings (page 82). Toss a dozen ears of corn on the grill as well. Pass out napkins and eat everything with your hands. Wash it down with a pitcher of Cucumber Honeydew Agua Fresca (page 90), spiked with gin, ideally.

- **Going big with 12 or more guests?** Make Cheeseburgers with Smoky Onions (page 85), shaped in advance, and handed over to the nearest person to grill while you prep the condiments. You'll get bonus points for homemade hamburger buns (page 298), although you've already won by serving hamburgers made with pastured beef. Ask guests to contribute assorted salads and fresh fruit for dessert. If you have any wiggle room in the budget, prepare a pitcher of Stone Fruit Sangria the day before (page 133) and settle back for a beautiful evening.

GRILLING 101

The grill isn't just for steaks anymore. Grill your salads, toast the burger buns, get some blackening on that fish, and while you're at it, grill your dessert on the embers. Here are a handful of tips I've gleaned from restaurants, home and just standing by the barbecue at gatherings and chatting up the grill master.

TOOLS

Start with the right tools. You can get by with just a pair of tongs, but the rest of these items come in handy, too.

- Long-handled tongs
- Flexible offset spatula
- Lighter wand
- Grill pan or basket
- Silicone pastry/basting brush
- Aluminum foil
- Pepper mill

STEAK

- Bring your meat up to room temperature and rub steaks with oil before grilling. This will help keep the meat moist and prevent sticking on the grate.
- Season steaks with salt and pepper just before grilling.
- Preheat your grill thoroughly. Sear the steaks on one side for about 2 minutes. Flip and cook for an additional 2 minutes.
- Keep the lid closed to allow heat to build up all around the meat. Move the steaks to a cooler part of the grill, turning them 60 degrees for diamond-pattern grill marks. Continue to monitor until the desired doneness is reached.
- Use a meat thermometer in the thickest part of the steak, and remove the steaks from the grill when they're about 5°F (2 or 3°C) below the target temperature. A rare steak is 125°F (48°C), so remove it when it's 120°F (50°C).
- Allow steaks to rest for 5 minutes before enjoying.

VEGETABLES

- Use vegetables of equal size (or cut as needed) to ensure equal cooking time.

- Brush oil on the vegetables to keep them from sticking to the grill or grill basket.

- Keep an eye on the grill if you're unsure of cooking time. Vegetables should be tender when pierced but not falling apart.

- Vegetables require varied cooking times. Group them according to required grill time, beginning with those that cook the longest. Firmer vegetables, such as root crops (carrots, sweet potatoes and beets) need low, even heat for at least 10 minutes per side. Less dense produce such as asparagus and young green beans can be cooked over moderately high heat for 4 to 5 minutes.

- If threading vegetables on bamboo skewers, soak the skewers in water for at least 30 minutes before using to prevent the wood from burning.

- Keep the grill cover closed to help prevent charring before vegetables are cooked through.

GREEN SALADS

- Romaine, radicchio, endive, iceberg, kale and chard can all be grilled. A little char on the lettuce slightly caramelizes its natural sugars and heightens the flavors of grilled greens. The contrast of charred edges, soft leaves and crunchy cores makes for a salad crammed with delightful textures. Stick with varieties that can be cut into wedges with the core still intact, so the greens hold together on the grill.

- Toss or brush greens lightly with olive oil and sprinkle with salt.

- Serve grilled salads warm and keep the vinaigrette light.

HAMBURGERS

- Season the meat generously with salt, pepper and your favorite additions, but take care not to handle it too much or the burgers will be tough.

- Shape patties quite thick (3/4 inch/2 cm) so you can get a good sear on the outside before they are cooked through.

- Preheat the grill and cook burgers for about 4 minutes on one side. Then flip, add cheese if using, and finish.

- Let burgers rest for 5 minutes before eating. This rest makes a big difference in how moist the burgers will be.

FRUIT

- Choose firm, unblemished fruit that is not quite ripe but is yielding.

- Be sure to brush the grill clean, and scrape off any charred meat or fish remains.

- Keep a close eye on the fruit, as their natural sugars can cause them to burn quickly if left unattended.

- Serve grilled fruit while still slightly warm to fully capture the flavor of the fruit.

WHOLE FISH

- Plan for approximately 8 ounces (250 g) of fish per person.

- Rub olive oil on the fish inside and out. Season it generously inside and out with salt. Stuff a few sprigs of fresh herbs into the cavity; I lean toward dill, thyme, oregano and parsley.

- Diagonal cuts into the flesh will promote even cooking, but small, skinny fish cook fine without.

- Dampen a paper towel with oil, and using tongs, rub it across the grate immediately before placing the fish on it.

- Grill for approximately 5 minutes per side, or longer depending on the size of the fish.

- Finish with a squeeze of lemon and chopped fresh herbs.

GRILLED GREEN BEAN AND PORTOBELLO SALAD WITH FETA

Tossed in olive oil, sprinkled with salt and slightly charred on the grill is my preferred way to enjoy fresh green beans. A topping of creamy feta brings a flavor punch, and meaty portobello mushrooms round out this salad. Cherry tomatoes make a good substitute for the mushrooms if they are ripening in your garden right now. And of course any variety of basil will do, although Thai is my first choice for its distinctive anise-like flavor.

SERVES 4

3 spring onions or new green onions

¼ cup (60 mL) olive oil, divided

3 portobello mushrooms

1 pound (500 g) new green beans, trimmed

½ teaspoon (2 mL) sea salt, divided

½ cup (125 mL) crumbled feta

Leaves from 2 sprigs Thai basil

1 tablespoon (15 mL) balsamic vinegar

1. Preheat grill to 400°F (200°C).

2. Coat spring onions in olive oil and place on the grill. Grill for about 10 minutes or until lightly charred and softened. At the same time, grill mushrooms for 7 to 8 minutes, until they soften. Remove onions and mushrooms from grill. Cool mushrooms slightly, then cut each one into 4 thick slices. Set aside onions and mushrooms.

3. Toss green beans with 1 tablespoon (15 mL) of the olive oil and ¼ teaspoon (1 mL) of the salt. Place in a grill basket and grill for 5 minutes, turning occasionally, until beans are floppy and lightly charred in places.

4. Heap green beans and sliced mushrooms on a serving platter. Chop grilled onions and sprinkle over the salad. Garnish with feta cheese. Tear basil with your fingers and sprinkle over the salad.

5. In a small bowl, whisk together remaining olive oil, ¼ teaspoon (1 mL) of salt and the balsamic vinegar. Drizzle dressing over the salad and serve at once.

PEACH-GLAZED GRILLED SALMON FILLETS

Wild salmon runs in July, and I can recall, as a teen, balancing on a rock overlooking Moricetown Canyon in the heart of British Columbia and watching the relentless sockeye and coho attempting to navigate the falls. They flashed silver in the sun as they leapt out of the water, then disappeared again in the white foam. Salmon is one staple I introduced to our family table, and now everyone is a fan.

This recipe, with its tangy peachy barbecue sauce, won over my children to fish and continues to be a family favorite. Wild salmon is less fatty than farmed, but it still yields those irresistible crispy edges when grilled. It is best enjoyed while still medium pink at the very center.

SERVES 4

4 skin-on wild sockeye salmon fillets (6 ounces/175 g each)

1 teaspoon (5 mL) olive oil

¼ cup (60 mL) Roasted Peach Barbecue Sauce (page 81)

2 green onions, sliced

1. Preheat grill to 400°F (200°C).

2. Rub salmon fillets all over with olive oil and grill, skin side up, for about 4 minutes. With an offset spatula or tongs, carefully flip the salmon.

3. Brush generously with peach barbecue sauce. Grill for another 4 to 6 minutes, until the fish is light pink and firm to the touch. Carefully transfer to a serving platter.

4. Garnish with sliced green onions. Serve at once with additional barbecue sauce.

ROASTED PEACH BARBECUE SAUCE

While I love everything barbecue sauce stands for—lazy summer meals, finger-licking food and grilled goodness of all kinds—I skip the processed version as often as possible in favor of a homemade variety that is superior, and easy to make.

To me, it makes perfect sense to pair summer cooking with sweet summer produce, and this peachy sauce proves undeniably that the marriage is a lasting one. Charred peaches lend a sweet smokiness to this quick stovetop barbecue sauce. Cider vinegar provides the required tang, and roasted garlic and onion round out the flavor. The sauce is irresistible, even for selective palates. You'll want to keep a jar on hand all summer long, and perhaps even freeze a few for winter.

MAKES 4 CUPS (1 L)

1. Preheat oven to 425°F (220°C).

2. Wash peaches and cut in half, removing the pit. Place peach halves and onion, cut side up, in a small cast-iron skillet or baking dish; add garlic cloves and drizzle everything with olive oil. Roast for 25 minutes or until fruit is mushy and caramelized but not burned, giving the pan a shake every 10 minutes or so to move the fruit around.

3. Meanwhile, in a large, heavy saucepan, combine cider vinegar, sugar and honey; stir over medium-high heat until sugar is dissolved. Stir in tomato paste, apple juice, Dijon and pepper. Add the roasted ingredients and simmer together for 20 minutes, stirring often. The peaches, garlic and shallot will soften even more.

4. Blend sauce with a handheld blender until smooth. Alternatively, transfer sauce to a blender and purée. Add salt and taste for seasoning; add additional salt if desired. Ladle barbecue sauce into clean jars and top with lids.

2 large or 3 small ripe peaches

½ sweet onion, peeled

2 garlic cloves, peeled

1 tablespoon (15 mL) olive oil

½ cup (125 mL) cider vinegar

2 tablespoons (30 mL) dark turbinado sugar

2 tablespoons (30 mL) honey

1 can (5½ ounces/156 mL) tomato paste

½ cup (125 mL) apple juice

1 tablespoon (15 mL) Dijon mustard

½ teaspoon (2 mL) black pepper

½ teaspoon (2 mL) salt

STORAGE
This sauce will keep, refrigerated, for up to 2 weeks or in the freezer for up to 1 year.

TIM'S ASIAN FUSION WINGS

My friend Tim (and this cookbook's photographer) is the strong, silent type when it comes to grilling. One minute he'll be surrounded by a shroud of smoke, dabbling in sauces and maneuvering coals. The next minute he'll appear with a heaping bowl of fall-off-the-bone wings that are so good they quiet all conversation around the table. I've finally persuaded him to share his recipe for these finger-licking morsels.

The method for cooking the wings is just as important as the recipe itself. The trick to get desirably tender wings is to grill them at a fairly low indirect heat (350 to 375°F/180 to 190°C). This keeps them moist and avoids burning the skin or the sugars in the sauce.

SERVES 8 TO 10 AS APPETIZERS

For the marinade

¼ cup (60 mL) barbecue sauce or Roasted Peach Barbecue Sauce (page 81)

3 tablespoons (45 mL) ketchup

2 tablespoons (30 mL) sesame oil

2 to 3 teaspoons (10 to 15 mL) Sriracha (depending on how spicy you want the wings)

3 tablespoons (45 mL) raw cane sugar

Sprinkle of white pepper

⅔ cup (150 mL) soy sauce

4 pounds (2 kg) chicken wings, tips removed, cut in half at joint

For the sauce

1 cup (250 mL) red wine

2 tablespoons (30 mL) barbecue sauce

2 tablespoons (30 mL) ketchup

2 tablespoons (30 mL) honey

2 tablespoons (30 mL) soy sauce

1 tablespoon (15 mL) raw cane sugar

1 tablespoon (15 mL) sesame oil

¼ cup (60 mL) bourbon (optional)

1. MAKE THE MARINADE Mix barbecue sauce, ketchup, sesame oil, Sriracha, sugar and white pepper together until sugar is well mixed in. Add soy sauce and stir until uniform.

2. Put wings into a sturdy resealable freezer bag and add three-quarters of the marinade. Chill for at least 4 hours or overnight. Refrigerate the remaining marinade.

3. GRILL THE WINGS Preheat grill to 400°F (200°C). If you have a charcoal kettle-style barbecue, set up the fire so you have hot coals on two opposite sides of the drum.

4. Remove wings from marinade (discard the marinade) and place the wings over indirect heat, avoiding the direct heat over the coals. This will ensure a consistent and even flow of heat. Cover the grill and cook wings, basting with reserved marinade every 10 to 15 minutes, until wings are cooked through and falling-off-the-bone tender, 50 minutes to 1 hour. Maintain the temperature of the fire with additional coals as needed.

5. MEANWHILE, MAKE THE SAUCE In a small saucepan or stainless steel bowl placed on the hottest part of the grill, reduce the red wine by about half. Add barbecue sauce, ketchup, honey, soy sauce, sugar and sesame oil. Cook on a part of the grill with low heat until the sauce thickens. Stir in the bourbon, if using. Keep warm.

6. Serve wings hot with the red wine sauce on the side as a dipping sauce or poured over top as a glaze.

CHEESEBURGERS WITH SMOKY ONIONS

Burgers are my choice for many of our backyard barbecues, especially when we're hosting a big group of friends. The patties (and the hamburger buns) can be made in advance, the condiments assembled just before we eat, and then all the action happens around the grill. Caramelized onions, sweet cheddar and a tender burger unite for a truly memorable meal.

We like to keep our patties simple: grass-fed beef, an egg to keep the meat moist, a dab of Dijon for mild spiciness, and salt and pepper. Chilling the patties gives the meat a chance to rest after they're shaped, which results in a tender burger. It also allows the salt to penetrate the beef for a full-flavored burger. Homemade condiments take the burger over the top, so serve these with Cucumber and Bell Pepper Relish (page 86) and mayonnaise (page 35).

SERVES 6

1. In a medium bowl, beat egg, Dijon, salt and pepper together with a fork. Add ground beef and use a clean hand to gently incorporate the egg mixture into the beef. Don't overmix or the burgers will be overly dense. Shape the meat into 6 patties, keeping them quite thick (¾ inch/2 cm). Place on a tray, cover with plastic wrap and refrigerate for up to 6 hours.

2. Preheat grill to 400°F (200°C) or build a medium-ash charcoal fire.

3. Peel onion and trim ends. Cut in half crosswise, then slice each onion half into 3 circles; try to keep the rings intact. Brush onions on both sides with olive oil. Place onions and burger patties on the grill and cook over indirect heat for about 5 minutes. Both should get some grill marks. Flip burgers and onions and cook for another 3 to 5 minutes, or until the burgers have reached your desired doneness.

4. Transfer burgers to a platter and let rest for about 5 minutes. Top each burger with a slice of cheese and a grilled onion. Slice hamburger buns in half and lightly toast on the grill, 1 minute per side. Build burgers by placing the lettuce on the bottom (to keep the bun from getting soggy), followed by tomato and finally the cheeseburger with smoky onions. Serve at once with plenty of homemade mayonnaise and relish.

1 egg

1 teaspoon (5 mL) Dijon mustard

½ teaspoon (2 mL) salt

¼ teaspoon (1 mL) black pepper

1½ pounds (750 g) lean ground grass-fed beef

1 large sweet onion, such as Vidalia

1 teaspoon (5 mL) olive oil

6 large slices white cheddar cheese

6 Buttermilk Oat Hamburger Buns (page 298)

6 large lettuce leaves

1 large tomato, sliced

CUCUMBER AND BELL PEPPER RELISH

Relish has always been the squeeze bottle I avoid on the condiment table, with its iridescent green chunks and watery pea-green liquid. *Non, merci!* However, this homemade sweet relish is an entirely different garnish with its zippy tang and sweet crunchiness. Try it once and you'll be certain to add this to your must-make list every summer. We keep several jars in the pantry year-round and heap it on everything from salmon burgers to beef lettuce wraps.

MAKES 3 (1-PINT/500 ML) JARS

2 pounds (1 kg) pickling cucumbers

¼ cup (60 mL) pickling salt

1 tray of ice cubes

2 red bell peppers

1 large sweet onion, such as Vidalia

1½ cups (375 mL) cider vinegar

1 cup (250 mL) raw cane sugar

2 tablespoons (30 mL) yellow mustard seeds

1 teaspoon (5 mL) celery seeds

1 teaspoon (5 mL) coriander seeds, slightly crushed

1 teaspoon (5 mL) granulated garlic

STORAGE
Relish will keep on a pantry shelf for up to 1 year. Remove rings and label the jars with the date.

1. Wash cucumbers and trim ends. Grate in a food processor or on a box grater. In a medium bowl, layer shredded cucumber, pickling salt and ice cubes. Cover with a tea towel and refrigerate overnight. This technique draws the moisture out of the vegetables and helps to produce a pickle with a good crunch to it.

2. In the morning, drain shredded cucumber in a colander. Rinse well under cold running water, squeezing the cucumber as you go to release as much brine as possible. Working in batches, gather the cucumber in your hands and give it a final squeeze to remove as much water as possible. Place in a bowl or large measuring cup. You should have about 2½ cups (625 mL).

3. Review canning basics on page 146 and prepare a hot water bath with three 1-pint (500 mL) jars and lids according to step 2 on page 147.

4. While your processing water is coming to a boil, seed and core the red peppers. In a food processor with a slicing attachment, shred red peppers and onion into slivers.

5. In a large, heavy pot, combine red peppers, onions, vinegar and ½ cup (125 mL) water. Bring to a boil, then reduce heat and simmer for 15 minutes, stirring often. Stir in sugar, mustard seeds, celery seeds, coriander seeds and granulated garlic. Bring back to a boil and stir until sugar is dissolved, about 1 minute.

6. Gently tip drained cucumbers into the pot and use a wooden spoon to distribute them evenly in the liquid. Simmer for 5 minutes. The cucumbers will change color from bright to dull green, which is normal. Remove from heat.

7. Working with one jar at a time, remove jar from hot water and place a wide-mouth funnel into the top. Using a ladle, fill jar with relish, leaving ½ inch (1 cm) headspace. Use a wooden chopstick or plastic straw to evenly distribute the vegetables and eliminate air bubbles. Seal the jar. Repeat with remaining jars.

8. Process for 10 minutes in hot water bath according to steps 4 and 5 on page 147. Wait at least 1 week before eating to allow relish to cure.

GRILLED STONE FRUIT SALAD

I brought this salad to a Father's Day barbecue one year, where it was met with a lukewarm reception. Until everyone tasted it, that is, and declared grilled fruit salad the perfect summer dessert: light, refreshing and bright with flavor. Grilling brings out the natural sweetness of fruit, as well as adding a subtle smoky taste. After its time over the heat, the stone fruit is refreshed with a squeeze of citrus juice and a grating of zest. Serve with vanilla ice cream for a true summer treat.

Choose stone fruits that are still firm, so they won't turn to mush when you grill them. Cherries can be halved and pitted, but put them in a grill basket or you'll lose them in the coals.

SERVES 6

An assortment of fresh stone fruit:
  2 each of peaches, plums,
  nectarines and apricots
1 teaspoon (5 mL) olive oil
Pinch of sea salt
1 pint fresh raspberries (optional)
2 limes
3 tablespoons (45 mL) liquid honey

VARIATIONS
Chopped or torn mint is an excellent flavor pairing with grilled fruit. A few leaves are often enough, as you don't want the mint to overpower the fruit. Wrap servings of fruit salad in a crêpe and top with whipped cream or homemade yogurt (page 301) for a pretty brunch dish.

1. Preheat grill to 425°F (220°C). Wash fruit and cut in half, removing the pits. Cut peaches into quarters. Place all the fruit in a large bowl and toss with olive oil and salt.

2. Transfer fruit to the grill. You may want to use a grill basket for smaller fruits. Grill for 2 to 3 minutes per side or until the natural sugars have caramelized and the fruit shows some grill marks. It doesn't have to cook completely, merely warm through and get a bit of char.

3. Remove fruit to a cutting board. Cut into large chunks and place in a serving bowl. Add fresh raspberries, if using.

4. Zest both limes over the fruit. Squeeze the juice of 1 lime over the fruit. Drizzle honey over the fruit. Toss gently and serve while still warm.

KIDS CAN
learn about eco
awareness by composting

In second grade, Noah had a marvelous teacher who was most thorough in teaching about environmental issues. Our son was so attentive to the needs and hurts of the Earth that for a while he berated us for everyday necessities such as driving our car and using electricity.

We finally had to point out all the ways that we *were* making an effort to be environmentally conscious at home, both indoors and out. We started with the loathed compost bucket that he and his brother took turns emptying into the bins at the back of the property. We moved on to recycling, our rain barrels (page 131) and the garden. Even the campfire, where we occasionally grilled or baked food in the ashes using wind-felled trees instead of a propane barbecue, was a lesson in earth matters. Eventually we appeased him, and now he eagerly participates in light chores around the homestead.

Since we sort our compost, recycling and garbage at the source, it's been important to teach the children what goes where. We compost three seasons of the year, and it dramatically cuts down on our garbage output, not to mention it provides us with rich fertilizer for our garden and food for our chickens.

So, what can you compost? Here's a general idea. The kitchen generates most of the indoor compost, with the occasional stack of newspaper, and the garden and yard provide most of the rest.

- Fruit and vegetable peels and scraps
- Bits of paper, napkins, etc.
- Tea bags
- Coffee grounds and paper filters
- Egg shells
- Peanut shells

- Houseplant trimmings
- Garden trimmings
- Grass
- Leaves
- Pine needles
- Decaying wood

We leave out anything that will attract pests, such as bones, dairy and cooked food. When we add kitchen scraps, we add a layer of leaves, mulch or yard trimmings to bury them. Layering the scraps helps them decompose faster as well as keeping odors down and pests at bay.

Even the smallest of yards has space for a compost bin. If you live in a condo or apartment, some Canadian cities collect organic and other compost material along with recycling and garbage. Check with your municipality for details.

CUCUMBER HONEYDEW AGUA FRESCA

After a certain tree fell on our garden one summer, the cucumber was the only vine to survive. It bounced back and thrived. Garden produce never tasted so good as our redemptive harvest that year, and this recipe was among our favorites featuring the stalwart cucumber. Making agua fresca is a great way to infuse summer drinks with seasonal flavors, use local produce and skip the artificial ingredients contained in most store-bought beverages. For a summery cocktail, add a splash of gin.

MAKES 6 CUPS (1.5 L)

1 ripe honeydew melon

2 cucumbers, washed

¼ cup (60 mL) lime juice (about 3 limes)

Pinch of salt

2 tablespoons (30 mL) liquid honey (optional)

STORAGE

Agua may be prepared ahead without the ice and kept refrigerated for up to 6 hours. Just before serving, add ice and stir well.

1. Slice honeydew in half lengthwise and remove the seeds. Cut into 1-inch (2.5 cm) slices, then remove the skin with a paring knife. Trim ends from cucumbers and coarsely chop.

2. Combine melon and cucumber in a blender and blend until smooth. Pour into a fine-mesh sieve or cheesecloth and let drain for at least half an hour. Discard the pulp. You should have about 4 cups (1 L) of bright green juice.

3. Pour the juice into a pitcher and add the lime juice, salt, 2 cups (500 mL) of water and 2 cups (500 mL) of ice. Stir well. Taste, and add honey for sweetness if desired. Serve garnished with a few slices of cucumber and lime.

5
DAYTRIPS

Quick Pickled Gingered Baby Carrots • Sugar Snap Pea, Tomato and Orzo Salad •
Backpacker's Banh Mi • Gingered Beef and Cheesy Bean Burritos • Orangette Chocolate
Oat Bars • Maple Marshmallows • Roasted Cherry Molasses Cookies •
Cold-Brewed Iced Coffee • Cold-Brewed Iced Tea

Nothing stimulates the appetite like the great outdoors, which is why it's important to pack a well-rounded meal or three when you're daytripping. Whether you are sitting lakeside or perched on a peak with a terrific view, eating under the open sky is a fun opportunity to mix up the typical dinner-table fare.

Danny and I didn't always live on a third-of-an-acre homestead. As newlyweds, we crammed ourselves, Danny's bulky engineering textbooks and our wedding presents into a third-story apartment in the heart of Montreal's Plateau district. We were frequent daytrippers in those days, seeking to escape the city and explore the surrounding countryside: wineries to the south, orchards to the north and plenty of farm stands and flea markets along the way.

With fellow hiking friends, we planned excursions to each of the small mountain ranges within driving distance of the city, packing the various necessities, including some nourishing meals. I'll never forget the time I left my hiking boots at home—but remembered our generous lunch. I had to trek ten kilometers in my Birkenstocks through rock, forest and bog, but boy did we eat well. Crusty baguettes sliced and crammed with smoked meat, pints of strawberries from roadside stands, and stacks of homemade molasses cookies.

I've always been a planner, which is why most of the recipes in this chapter can be prepared the night before. Now we're a family of five, it pays to be organized so nothing of importance gets left behind. Danny and I split up the tasks: he packs the large camping essentials, like the tarp, ax and maps. I pack an enormous cooler with food and drink, and also think to bring dry clothes, bug repellent and my favorite pocketknife. The children run around like crazy in the excitement of the moment but are ultimately responsible for life jackets, sand toys and a hat on their head. We don't always succeed, but every summer we try hard to team up on packing the station wagon.

Trail food can be as simple as a bag of trail mix and an apple, but with a little planning, it's easy to elevate a hiker's lunch into something that both refuels and satisfies. Orangette Chocolate Oat Bars (page 103) provide energy and sustenance, not to mention holding up well *en route*. Backpacker's Banh Mi (page 98) can be consumed while on the go, either in the car or on the trail. Once you've reached your destination and built a fire (page 110), Gingered Beef and Cheesy Bean Burritos (page 100) nestle up together on the coals for a satisfying hot meal at the end of a long day. Of course, any summer's eve around a campfire wouldn't be complete without a s'more. For this occasion, I pack homemade Maple Marshmallows (page 104), thin squares of dark chocolate and a sleeve of graham crackers.

I go along with a lot of things just for the food—Super Bowl parties and wedding showers both come to mind—but good eats are not a requirement to get me out into nature. I'm happy with just the sun filtering through the trees, showering diamonds on our reflections in a quiet stream as we hear bullfrogs begin their evening chorus. A well-packed food hamper is the icing on the cake. This chapter has everything you need for a well-planned and delicious daytrip.

QUICK PICKLED GINGERED BABY CARROTS

I'm not sure how these homemade pickles can have such an addictive quality to them, but perhaps it is because they have such a refreshing crunch. Or maybe because the ingredient list is short and they are a cinch to make. After one batch you'll see for yourself how utterly irresistible they are and soon you too will be tossing these pickled carrots into salads, tucking forkfuls into sandwiches and wrapping them up in rice paper.

MAKES 1 (1-PINT/500 ML) JAR

1. Combine rice vinegar, sugar, sea salt and 1/2 cup (125 mL) water in a small saucepan. Bring to a boil, stirring to dissolve the sugar. Remove from heat and add the ginger slice. Cover and let infuse while you prepare the carrots.

2. Slice carrots into thin slabs, and then cut those slabs into 2-inch (5 cm) matchsticks. Pack carrots into a clean 1-pint (500 mL) wide-mouth jar.

3. Pour vinegar brine over carrots and seal the jar. Allow carrots to cool completely at room temperature and then refrigerate. Pickle for 24 hours before consuming.

3/4 cup (175 mL) rice vinegar

2 tablespoons (30 mL) raw cane sugar

1 teaspoon (5 mL) sea salt

1/4-inch (5 mm) slice fresh ginger

8 ounces (250 g) baby carrots, scrubbed

VARIATION
For Pickled Daikon, replace half or all of the carrot with daikon radish cut into matchsticks.

STORAGE
These pickles will keep in the refrigerator for up to 4 weeks.

SUGAR SNAP PEA, TOMATO AND ORZO SALAD

Delicious as a main dish as well as a side, this is our go-to summer pasta salad. I may change up the fresh garden herbs, add asparagus or substitute feta cheese for the Parmesan, but no matter the variation, it's always gobbled up. Slow-roasted tomatoes are flavor-packed little morsels that add a dynamic bite and a pop of color to the salad. I am convinced this salad is even better after an overnight chill to let the flavors meld together, so make extra for leftovers. The sugar snap peas won't be as bright in color, but the flavors sure will sing. Pair it with campfire-grilled lamb sausages for a Mediterranean-style cookout.

SERVES 4 TO 6

1. Preheat oven to 275°F (140°C).

2. Slice tomatoes in half end to end and place them cut side up on a rimmed baking sheet. Season with sea salt and freshly ground black pepper and drizzle with 1 tablespoon (15 mL) of the olive oil. Slowly roast for 4 hours; the tomatoes will collapse but not completely dry out. Cool the tomatoes on the baking sheet. (Tomatoes may be roasted up to 3 days ahead. Refrigerate in an airtight container.)

3. Bring a large pot of salted water to a boil. Meanwhile, trim the ends of the snap peas and slice them into 1/4-inch (5 mm) rounds. Add the orzo to the boiling water. Cook, stirring occasionally, for 7 1/2 minutes. Add the snap peas and cook for an additional 30 seconds. Drain orzo and peas well, then transfer to a baking sheet and spread out to cool completely.

4. Zest lemon into a large bowl; juice it into the bowl. Finely chop basil and add it to the bowl. Grate garlic into the bowl using a microplane, or crush it in a garlic press. Add the sea salt, pepper, and remaining 3 tablespoons (45 mL) olive oil. Mix well until dressing is smooth and a little creamy.

5. Add cooled pasta and peas and mix well with the lemon-basil vinaigrette. Toss in the roasted cherry tomatoes, Parmesan and pine nuts. Mix well again to combine. Taste for seasoning and adjust if necessary. Serve at room temperature.

1/2 pint (250 mL) red cherry tomatoes

Sea salt and freshly ground black pepper

4 tablespoons (60 mL) extra-virgin olive oil, divided

1 cup (250 mL) sugar snap peas

1 cup (250 mL) orzo pasta

1 small lemon, scrubbed

10 to 12 large fresh basil leaves

1 small garlic clove

1/2 teaspoon (2 mL) sea salt

1/4 teaspoon (1 mL) freshly ground black pepper

1/4 cup (60 mL) freshly grated Parmesan cheese

1/4 cup (60 mL) pine nuts, toasted

STORAGE
This salad will keep in an airtight container in the refrigerator for up to 2 days.

BACKPACKER'S BANH MI

There's something about getting out in the great outdoors that leaves me completely famished. I've learned to satiate hiking-induced hunger by packing one of the most satisfying sandwiches around—the banh mi. It has crunch and crust, sauce and spice, and it packs in enough protein to get you back down the mountain. My version is by no means authentic, but the point is to get a lunch together and get out the door as quickly as possible. So I buy my pork and pâté, but make my carrot pickles a few days ahead (page 95). It's a compromise I can live with, especially when I'm taking in the view on a warm summer day.

I'm happy with how the baguette holds up on a hike, but if you are serving these at home, you may want to go with a softer submarine-like roll.

SERVES 4

1 tablespoon (15 mL) sour cream

1 tablespoon (15 mL) mayonnaise (page 35)

1 teaspoon (5 mL) Sriracha

1 crusty baguette

1 jalapeño pepper

2 mini cucumbers

4 ounces (125 g) country-style pâté

8 ounces (250 g) thick-cut deli roast pork

½ cup (125 mL) Quick Pickled Gingered Baby Carrots (page 95)

¼ cup (60 mL) fresh cilantro leaves

1. Stir together sour cream, mayonnaise and Sriracha in a small bowl. With a sharp bread knife, slice the baguette from end to end like a large subway sandwich, but don't cut it all the way through. Generously spread the Sriracha mayonnaise on both cut sides of the loaf.

2. Thinly slice jalapeño in rounds. Slice cucumbers in quarters lengthwise. Spread pâté along the bottom of the bread and top with roast pork. Making sure all ingredients are fairly evenly distributed, lay cucumber strips on the pork and top with pickled carrots. Tuck in cilantro leaves and jalapeño slices.

3. Cut baguette in half crosswise and then in half again to yield 4 large sandwiches. Wrap in parchment paper and toss in your backpack. Eat with gusto.

KITCHEN TIP

If the mornings before your hike are as rushed as mine, you won't have time to go out for a fresh baguette. Buy one in advance, slice it in half lengthwise and freeze it wrapped in plastic wrap. Thaw it slightly just before you leave, and build your banh mi on a partially frozen loaf. This will keep your meats and greens cooler for longer as you trek to your destination.

GINGERED BEEF AND CHEESY BEAN BURRITOS

These zesty, hearty burritos are one of our campfire staples, wrapped in foil and baked in the ashes until toasty. The outer edges of the tortilla get crispy, while the filling bakes into melted cheesy deliciousness. They can also be heated over coals on the barbecue for a similar smoky flavor. Although you can use any flour tortilla, we fill homemade tortillas (page 294) with a gingered beef and bean filling and add a generous helping of cheddar cheese. With a side of salsa, sour cream and guacamole, there is nothing lacking on our campout.

I make these burritos mildly spiced for the children but you can spice them up as much as you like with additional chili powder. The amount of ginger may seem insignificant, but you'll be surprised at how it enhances the overall mild heat.

SERVES 8

1 tablespoon (15 mL) olive oil

1 pound (500 g) ground grass-fed beef

1 small onion, finely chopped

1 can (14 ounces/398 mL) pinto or black beans, drained and rinsed

2 garlic cloves, minced

1 teaspoon (5 mL) salt

1 teaspoon (5 mL) ground cumin

1 teaspoon (5 mL) chipotle chili powder, or to taste

½ teaspoon (2 mL) dried oregano

½ teaspoon (2 mL) grated peeled fresh ginger

8 Soft Wheat Flour Tortillas (page 294) or 8-inch (20 cm) whole wheat tortillas

2 cups (500 mL) grated cheddar cheese

STORAGE

Cooked filling will keep in the freezer for up to 3 months. Filled burritos can be wrapped in foil and refrigerated overnight or frozen for up to 3 months. Reheat from frozen in a 400°F (200°C) oven for 30 minutes.

1. MAKE THE FILLING   Heat a large cast-iron skillet over high heat and add the olive oil. Sear beef, breaking the meat apart with a wooden spoon, for about 5 minutes or until the meat is browned and broken up. Drain off excess fat or liquid.

2. Stir in onion. Cook over lowest heat for another 5 minutes, until onions are soft.

3. Add beans, garlic, salt, cumin, chili powder, oregano, ginger and ½ cup (125 mL) water; stir to combine. Cook mixture for 5 minutes over medium heat, stirring occasionally. The water will evaporate and the meat will begin to crisp slightly on the bottom. Turn off heat and taste the filling. Add more salt or chili powder to suit your tastes. Let the filling cool, then either transfer to containers to freeze or prepare burritos.

4. TO ASSEMBLE   Place 8 sheets of foil, each about 1 foot (30 cm) square, on the countertop. Place a tortilla in the middle of each sheet; place ¼ cup (60 mL) of the grated cheese in the center of each tortilla. Divide the beef filling between the tortillas. Roll halfway, tuck in the filling, then fold over the sides and continue rolling into a burrito. Wrap each burrito tightly in foil using a similar procedure.

5. Cook burritos over smoldering coals away from the main flame for 4 minutes. Flip and cook for another 4 to 5 minutes. Remove from heat. Allow to cool slightly and serve hot. Alternatively, grill over indirect heat on a barbecue for at least 10 minutes per side. Keep the grill covered.

HOMESTEADING

Common Sense for Backyard Vegetable Gardening

Each summer brings new challenges in the garden, yet every failed crop leads to a lesson learned. I've had a few of those in my time, but along the way I've also learned so much about backyard vegetable gardening. Here are my best tips.

- Pay attention to sun and shade requirements and your garden will thrive. A basic rule is that if you grow a plant for the fruit or the root, it needs full sun. If you grow it for the leaves, stems or buds, shade is just fine.

- If you plant it, they will come—garden pests, that is. Edging plots with "spicy" flowers such as marigolds and nasturtiums helps to keep critters out, but keep flowers pruned back so they don't get out of hand.

- Grow an assortment of herbs in pots or planters on the back patio. They thrive in containers and are easily accessible for cooking and grilling.

- Water your garden in the morning or evening, never in the heat of the day. It gives the water a chance to seep down to the roots instead of evaporating on the surface of the soil.

- Mulch the garden beds to keep the weeds down. Use leaves, compost, woodchips or straw.

Don't forget that kids can plant a garden too. Every spring I involve my boys, and together we plant produce that will capture their imaginations and tickle their palates.

- Begin indoors, with simple seed-germination projects. This offers plenty of teaching moments and builds excitement for summer planting.

- Decide together what to grow, but lean toward aboveground vegetables, meaning no root crops. Kids will be more enthusiastic about gardening when they can watch their plants and produce form and grow.

- Vegetables like peas, cucumbers and beans are fast growing and good for kids. Plus, there is always the pick 'n' eat factor that is so attractive.

- Don't worry about spacing in the beginning. Let the children go nuts with the seed packages and thin later.

ORANGETTE CHOCOLATE OAT BARS

A simple recipe for prunes stewed with oranges and cinnamon from the food memoir *A Homemade Life*, by Molly Wizenberg, aka Orangette, inspired these grab-and-go bars. After the tenth time I topped yet another bowl of those stewed prunes with granola and a handful of almonds, it occurred to me that the whole combination would make a marvelous granola bar. My hunch was right. Dark chocolate melts into the soft prunes to complement the fragrant orange slices. Oats provide the bulk of the bar, and slivered almonds lend a welcome crunch. These energy-giving bars are an ideal snack for day hikes or biking excursions thanks to their portability. They hold up well in a tin and stay soft for up to three days should you get lost in the woods. But that's not going to happen now, is it?

MAKES 12 GRANOLA BARS

1. Place prunes in a medium saucepan and sprinkle with sugar. Cut orange in half from top to bottom. Squeeze the juice of one half over the prunes. Lay the other half down on its cut side and slice crosswise into very thin half-moons; remove any seeds and add oranges to the prunes. Add just enough water to barely cover prunes. Bring to a very low simmer over medium heat; the water should be barely moving. Reduce heat to low and simmer very gently, uncovered, for about 45 minutes. The water will mostly evaporate and the fruits will become tender but still hold their shape.

2. Meanwhile, preheat oven to 325°F (160°C). Grease a 9-inch (23 cm) square baking pan and line with parchment paper, leaving an overhang on two sides.

3. Spread rolled oats on a rimmed baking sheet and toast in the oven for 5 to 7 minutes, until the oats take on a slightly golden hue. Cool. Repeat with almonds, but do not mix the two ingredients. Leave the oven on.

4. Place the hot prunes and oranges and any liquid in a food processor. Add chopped chocolate and salt. Process until the mixture is smooth and chocolate has melted. Add toasted oats and pulse 6 or 7 times to combine and partially chop the oats. Add almonds and pulse just once to combine.

5. Using a sturdy rubber spatula, scrape the mixture into the prepared pan. Spread it evenly to the four corners of the pan. Bake for 25 to 30 minutes or until firm to the touch. Cool bars in the pan for 10 minutes. Invert onto a rack and peel off parchment. Let cool completely, then cut into 12 bars.

8 ounces (250 g) pitted prunes

½ cup (125 mL) raw cane sugar

1 orange, scrubbed

2½ cups (625 mL) old-fashioned rolled oats

¾ cup (175 mL) slivered almonds

4 ounces (125 g) dark chocolate, chopped

½ teaspoon (2 mL) salt

STORAGE
These bars will keep in an airtight container for up to 3 days or in the freezer for up to 2 months.

MAPLE MARSHMALLOWS

I began experimenting with homemade marshmallows right around the time we dug a fire pit in our backyard, and it became apparent that our future would hold many fireside evenings with the children. Admittedly, the final recipe has turned Danny and me (and many of our friends) into marshmallow snobs, but we're okay with the moniker.

At Christmas time I like to flavor the 'mallows with peppermint, and for birthdays I dip them in dark chocolate, but by far maple is the most popular flavor. In spring, I replace the water in the recipe with fresh sap from our maple trees and dub them Double Maple. But no matter the flavor, they always end up toasted and sandwiched between graham crackers with a sliver of dark chocolate: the taste of summer evenings defined in a sticky mouthful.

MAKES 24 (1-INCH/2.5 CM) MARSHMALLOWS

1 tablespoon + 2 teaspoons (25 mL) plain gelatin

1 cup (250 mL) granulated sugar

1/3 cup (75 mL) pure maple syrup

Pinch of salt

1/2 teaspoon (2 mL) pure maple extract

Icing sugar, for dusting

STORAGE

These marshmallows will keep in an airtight container at room temperature for up to 2 weeks.

1. Line a 9-inch (23 cm) square baking pan with plastic wrap and brush lightly all over with vegetable oil. Pour 1/4 cup (60 mL) cold water into the bowl of an electric mixer fitted with the whisk attachment. Sprinkle with the gelatin. Let stand for 10 minutes.

2. Combine granulated sugar, maple syrup, salt and 2 tablespoons (30 mL) water in a small saucepan. Bring to a boil and boil rapidly for 90 seconds, stirring occasionally.

3. With the mixer on medium speed, slowly pour boiling syrup into gelatin. Increase speed to high and beat marshmallow for 8 minutes. Add maple extract and beat to combine.

4. Scrape marshmallow fluff into the greased pan and spread as evenly as you can with a spatula. Lightly oil another sheet of plastic wrap and place it over the marshmallow in the pan. Smooth the top with your hands and press the marshmallow into the corners of the pan.

5. Let marshmallow set for about 6 hours at room temperature; overnight is even better. Remove top layer of plastic wrap and dust marshmallow with icing sugar. Invert pan onto a cutting board and remove bottom layer of plastic wrap.

6. Dust marshmallow slab with icing sugar. With a sharp chef's knife, cut into strips about 1 inch (2.5 cm) wide. Rotate cutting board and cut marshmallows again into 1-inch (2.5 cm) cubes. Dredge each piece of marshmallow in icing sugar.

ROASTED CHERRY MOLASSES COOKIES

In this recipe, a classic molasses cookie is a complementary match for a slow-roasted summer stone fruit. Before you dismiss them as too much work, what with pitting cherries and all, give them a try—you'll discover a spicy treat that is simply scrumptious. Studded with sweet roasted cherries, these cookies stay soft for several days, making them ideal candidates for a weekend summer road trip.

MAKES 30 COOKIES

1. Position oven racks in the middle and lower levels of oven and preheat oven to 300°F (150°C). Line a rimmed baking sheet with parchment paper.

2. Wash, stem and pit cherries. Cut cherries in half and spread them out in a single layer on the baking sheet. Roast for 1 hour 30 minutes to 1 hour 45 minutes, or until the cherries are partially dried but still soft. Cool on the baking sheet. You will have about ¾ to 1 cup (175 to 250 mL).

3. Increase oven to 350°F (180°C). Line two rimmed baking sheets with parchment paper.

4. In a large microwavable bowl, melt butter. Beat in molasses with a wooden spoon or spatula. Pour in sugar and mix well. Lightly beat egg and stir it into the molasses butter.

5. In a smaller bowl, sift flour with ginger, cinnamon, allspice, salt and baking soda. Add to the wet mixture and stir just until combined. Add roasted cherries and stir to combine. The dough will be very soft.

6. Drop dough by tablespoonfuls onto the baking sheets, 8 cookies per sheet. Bake, rotating the baking sheets from top to bottom rack halfway through the baking time, for 12 to 14 minutes, depending on how soft you want them—a shorter cooking time yields a softer cookie. Cool for a few minutes on the pan, then transfer to a rack to cool. Repeat with remaining dough.

3 cups (750 mL) cherries (preferably Rainier, but Bing will work)

¾ cup (175 mL) unsalted butter

⅓ cup (75 mL) molasses

1 cup (250 mL) raw cane sugar

1 large egg

2 cups (500 mL) all-purpose flour

1 teaspoon (5 mL) ground ginger

1 teaspoon (5 mL) cinnamon

½ teaspoon (2 mL) ground allspice

½ teaspoon (2 mL) sea salt

½ teaspoon (2 mL) baking soda

STORAGE
These cookies will keep in an airtight container for up to 5 days or in the freezer for up to 3 months.

COLD-BREWED ICED COFFEE

Aside from a tall glass of water, cold-brewed iced tea and coffee may be the simplest beverages you can make over the summer. I'm seldom without at least one of these drinks in the fridge from June to September, awaiting company to drop over or to fuel my day's hike. Why boil water to make coffee, only to cool it down again over ice? "Cold-brewed" means coffee that is steeped in cold water for about 12 hours. All that is left to do is simply strain and savor. Because of the lengthy brew time, cold-brew requires some planning, but that is the only downside.

SERVES 6

1 cup (250 mL) coarse coffee grounds

About 4 cups (1 L) cold filtered water, plus more for serving

Ice cubes

Milk, to taste (optional)

Sweetener, to taste (optional)

1. Pour coffee grounds into a 1-quart (1 L) jar. Fill jar to the very brim with cold filtered water. Cover and let steep in the refrigerator for 12 hours.

2. Strain steeped coffee through a coffee filter, a fine-mesh sieve or a sieve lined with cheesecloth. Alternatively, pour contents into a 4-cup French press and slowly plunge the coffee. Now you have iced coffee concentrate.

3. To serve: In a tall jug, mix equal parts coffee concentrate and cold filtered water. If desired, add milk and sweetener. Top with ice and serve, or pour into a thermos and add it to your backpack or camping cooler.

KITCHEN TIP
Dilute a little concentrate with water, then pour into ice cube trays and freeze. Add iced coffee cubes to your next iced coffee and enjoy it full strength.

STORAGE
This concentrate will keep in the refrigerator for up to 1 week.

COLD-BREWED
ICED TEA

In the scorching midsummer weeks, I make this delicious tea in a gallon jar to ensure there is always some around, and yet it still disappears quickly. I enjoy it daily with a little maple syrup, a squeeze of lemon and ice. Serve it for your next summer soiree alongside a pitcher of fresh mint to garnish.

SERVES 8

1. Place tea bags in a half-gallon (2 L) jar or jug. Fill with cold filtered water. Cover and let steep in the refrigerator for 12 hours. Remove tea bags.

2. To serve: Pour into a glass. Add a slice of lemon if desired. Add sweetener if desired. Top up with ice. If you are transporting the tea for a daytrip, pour it into a thermos or a recycled plastic bottle and chill until departure.

4 tea bags
8 cups (2 L) cold filtered water
Lemon slices (optional)
Sweetener, to taste (optional)
Ice cubes

STORAGE
This drink will keep in the refrigerator for up to 5 days.

KIDS CAN
learn basic fire-starting skills

At a summer camp competition when I was about twelve, we had to build a fire with a single match, fetch water from a nearby lake and bring it to a boil in a can over our fire. The first camper with a rolling boil in his or her tin can won the challenge. I didn't win, but I was the only girl to get a roaring fire started.

Children, boys especially, have a natural curiosity about fire. Instead of squelching it, why not teach them the basics of fire building, tending and safety? While you are building their confidence and teaching responsibility, lend them your Swiss Army knife and teach them to whittle and carve, too. After that? Dig for worms and bait a fishing hook. Before long they will be cooking the day's catch for you.

Nowadays some preteens have unsupervised access to YouTube and the rest of the Web through smart phones and tablets, but parents are reluctant to hand over a box of matches or a pocketknife even under supervision. Why not spark their imaginations with age-old tasks that have been keeping hands busy for forever? Of course it is important to remember that each child matures differently, and as parents we have to determine whether each is ready to be entrusted with the tasks of fire building, fishing and wood carving.

Fire-starting basics

Start your fire in a fire pit. Avoid unnecessary destruction and scorching by using the provided fire pits in a campsite. If you are roughing it, build your fire on soil, and form a ring around the fire pit with rocks.

Have a wind barrier. Most fire pits are dug into the ground to provide a natural barrier, or have one built around them from a metal ring, rocks or brick. This will protect the area around the fire from wayward sparks, but it will also protect the fire from wind, causing it to burn slower, which is ideal for cooking.

Clear the area around the fire pit of dried leaves, dead grass and sticks. Be sure no overhead branches are low enough to catch fire. Fetch a bucket of water and have it nearby at all times, should you need to quickly douse the flames for any reason.

Gather the fire starter. This is a perfect job for little helpers. Assemble dried leaves or moss for the tinder, and small sticks and twigs for the kindling.

Use dry, dead wood for clean burning. For the best burn, always use dry wood, not green wood. If no dry wood is readily available, fetch it from the campsite office or from a nearby general store.

Build the fire teepee-style. Begin with the tinder in the middle of the fire pit and lay the kindling on top in teepee-style. Start with the smallest twigs and work up to the larger ones. Finally, place your dry logs around the outer edges. Light a match or two to the tinder in the center of the teepee.

Grade your coals. Use a stick or your tongs to maneuver the coals into a higher level at the back end of the fire pit and lower level at the front. This will give you the equivalent of High, Med and Low heat settings. Or level the coals to your preference and move the still-flaming logs and tinder to the back.

Burn garbage such as paper plates, used napkins and food scraps, but never toss Styrofoam, plastic or aluminum foil into the fire.

6
HARVEST DINNER

Summer Squash and Parmesan Galette • Quick Marinated Golden Beets • Caprese Salad with Fresh Thyme Drizzle • Corn on the Cob with Chili Basil Brown Butter • Lemon Oregano Roast Chicken • Blueberry-Peach Mascarpone Trifle • Stone Fruit Sangria

"Tell us about when Auntie Miranda ate your very first strawberry!" my boys occasionally ask me. Their eyes twinkle and they giggle as I recount the tale of my first solo gardening attempt as a child, and the pesky baby sister who crawled into the patch when I wasn't looking and plucked the first fruits of my labor. She couldn't resist the ripening red berry, and I learned the lesson early to watch for garden predators, although she was the cutest I ever did see.

I always had my hands in the dirt in the family garden when I was growing up, because my mother required a certain number of hours each week from each of us children. We thinned the carrots, pruned the cucumbers or—most loathsome of all—weeded. It was drudgery back then, kneeling in the hot earth. Funnily enough, as soon as I became a mother myself, a garden of my own was high on the priority list.

It started with pots of herbs on the partially shaded back balcony of my minuscule third-floor apartment in Montreal. They grew mightily, despite the pesky back-alley squirrels that would bury their nuts in my soil. When Danny and I bought our first house, the basil and parsley expanded to include tomatoes, zucchini and Swiss chard. I wanted my children to make that key connection between field and fork, so I involved my young boys in the sowing that summer, purposely planting vegetables that would capture their imagination. Sure enough, they were in the garden every day, exclaiming over the reach of the beans, the height of the corn and the girth of the pumpkins.

Our plot was crowded and sloppy, and plants were often trampled before they had a chance to mature, but we made the best memories. That season was truly essential to get the boys hooked on vegetable gardening. Mateo was disappointed that my rainbow chard did not, in fact, grow in every color of the rainbow, but their bright stems charmed him all the same. I've seen how growing their own vegetables has helped curb my sons' fears of new foods. Now they love big summer salads as much as their parents do. I believe kids are simply unaware of the effort that goes into producing fruits and vegetables if they are not exposed to gardening and harvesting. Also, what better way to explain seasonal eating than by observing it first-hand as the seasons change?

Today my backyard garden is nourished, but sometimes neglected. It's wild, yet still yielding. Every year is a learning experience, with mistakes and triumphs recorded and lessons heeded. My love for tender new lettuce leaves, sweet baby carrots and an abundance of fresh herbs propels me to plant every spring, even though that initial push to get the crops planted—four raised garden beds, front flower beds, hanging baskets and deck pots—feels like a superhuman accomplishment every season.

As any homesteader can attest, there are mishaps in the garden along the way, most of which are unpredictable. Who could have foreseen that a small tornado would whip through our neighborhood on a scorching July afternoon and topple a hundred-foot willow tree onto just-ripening tomatoes and flowering beans? Some plants survived the crushing weight of all those branches that took out three sections of fence, but there was much less of a harvest that autumn. We learned about garden regrowth and recovery, and discovered the silver lining in the setback: now the raised beds bask in several more hours of sunshine a day, an advantage that directly translates into more produce for us. I guess I can put sweet peppers on the planting list for next spring after all.

DINNER IN THE GARDEN

Every year, in late August, we host a harvest dinner, complete with rented stemware and matching tablecloths. The event coincides with my birthday, but I don't care for presents or candles; I just want as many of my friends as possible around one long table out by the garden.

It is a communal effort. It has to be. Danny looks after the lawn care, lugs our tables outdoors and rounds up every chair we own: twenty-three. The children scrub new potatoes and shuck corn on the cob down by the compost heap. I massage a fresh herb marinade into free-range chickens and roast them until their skin is crispy (page 126). My sister opens jars of pickles and cuts fat slices of deeply hued tomatoes for the salad. Our menu highlights all that is sweet and good in the prime of summer: tender ears of corn, plump tomatoes, summer squash and wild berries. Selections from the herb garden shine in every dish—thyme, oregano, basil, mint and dill—further enhancing the season's best.

Friends trickle into the yard as the heat of the day is fading away, bringing desserts that quickly fill up an entire side table: warm cherry clafoutis, a streusel-topped apple cake and other seasonal sweets. They help themselves to a glass of Stone Fruit Sangria (page 133) and a wedge of warm Summer Squash and Parmesan Galette (page 119). The older children skip off to play on the swings and scope out the enormous tent we've set up for them. The toddlers tumble down the lawn to the chicken coop and poke grass through the wire at the hens.

Soon we take our places around the long table. Danny pours the wine and I carve the Lemon Oregano Roast Chicken (page 126). We gather to celebrate the season—a pause, amid the nonstop action that is summer life with active young children and demanding jobs, to relish our family food life. We toast the harvest, good health and the chubby-faced babies who have joined us this year. The children eat at their own table on the grass, screeching with laughter at each other's funny faces. Before long they abandon their overturned wine box seats and scatter for a scavenger hunt. The last light of the day is bathing the forest in golden tones as they disappear into the trees, hunting for feathers, moss and wild berries.

Around our table, a few of the babies have been lulled or nursed to sleep, and we savor jars of cold creamy trifle layered with soft peaches and sweet wild blueberries (page 129). Behind us, the hens climb their ramp like obedient children and disappear to roost for the night. As the early fireflies blink and the old toads by the back stream raise their voices in chorus, Mateo crosses the lawn in a blur and plants himself next to my chair. There are smudges of dirt—or is it chocolate?—on his flushed cheek. "But Mama! We forgot the most important thing! We forgot to sing 'Happy Birthday' to you."

Always the thoughtful one! I hug him close and murmur that it is okay, that I'm perfectly content in the moment, surrounded by friends and family lingering around the table on a warm evening.

Actually, I can't think of a better way to bid late summer adieu.

SUMMER SQUASH AND PARMESAN GALETTE

If you ever want to feel like an accomplished gardener, find a sunny corner where you can plant one or two summer squash and then sit back and reap the harvest for all of August and well into September.

Zucchini plants are prolific producers, and before you know it, you'll be searching for recipes and new ways to keep the extra squash from going the way of the compost heap. This tart is among the most simple and delicious uses of them all. It will have zucchini naysayers reaching for a second slice and devotees asking for the recipe. It doubles and triples well, but is best enjoyed on the same day it is made.

SERVES 4 AS AN ENTREE, 6 AS AN APPETIZER

1. On a floured surface, roll puff pastry into a 12- × 5-inch (30 × 12 cm) rectangle ¼ inch (5 mm) thick. Slide onto a rimmed baking sheet and refrigerate while you prepare the zucchini filling.

2. Preheat oven to 400°F (200°C).

3. Melt butter in a small skillet over medium heat. Add onion and cook for 5 minutes, stirring occasionally.

4. Meanwhile, trim ends from zucchini and slice into coins about ¼ inch (5 mm) thick. Reserve a handful (about ½ cup/125 mL) for the topping. Add the rest to the onions. Sauté zucchini coins over medium heat for about 8 minutes. They will wilt and release much of their moisture, which will evaporate. Add the chopped dill in the last minute of cooking. Remove from heat and cool the vegetables while you prepare the filling.

5. In a medium bowl, beat together egg, mayonnaise, lemon zest, salt and pepper. Stir in panko and Parmesan. Add the sautéed vegetables and combine well. Spread filling over the puff pastry, leaving a ½-inch (1 cm) border around the edge.

6. Layer reserved raw zucchini on top. Drizzle with olive oil. Bake for 35 minutes or until the pastry is puffed and golden brown. Cool for a couple of minutes, then garnish with fresh dill if desired. Slice into wedges and serve warm or at room temperature.

5 ounces (150 g) puff pastry

1 tablespoon (15 mL) salted butter

¾ cup (175 mL) finely chopped sweet onion (about ½ medium onion)

2 small zucchini (preferably 1 yellow and 1 green; about 7 ounces/200 g)

1 tablespoon (15 mL) chopped fresh dill, plus more for garnish

1 large egg

2 tablespoons (30 mL) mayonnaise (page 35)

1 tablespoon (15 mL) lemon zest

¼ teaspoon (1 mL) salt

¼ teaspoon (1 mL) freshly ground black pepper

¼ cup (60 mL) panko crumbs

¼ cup (60 mL) grated Parmesan cheese

1 teaspoon (5 mL) extra-virgin olive oil

STORAGE

This galette will keep, sliced and tucked into an airtight container or well wrapped in plastic wrap, in the refrigerator for up to 1 day. Reheat in a 350°F (180°C) oven for 10 to 12 minutes before serving.

QUICK MARINATED GOLDEN BEETS

I suppose you could call me a pickled beet snob, because this recipe produces the only variety I can stand behind. I don't care for the traditional sweet version, the ones that smell like cloves and dye your teeth pink. Instead, I wholeheartedly embrace their golden counterpart, lightly pickled in a rice vinegar brine. I like to finely chop the beets and fold them into a tartare or tuna salad. Thinly sliced, they dress up a sandwich and contribute a zesty tang. Slice them into wedges and pair them with endive, pears and walnuts for a quick salad. And I highly recommend them straight from the jar, preferably with a pickle fork.

MAKES 2 (1-PINT/500 ML) JARS

1½ pounds (750 g) baby golden beets
½ cup (125 mL) raw cane sugar
1 teaspoon (5 mL) sea salt
2 cups (500 mL) rice vinegar

STORAGE
These beets will keep in the refrigerator for up to 3 months.

1. Place baby beets, untrimmed, in a medium pot and cover them with 2 inches (5 cm) of cold water. Partially cover and bring to a boil over high heat. Reduce heat and simmer until beets are tender when pierced with the tip of a knife, about 1 hour.

2. Combine sugar, salt and rice vinegar in a medium saucepan. Bring to a boil, stirring until sugar is dissolved, then remove from heat. Keep hot. Thoroughly wash and dry two wide-mouth 1-pint (500 mL) jars and lids.

3. When beets are cooked, drain them, and working under cool running water, slip the skins off by rubbing them gently. Trim the ends of the beets with a paring knife. Divide beets between the jars. You may want to cut them in half, depending on how "baby" they really are.

4. Pour the hot vinegar brine over the beets and seal jars. Leave to cool on the counter, then place them in the refrigerator.

CAPRESE SALAD WITH FRESH THYME DRIZZLE

When you eat with the seasons, there is an inevitable lineup of dishes that absolutely must come into rotation a handful of times before they leave for another whole year. This salad, featuring sweet cherry tomatoes and heaps of fresh, fragrant thyme, is one of those essential eats. Among many other things, Montreal chef Philippe de Vienne introduced me to *salmoriglio*, an intense dressing of pulverized herbs, garlic, sea salt and olive oil, balanced with fresh lemon juice. It is a condiment I prepare frequently over the summer, spooning it on top of grilled fish, brushing it onto steamed corn and drizzling it over warm garden tomatoes. In this recipe, featuring fresh thyme, the sauce elevates a simple Caprese salad and adds a welcome punch of flavor to the mild mozzarella.

SERVES 6

1. Using a small mortar and pestle, grind thyme and salt together until it is a dark green paste. Add garlic and pulverize again. Drizzle in lemon juice and olive oil and mix to combine. Finish the dressing by sprinkling with black pepper.

2. Slice cherry tomatoes in half and in a medium bowl toss them with 2 tablespoons (30 mL) of the dressing. Arrange tomatoes on a platter or in a serving bowl. Tear apart fresh mozzarella and arrange it over and around the tomatoes.

3. Drizzle salad with remaining dressing and top with more fresh thyme if desired. Serve at room temperature.

VARIATION
For a delicious take on Greek salad, substitute fresh oregano for the thyme and round out the salad with Kalamata olives, sliced cucumbers and slivers of red onion.

2 tablespoons (30 mL) packed fresh thyme leaves, plus more for garnish

½ teaspoon (2 mL) sea salt

1 small garlic clove, peeled

1 tablespoon (15 mL) fresh lemon juice

3 tablespoons (45 mL) extra-virgin olive oil

¼ teaspoon (1 mL) freshly ground black pepper

2 pints (1 L) cherry tomatoes of all colors

8 ounces (250 g) fresh mozzarella or buffalo mozzarella

CORN ON THE COB WITH CHILI BASIL BROWN BUTTER

Fresh sweet corn needs little embellishment during its summer reign, but occasionally it is worth the effort to dress up the traditional daub of butter. In this recipe, the butter is browned to give it a nutty flavor that pairs splendidly with the tender corn. A touch of heat from a fresh chili awakens the taste buds even more, while a sprinkling of fresh basil brings the focus back to the garden. My three children cut their teeth (literally) on our local sweet corn, and it remains a firm favorite every August.

SERVES 4

4 ears of sweet corn

2 teaspoons (10 mL) sea salt, plus more for sprinkling

2 tablespoons (30 mL) salted butter

½ red serrano chili

2 tablespoons (30 mL) chopped fresh basil (about 12 large leaves)

VARIATION
For a milder heat, use a jalapeño pepper. For even more heat, reach for a fiery Thai chili.

KITCHEN TIP
The natural sugars in corn begin to break down as soon as the ear is harvested, so for tender sweet corn, buy it as fresh as possible and plan to cook it the same day.

1. Shuck corn and trim ends. With a sharp chef's knife, cut each cob in half. Place in a large pot and cover with cool water. Sprinkle 2 teaspoons (10 mL) salt into the water and bring to a boil over high heat.

2. Meanwhile, melt butter in a small saucepan over low heat. Cook for about 5 minutes, or until it is dark golden in color and has a pleasant, nutty aroma. Do not let it burn. Remove from heat.

3. Remove seeds from the chili and slice into strips. Add chili to the browned butter and let it infuse while the corn cooks.

4. As soon as the water is boiling, set a timer and cook for 5 minutes if the corn is very fresh, 7 minutes if it is not as tender. Transfer the corn to a serving dish.

5. Stir chopped basil into the chili brown butter. Drizzle butter over corn and gently toss. Serve hot, sprinkled with a little sea salt.

LEMON OREGANO ROAST CHICKEN

Roast chicken may seem an odd choice for a sit-down summer dinner party, but I make it because of its sheer simplicity and its ability to feed a crowd with minimal effort. In the past I have been tied to the barbecue, going for the perfect doneness and grill marks, with stinging eyes and singed fingertips. No, I'd rather sip sangria with my guests, thank you very much. Roasting one or four chickens requires about the same amount of effort and time, and everyone is a fan of this comfort food. Besides, my overgrown oregano patch would never get under control were it not for this recipe that uses it in abundance.

I marinate my chickens overnight, which makes for both succulent birds and less work for me on party day.

SERVES 6

½ cup (125 mL) loosely packed fresh oregano leaves

Zest of 2 lemons

Juice of 1 lemon

4 garlic cloves, peeled

2 tablespoons (30 mL) olive oil

1 tablespoon (15 mL) sea salt

1 teaspoon (5 mL) freshly ground black pepper

1 whole organic chicken (about 5 pounds/2.2 kg)

1. In a small food processor, combine oregano, lemon zest, lemon juice and garlic. Pulse a few times until mixture looks like pesto. Add olive oil, salt and pepper. Pulse to combine.

2. Pat chicken dry with paper towel. Rub about half the lemon-oregano marinade all over the chicken. Gently lift the skin on either side of the neck and rub plenty of marinade directly onto the breast meat, under the skin. Don't forget to get some inside the cavity. Refrigerate for 2 to 8 hours, uncovered, to allow marinade to infuse the meat. If marinating overnight, place the bird in a large resealable freezer bag and seal.

3. Remove chicken from fridge about an hour before cooking. Bringing the meat up to room temperature (about 70°F/21°C) will both cut down on the cooking time and ensure the meat cooks evenly. Preheat oven to 450°F (230°C).

4. Place chicken in a roasting pan, breast side up, and roast for 10 minutes. Reduce heat to 400°F (200°C) and roast for an additional 1 hour and 30 minutes to 1 hour and 45 minutes, checking for doneness after 1¼ hours. Test for doneness in any of the following ways: juices run yellow, not pink, when drumstick is pierced; the drumstick wiggles freely at the joint when manipulated; or a meat thermometer registers 170°F (75°C) when inserted into the thickest part of the thigh (but not touching the bone).

5. Transfer chicken to a platter or cutting board, cover loosely with foil and let stand for 20 minutes before slicing. Carve at the table, or portion the chicken and arrange the meat on a platter. Serve hot.

BLUEBERRY-PEACH MASCARPONE TRIFLE

Once upon a time, my mother, sisters and I competed in a reality cooking show that was televised nationally on Food Network Canada. As a nod to our British heritage (on my father's side) and the season (it was August), we prepared a peach trifle for dessert, only the stone fruits provided by the production team were rock hard—so hard, in fact, that my sister Haidi cut herself while trying to pit them. Despite hand-whipped cream and a dreamy white chocolate mascarpone mousse, the flavor of those unripe peaches just never came through. We lost the challenge, to a sticky Nutella-banana concoction our competitors produced.

This is my redemptive recipe. It combines the best of midsummer fruits and pairs them with a decadent white chocolate mascarpone mousse in an elegant dessert. Wild blueberries are prolific at the local markets here in Quebec, but if you must use cultivated, be sure to wash and dry them well beforehand. And for goodness sake, buy the best peaches available. The trifle refrigerates overnight to allow the flavors to develop and to help the cream set up.

SERVES 6

1. Wash and dry 6 half-pint (250 mL) wide-mouth jars or ramekins. Remove skin from peaches using a vegetable peeler or a sharp paring knife. Quarter each peach, remove the pit, and slice each quarter into 1/2-inch (1 cm) wedges.

2. Melt butter in a large skillet over medium-high heat. Add the peaches, toss once or twice to coat with butter, and then spoon in 1 tablespoon (15 mL) of the honey and 1 tablespoon (15 mL) of the Grand Marnier. Cook, turning occasionally, for about 3 minutes, even less if the peaches are very ripe. You don't want them to turn to mush. Transfer peaches and their juices to a plate and let cool completely.

3. In a medium microwavable bowl, combine 1/4 cup (60 mL) of the cream and the white chocolate chips. Cook on medium power for about 1 minute, until the chocolate is melted. Whisk until smooth. Whisk in mascarpone until mousse is smooth and cool to the touch. Set aside.

continued...

3 large ripe but firm peaches

1 tablespoon (15 mL) unsalted butter

2 tablespoons (30 mL) liquid honey, divided

2 tablespoons (30 mL) Grand Marnier or other orange-flavored liqueur, divided

1¼ cups (300 mL) heavy (35%) cream, divided

1/3 cup (75 mL) white chocolate chips (2 ounces/60 g)

1/2 cup (125 mL) mascarpone, at room temperature

3 tablespoons (45 mL) orange juice

6 ladyfingers

1 cup (250 mL) wild blueberries, plus more for garnish

4. Combine orange juice and remaining 1 tablespoon (15 mL) Grand Marnier in a shallow bowl. Break ladyfingers in half crosswise, dip and roll in the juice, then place in the bottom of the jars, 2 halves per jar. Divide the cooled peaches and the pan juices evenly among the jars. Evenly divide the white chocolate mascarpone mousse among the jars. Finally, divide the blueberries among the jars.

5. Seal the jars and refrigerate for at least 6 hours or overnight. The white chocolate mousse will thicken and the flavors will come together.

6. Just before serving, whip the remaining 1 cup (250 mL) cream to soft peaks. Fold in the remaining 1 tablespoon (15 mL) honey and taste. Add more honey if desired. Uncover the trifles and top generously with the honey whipped cream. Serve at once, garnished with additional blueberries if desired.

VARIATION
If you prefer an alcohol-free dessert, use orange juice in place of the liquor.

KITCHEN TIP
Trifles will keep, covered and refrigerated, for up to 2 days.

HOMESTEADING

Installing Rain Barrels

Capturing rainwater to use in our garden is just one small way we are making a positive impact on the environment. Rainwater is free of chlorine and fluoride additives. Rainwater also lowers the pH of the soil, giving plants more access to nutrients.

Here are a few things to think of when considering rain barrels for your property.

Use: Our rain barrel is strictly for garden use and providing water for the chickens. If you plan on drinking your water, there are many other considerations, such as filtration and disinfection, as well as your roof composition to think about (asbestos tiles, anyone?).

Overflow: Depending on the size of your roof and the amount of rain you get, the barrel can fill within minutes. An overflow connection allows you to direct the excess water away from your house and foundation, a really smart idea.

Size: We live in a fairly humid area, so we are using our 55-gallon (208 L) barrel just to "top up" our garden if we have a dry week or two. If you want to irrigate exclusively with rainwater, you will have to analyze the historical rainfall for your area, as well as your usage requirements, and become familiar with terms such as "evapotranspiration rate."

Location: Your barrel can be buried or sit above ground, but you also have to consider where you're going to put it. We chose an aboveground model that is gravity-fed, and anchored it right next to the house under a modified downspout, but this could be a problem if you want to collect large amounts of rainwater or irrigate with devices that need extra power. An underground cistern will certainly hold more, but it will cost more as well. You also want to ensure that any overflow is routed far away from your foundation, especially if you have a basement.

Top mesh and cover: This is important to keep leaves and other natural debris from entering your barrel and making "tea," as well as preventing the barrel from becoming a mosquito farm. I was very concerned about the safety of our children, but our barrel has a child-, pet- and pest-proof lid.

Maintenance: In summer, if your barrel is becoming infested with algae or mosquitoes, you'll need to maintain it regularly by keeping it clean with a quick scrub and rinse and making sure the wire mesh is intact. In winter, because we get freezing temperatures, we have to prevent the barrel from expanding with ice and breaking. It's best to remove the spout, clean out the barrel, invert it, and then reattach the old downspout and attachments to let the snowmelt and ice melt stay far away from the house's foundation.

Sourcing: Our rain barrels are originally from Greece, used to import pickled peppers and olives. Ironically, these upcycled barrels are now watering my cucumbers. Some municipalities provide barrels for a nominal charge, and ours will reimburse the cost up to $70. To find recycled plastic barrels locally, visit www.gardenwatersaver.com.

STONE FRUIT SANGRIA

I made a large batch of this sangria for our very first harvest dinner years ago. It was full of sweet peaches, halved cherries and sliced plums, and was a big hit with guests, especially those boozy bits of fruit at the bottom of their glasses. At some point, we started feeling the effects, and as darkness fell, we thought it would be great fun to build a bonfire. However, we had no fire pit at the time. Someone suggested we use our old garden wheelbarrow, and so we laid a fire in the bottom. For a time, all was well. But that was before the smell of burning rubber filled the air and the wheelbarrow's tire exploded, causing us to leap into action and douse the fire. Allow me to point out that this was a group of, ahem, engineers who devised this brilliant plan. Perhaps we can blame the sangria for the oversight.

SERVES 10 TO 12

1. Wash all the fruit. Cut stone fruits in half and remove pits. Lay plums, peaches and apricots on their cut side and slice them into thin half-moons. Very thinly slice lime and lemon (a serrated knife works best).

2. In a large pitcher or 8-cup (2 L) glass jar, combine sliced stone fruit, sliced citrus and cherry halves. Add wine, honey, triple sec and lime juice. Stir well, then cover and refrigerate overnight.

3. Just before serving, stir in Aranciata and mint leaves. Serve with plenty of ice.

4 plums

2 peaches or nectarines

2 apricots

1 lime

½ lemon

2 cups (500 mL) halved and pitted cherries

1 bottle (750 mL) rosé wine

½ cup (125 mL) liquid honey

½ cup (125 mL) triple sec or other orange-flavored liqueur

2 tablespoons (30 mL) fresh lime juice

2 cans (11.15 ounces/330 mL each) San Pellegrino Aranciata or soda water

1 cup (250 mL) torn fresh mint, plus more for garnish

KIDS CAN
be part of the harvest
dinner, too

Have you ever attended a summer party and barely enjoyed a bite of food because the kids kept you so busy? As parents of young children, we're always making sure they get a balanced meal, looking out so they don't spill their drink, and keeping them out of trouble in general. Well, I've tested a few theories for my backyard barbecues and dinners and come up with a list of ideas for keeping both kids *and* their parents happy.

- Set up a tent and create a designated "Kids' Corner." Stock it with games, balloons and balls.

- Include your kids in the setup and preparation. Get out their sets of markers and encourage them to make up "Kids' Corner" and "Lemonade" signs. Having helped with setup, they can help their friends find a drink, a napkin or a snack.

- Set up a snacking station with finger food that appeals to children, and let them graze all evening long. The advantage is that the parents don't have to monitor (much), and the children eat when they are hungry.

- Prepare wraps, cold chicken, cheese and crackers, plenty of vegetables and fruits—basically any favorite self-serve foods that can be eaten in-hand.

- Ditch the juice boxes (too much sugar) and serve homemade lemonade (page 57) or ice water in a plastic pitcher or small camping jug with a spigot. The camping jug not only keeps the beverage cold but it is spill proof, too.

- Set a paper towel roll in a can for sticky fingers and eliminate the problem of napkins blowing away in the wind. Better yet, provide a hand-washing station in a basin with plenty of soap and towels.

- Serving a hot meal? Dish up plates for kids and feed them 15 minutes before your dinner, so parents can supervise without their own food getting cold.

- No seating? No problem. Provide a basket of quilts and blankets for children to spread on the grass, picnic-style.

- Plan a children's activity for when adults are eating. Hand out a list of items for a scavenger hunt or arrange a treasure hunt.

- If you have a large group of kids, you may want to hire a tween or teen friend to come hang out with them. You'll find parents won't mind pooling a few dollars to pay the helper in exchange for a relaxing meal.

- Lastly, from what I've observed, eating plays second fiddle to games when our kids get together with their friends, so why not let them have fun? They can always eat a square meal tomorrow, but summer is fleeting; let them enjoy it while they can.

AUTUMN

7

JAM JARS

Baba's Sweet Mustard Pickles • Fall Fruit Chutney with Cashews and Currants • Strawberry-Honey Jam with Orange Zest • Cinnamon Applesauce • Peaches Preserved in Honey Syrup • Blueberry Cardamom Butter • Make-Ahead Currant Scones • Zucchini Cornbread

It was long ago, during my mother's canning parties, when I picked up my first bits of knowledge of preserving summer stone fruits. I can distinctly remember those warm afternoons, being sticky up to my elbows, surrounded by tubs of smooth, sweet-smelling peaches, steaming pots of simple syrup and endless chatter. Perched on stools around a long steel counter, my friends and I flicked the pits from the Okanagan fruits and stuffed them, cut side down, into jars. Back then canning wasn't as high on my teen interest list as, say, boys were, but I inadvertently picked up a few tricks along the way—such as tapping the jar gently but firmly on a towel-lined counter to remove unwanted air bubbles—as one is accustomed to do when a canning culture is passed down from generation to generation.

My mother's mother—my Baba—was a Ukrainian homesteader on the Canadian Prairies, as was her mother before her. Though Baba's attentions were divided between raising her three children and teaching at the local schoolhouse, she still put up the family garden's produce every summer in great big batches. The handwritten recipes in my mother's tattered cookbook prove it, listing quantities for as many as 20 quarts per batch. Canning is a powerful connection to the past—to culture, family and heritage. I feel that connection when I make Baba's pickles (page 149), knowing she also probably stayed up late slicing cucumbers and measuring spices. Although she has passed on, I know my grandmother would be happy I am carrying on the tradition.

None of us have to trace our lineage back very far before we find an ancestor who preserved nearly everything. If you're fortunate enough to have a parent or grandparent willing to pass along the knowledge, you may want to sit down with them to learn. On my last visit to my hairdresser, she thrilled me by announcing her plans to preserve fall produce with her grandmother. Rachel is as modern hipster as they come, but she tilted back on her heels and tapped her fingers with the point of her scissors, naming off the items they planned to make: pickled beets, spaghetti sauce, grape jelly and applesauce. She was keenly aware that her grandmother was getting on in years and she wanted to retain that knowledge gleaned only from years upon years of experience.

Of course, I can my own food for plenty more reasons than sentimental satisfaction. I've learned that the experience of opening a jar of cherry preserves in January is more than just practical: it's transporting. It is deeply rewarding to select your own top-quality produce and can it at its peak of ripeness. You can be sure that the flavor of your home-canned product will mirror the quality and care that you put into making it.

Canning at home can be financially rewarding as well. Buying produce in season when it is cheap and plentiful for preserving can be an economical way to stock your pantry. And you may be surprised to discover that those decadent yet pricy jams that you eye in the local whole foods store can be easily reproduced for pocket change.

Need one more good reason to can your own food? In my books, nothing says "I love you" quite like a jar of homemade preserves. Come Christmastime, we canners have the upper hand in the gift-giving department, as a well-stocked pantry of jams, jellies and pickles ensures a solid backup plan to cover everyone on the list, last-minute hostess gifts and all.

HOW TO MAKE CANNING WORK FOR YOU

My efforts are much more scaled back than in the homesteading days of my mother and her mother. I'm a firm believer in taking on only what is realistic for me. Because canning can take place year-round, there's really no need to burn out during one particular month. No matter the season, we can always find something delicious to pack away in jars. After the rush of summer produce with its berry jams and pickle pleasures, the fall brings a selection of apples and pears to be turned into sauces, butters and chutneys, and an assortment of tomato-based products. By the time that season is over, the winter citrus has arrived, begging to be preserved as marmalades and curds. Before you know it, the rhubarb is bursting forth and with it, springtime and strawberries.

They say if you don't know where you are going, you will probably end up somewhere else, and this certainly rings true when it comes to home preserving. If you don't have a game plan, the summer can easily pass you by with little or no canning accomplished, creating a fall scramble to put food up. The key to finding a balance in canning is to start small and pace yourself. Begin the season with a practical assessment of what you want to accomplish. Be realistic. The place to do this is in your kitchen, not at the market where the beautifully arranged produce can lead you down the wrong path, so to speak. Make a list of what you want to preserve, scaling it down to include what you and your family love to eat. Ask yourself these questions:

- What was popular in the household last winter?
- What is still sitting on my shelves now?
- What was the family's least favorite canned item last year?
- What was a pain in the neck to put up?
- What was best received as gifts?

If you are a beginner, perhaps start with two projects a month: one sweet, like a Strawberry-Honey Jam with Orange Zest (page 152), and something pickled, such as the simple asparagus (page 49). In the fall, try applesauce (page 155) and closer to Christmas, a fall fruit chutney (page 150).

Don't get ahead of yourself. It sounds obvious, but bears repeating: can what is in season *now*. Talk to growers to find out how much longer specific produce will be around the market and if prices are expected to lower. I usually can my tomatoes in the last week that they are available at the market, for example, because I can get a better deal per bushel if I wait until after the season has died down. Whatever you do, have a game plan before you go to the market. Don't buy produce just because it's a deal, unless you have a little wiggle room in your schedule and are feeling like branching out from your repertoire. In that case, by all means, pick up a basket of damson plums and transform them into something spectacular.

THE JAM SWAP

An early Saturday morning spent pitting cherries, a weekend peach-preserving blitz and a late-night salsa-making party with a friend are some of the pockets of time I use over the summer weeks to pack food into jars. It pays off in autumn, when I have a season's worth of canning efforts to swap with friends. Through a swap, you will gain a wide assortment of jams, jellies and preserves if you don't have a whole lot of canning experience or time. I organize an exchange every fall, and the attendance ranges from five to twenty-five. It's a thrilling way to wrap up summer with a nod to the gorgeous produce of the season.

On the morning of the swap, I bake several batches of currant scones (page 160) and set out the best teacups. A tasting is an integral part of the swap, and we must have accompanying tea and toast. Each attendee contributes a dozen jars for swapping and one jar for tasting. If there are a large number of guests, I divide up the preserves into sweet and savory. I pair salsas, pickles, chutneys and savory spreads with corn tortilla chips, crackers, sliced baguette and a few rounds of cheese. That leaves the warm scones to transport all the jams, jellies, marmalades and fruit butters into our bellies. Somehow, every single scone gets eaten every year. Over the course of the afternoon the teapot is emptied and refilled several times over. There are precious few tea parties nowadays; what better occasion to use grandmother's china teapot?

My favorite part is eavesdropping on all the conversations happening around the oh-so-popular tasting table. It is here where the absolute best tips are swapped and recipe notes exchanged. There are exclamations over the ideal consistency of the raspberry jam and the perfectly rosy hue of the rhubarb jelly. Attempts are made to guess every ingredient in the fall fruit chutney. Suggestions for sugar substitution are inevitably offered and accepted. The air is a blur of canning jargon and it is pure bliss.

Everyone takes pride in his or her efforts. You can see it in the way the jars are carried to the table and set out in rows, with an array of decorated tops. You can read it on the faces of these DIY enthusiasts, where a gleam in their eye means "Try mine!" When the last lingering taster has dipped a final spoon into the marmalade, dotted a scone with the golden conserve and savored the last crumb, we are ready to get down to the serious business of swapping. The dining room table is groaning under the weight of all the jam jars, but in a few minutes it is all over. Each guest holds a box featuring a dozen or so varieties of homemade preserves. It feels like Christmas and we've just been richly gifted.

Here's hoping the recipes in this chapter and sprinkled throughout the book will inspire you to make a connection with an age-old practice as you stash a few jars of preserves in your pantry.

HOMESTEADING

A Canning Primer

FIVE INSTRUCTIONS FOR THE BEST RESULTS

1. Follow the recipe. Don't experiment until you have several years of canning experience under your apron ties.

2. Start small. Don't take on more than a couple of recipes per season.

3. Work cleanly. Clear clutter, scrub your work area and be as neat as possible.

4. Equip yourself. See the list below and have everything out and at the ready before you begin.

5. Find a mentor. Seek out a canning mentor if possible and observe them prepare a canning project from start to finish.

EQUIPMENT FOR HOT WATER BATH CANNING

Get well organized before beginning any canning project. Here's what you will need.

- Mason-style canning jars with sealed canning lids called "flats" (or "snap lids") and "rings" are found at most grocery and hardware stores.

- A wide-mouth funnel makes filling jars with sauces or jams easier and less messy.

- For easy removal of lids and rings from boiling water, use a magnetized lid wand or tongs.

- Use a ladle for filling jars and a saucer for resting the inevitably sticky ladle on.

- A rack in a large pot allows hot water to circulate fully around the jars and protects them from the direct heat of the burners. I use a cake cooling rack that fits my pot.

- Make sure your large pot with a lid is tall enough that your jars will be covered by about 1 inch (2.5 cm) of water when you place them on the rack.

- Rubberized jar lifters are essential for removing slippery jars from their water bath.

- Use clean cloths to wipe down jars and lids.

SIMPLE STEPS FOR CANNING IN A HOT WATER BATH

Canning in a hot water bath heats the food to a temperature that will kill any microorganisms that may grow in your food and also creates a vacuum seal in the jar.

Step 1. Start right away. It is best to can your fruits and vegetables immediately after you harvest or buy them for the highest vitamin and nutrient concentration. Avoid iron, aluminum or copper products when preparing your fruits and vegetables, as these metals can cause your produce to discolor.

Step 2. Sterilize. Wash your jars, lid rings and flats in hot soapy water and rinse. Wash any utensils or tools you will be using for the recipe. Place the rack in a canning pot or a large stock pot and put the required number of jars (without their lids) on top. Fill the pot with water and bring to a boil. Boil for 10 minutes to sterilize the jars. Leave the jars in the hot water to keep them warm and to ensure they don't become contaminated before you seal them.

Place the lid rings on the counter. Put the flat lids in a small pot and cover with an inch (2.5 cm) or so of water. Bring to a simmer and keep warm while you prepare your recipe.

Step 3. Fill jars. Once your preserves are ready, use a rubberized jar lifter to remove the hot jars, one at a time, from the hot water bath, tip them to empty, and set them on a tea towel. Use a clean wide-mouth funnel and a ladle to fill the jars. Be sure not to fill the jars completely. Produce expands during the boiling process, so adequate headspace, about ½ inch (1 cm), at the top prevents the jar from leaking or expanding and breaking the seal. Make sure there are no air bubbles along the sides of the jar by tapping the jar gently on the tea towel or by passing a clean wooden chopstick around the contents. Also make sure the produce is submerged in the liquid. Wipe the rims of the jars with a clean cloth and cap with the flat sealing lids and rings. Turn the rings only fingertip tight, meaning a light twist with the tips of your fingers.

Step 4. Process in a water bath. Return the filled jars to the canning pot using your jar lifter, and place them so they are not touching each other. Be sure the water covers the top of the canning jars by at least 1 inch (2.5 cm). Return the water to a rolling boil. Start your timer when the first bubbles start and process for the length of time specified in your recipe.

Step 5. Let jars cool. When your timer goes off, remove your jars from the bath and place them on a wood- or cloth-covered surface to let them cool. Let them sit for a day to completely cool before tightening the rings. While cooling, your jars will start to pop, creating a vacuum seal. After they have cooled, press down on the center of each lid to ensure the jar has sealed completely. Any lids that don't dip down in the middle or that spring back have not sealed. Place them in the refrigerator and enjoy them first.

Step 6. Label and store. Label your jars with the contents and the date. Write directly on the lid with a permanent marker or download and print or purchase specialty labels. Remove the rings, as it is best to store the jars without them. Wipe down the jars with a damp cloth and store your preserves in a dark, dry place until you're ready to enjoy. One year is optimum, and I frequently store for up to two.

BABA'S SWEET MUSTARD PICKLES

When my mother was growing up on the Prairies, canning food in summer was essential for keeping the family well fed throughout the winter. Her mother, my Baba, didn't mess around with small batches of anything, and stored rows and rows of preserves in their cellar. These pickles are adapted from my Baba's recipe, scaled way down from the original yield of "20 Quarts" penciled in the margin of a tattered, handwritten cookbook of my mother's.

We dig into this pickle all summer long, setting out the vegetables at each barbecue, heaping them onto burgers, you name it. In the winter, I layer the cucumber slices into egg salad sandwiches and dice up the cauliflower for tuna salad. For a taste of summer on a chilly winter day, enjoy these mustard pickles straight from the jar, preferably with your grandmother's pickle fork.

A mandoline comes in handy for slicing the cucumbers evenly.

MAKES 3 (1-PINT/500 ML) JARS

1. Cut onion and bell pepper in half and slice into ¼-inch (5 mm) strips. In a large bowl, combine onion, red pepper, cucumbers and cauliflower florets. Sprinkle with pickling salt and toss to combine. Pack ice cubes in and around the vegetables. Cover with a tea towel and refrigerate for up to 12 hours or overnight. This technique draws the moisture out of the vegetables and helps to produce a pickle with a good crunch to it.

2. Review canning basics on page 146 and prepare a hot water bath with three 1-pint (500 mL) jars and lids according to step 2 on page 147.

3. Dump the pickles into a large colander to drain off the salt water. Run under cold water for about 1 minute and move the vegetables around to rinse them thoroughly.

4. In a large pot, combine sugar, vinegar and 1 cup (250 mL) water. Bring to a boil over high heat, stirring until the sugar is dissolved. Add mustard seeds, celery seeds, peppercorns and bay leaves. Mix dry mustard with 2 tablespoons (30 mL) water and add to the pot. Bring spiced vinegar back to a boil.

5. Gently tip the drained vegetables into the spiced vinegar and use a wooden spoon to distribute them evenly in the pot. Simmer for 5 minutes. The cucumbers will change color from bright to dull green. Remove from heat.

6. Working with one jar at a time, remove jar from hot water and place a wide-mouth funnel into the top. Using a slotted spoon, pack the jar with vegetables. Ladle or pour the vinegar into the jar, leaving ½ inch (1 cm) headspace and making sure to tuck 1 bay leaf into each jar. Use a wooden chopstick or plastic straw to evenly distribute the vegetables and eliminate air bubbles. Seal the jar. Repeat with remaining jars.

7. Process for 10 minutes in a hot water bath according to steps 4 and 5 on page 147. Wait at least 1 week to allow pickles to cure.

1 medium sweet onion, such as Vidalia or Walla-Walla, peeled

1 large red bell pepper, cored

6 cups (1.5 L) pickling cucumbers trimmed and sliced about ⅛ inch (3 mm) thick

2 cups (500 mL) small cauliflower florets

¼ cup (60 mL) pickling salt

2 trays of ice cubes

1½ cups (375 mL) raw cane sugar

1½ cups (375 mL) cider vinegar

1 tablespoon (15 mL) mustard seeds

1 teaspoon (5 mL) celery seeds

½ teaspoon (2 mL) peppercorns

3 bay leaves

1 teaspoon (5 mL) dry mustard

STORAGE
Pickles will keep on a pantry shelf for up to 1 year. Remove rings and label the jars with the date.

FALL FRUIT CHUTNEY WITH CASHEWS AND CURRANTS

I always thought chutney was complicated until my culinary mentor, Philippe de Vienne, presented me with a jar of dark chutney studded with whole cashews and claimed he cleaned out the pantry to make it. Boldly spiced, with a perfect balance of sweet and tang, that jar gave me confidence to experiment with what I had on hand. I hope this recipe, adapted from Philippe's so long ago, will inspire you to do the same. Don't be put off by all the chopping. Once that is done, you toss everything into one pot and most of your work is finished.

Chutney has the sweetness and consistency of jam, but is closer to relish thanks to the addition of vinegar and spices. It is the perfect medium for using up a surplus of fall fruit. We scoop our chutney onto lamb curries and spoon it alongside roast chicken. We also dollop it atop slices of sharp cheese on grainy crackers.

MAKES 6 (HALF-PINT/250 ML) JARS

1½ cups (375 mL) raw cane sugar

1½ cups (375 mL) cider vinegar

4 cups (1 L) chopped cored apples (use a variety that will keep its shape, such as Wolf River, Russet, Gala, Idared, Mutsu/Crispin, Fuji or Spy)

3 cups (750 mL) chopped cored Anjou or Bartlett pears

3 cups (750 mL) chopped onions

1 cup (250 mL) chopped pitted dates

1 cup (250 mL) dried currants

1 cup (250 mL) unsalted cashews, split in half

¼ cup (60 mL) poppy seeds

1 tablespoon (15 mL) minced peeled fresh ginger

2 teaspoons (10 mL) garam masala

½ teaspoon (2 mL) freshly ground black pepper

1 whole star anise

1 bay leaf

1. Review canning basics on page 146 and prepare a hot water bath with 6 half-pint (250 mL) jars and lids according to step 2 on page 147.

2. Combine sugar and vinegar in a large, heavy pot and bring to a simmer over medium heat. Stir until the sugar is dissolved. Add apples, pears, onions, dates, currants, cashews, poppy seeds, ginger, garam masala, pepper, star anise and bay leaf. Mix well to combine.

3. Simmer chutney, uncovered, for 30 minutes, stirring frequently. Reduce heat to low and cook for an additional 15 minutes. Stir the pot more often as chutney thickens. The ingredients will cook down and the liquid will evaporate, resulting in a thick chutney. Remove from heat and discard bay leaf.

4. Working with one jar at a time, remove jar from hot water and place a wide-mouth funnel into the top. Using a ladle, fill jar with chutney, leaving ½ inch (1 cm) headspace. Use a small spatula or plastic bubble remover to remove air pockets. Seal the jar. Repeat with remaining jars.

5. Process for 10 minutes in a hot water bath according to steps 4 and 5 on page 147.

STORAGE

Chutney will keep on a pantry shelf for up to 1 year. Remove rings and label the jars with the date.

HOMESTEADING

Host a Pantry or Food Swap

Not everyone in your circle of friends may be interested in canning, but you can still encourage whole foods and cooking from scratch by organizing a Pantry Swap. It works like a preserves swap, only guests bring homemade pantry, fridge or freezer items to exchange. It's a great way to diversify your pantry while trading resources, time and effort.

The concept is simple: invite guests to bring ten homemade items to swap. Kindly instruct them to label and list ingredients clearly, and package items neatly. Everyone leaves with an assortment of pantry items, prepared from scratch and made with care.

Here are some ideas for your next pantry swap:

- Jars of soup (try Roasted Carrot, Parsnip and Thyme, page 268)
- Pint (500 mL) jar of pancake mix (try dry ingredients for Buttermilk Buckwheat Pancakes, page 9)
- Sealed bags with 2 balls of pizza dough (page 292) each
- Quart (1 L) jar of Dark Chicken Stock (page 286)
- A loaf of homemade bread (try Everyday Sandwich Bread, page 296)
- 2-cup (500 mL) bags of granola (try Maple Walnut Granola, page 11)
- Box of 8 granola bars (try Orangette Chocolate Oat Bars, page 103)
- Bag of 12 Maple Marshmallows (page 104)
- Half-pint (250 mL) jar of barbecue sauce (try Roasted Peach Barbecue Sauce, page 81)
- Jar of dried wild mushrooms
- Bag of dried fruit
- Spiced nuts
- Refrigerator pickles (try Quick Marinated Golden Beets, page 120)
- Jar of muffin mix
- Bag of caramel corn (try Ice Cider Caramel Corn, page 230)
- 1 quart (1 L) chili (try Maple Pumpkin Chili, page 262)
- 1 quart (1 L) Mild Marinara Sauce (page 270)
- Half-pint (250 mL) jar of mincemeat (try Cranberry Pear Mincemeat, page 176)
- Half-pint (250 mL) jar of dry cocoa mix, with recipe (try Mexican Hot Cocoa, page 207)
- A half-dozen farm-fresh eggs
- Local honey in jars
- Handmade soap
- Fresh-pressed apple cider
- Half-cup (125 mL) jar of homemade vanilla extract

Check out Food Swap Network (www.foodswapnetwork.com) to see if there is a swap near you. If not, consider starting one of your own.

STRAWBERRY-HONEY JAM WITH ORANGE ZEST

Making jam and canning is most definitely therapeutic for me. It starts with the prepping of the fruit, a task I usually take to the back patio where I can watch the kids play and multitask in the most relaxed of ways. Then I put a large pot of water on to boil, and as it gurgles on the stove, I pad around the kitchen, gathering ingredients and tools, grateful for the time and space for the task at hand. I feel a connection— to food culture, to the past, to the countless homemakers before me who put up every summer. The fruit under my hands is ripe, luscious and deserving of respect. Plus, I know that the experience of opening a jar of strawberry jam in March is more than just practical—it's transporting. So a-jammin' I go.

This jam is neither boring, common nor inferior to jazzier conserves. Honey contributes a strong flavor and marries beautifully with the berries. While many sugar-free jams tend to be a tad on the thin side, this one holds up beautifully on the blade of a knife, thanks to an extended boiling time. I spoon this jam over vanilla ice cream and add it to yogurt, but my favorite way to enjoy it would have to be slathered on a warm scone (page 160).

MAKES 4 (HALF-PINT/250 ML) JARS

6 cups (1.5 L) chopped strawberries
Zest and juice of 2 oranges
2 boxes (57 g each) pectin crystals
1½ cups (375 mL) liquid honey

1. Review canning basics on page 146 and prepare a hot water bath with 4 half-pint (250 mL) jars and lids according to step 2 on page 147.

2. Mash the berries with a potato masher and place in a large, heavy saucepan with the orange zest. Add the pectin and stir with a wooden spoon to combine. Bring to a rolling boil over medium-high heat. Stir and boil for 1 minute.

3. Remove from heat. Add honey and orange juice; mix well. Return to heat and bring to a boil again over medium heat, stirring occasionally. Boil for 10 to 12 minutes, stirring frequently to be sure it doesn't scorch. Remove from heat and skim off foam. Let stand for a couple of minutes. The jam will thicken slightly and fruit will be well distributed.

4. Working with one jar at a time, remove jar from hot water and place a wide-mouth funnel into the top. Using a ladle, fill jar with jam, leaving ½ inch (1 cm) headspace. Seal the jar. Repeat with remaining jars

5. Process for 10 minutes in a hot water bath according to steps 4 and 5 on page 147.

STORAGE

Jam will keep on a pantry shelf for up to 1 year. Remove rings and label the jars with the date.

CINNAMON APPLESAUCE

Applesauce was my hook into home preserving. The velvety sweetness and alluring blush color of a homemade version leaves the bland canned sauces in the dust. Stirred into yogurt, baked into cookies or spooned over pancakes are just a few of the ways we enjoy our applesauce. This basic step-by-step tutorial is easy to make in large batches and well worth the effort. I use Cortland apples, which are quite sweet and one of my favorite local varieties. McIntosh are excellent for sauce as well, but really, almost any kind of apple can be used for applesauce. Try using a blend of varieties for a truly unique sauce.

MAKES 4 (1-PINT/500 ML) JARS

1. Wash apples thoroughly. This is a great job for little helpers, who can also help twist off stems. Don't peel the apples—apple skins add flavor and color to applesauce.

2. Using a sharp chef's knife, quarter all the apples. With a paring knife, remove the core. Toss quarters into a large, heavy pot. Add cider and cinnamon stick. Partially cover the pot and bring to a simmer over medium heat. Reduce heat to medium-low and allow apples to cook down slowly, 20 to 30 minutes, stirring occasionally and keeping an eye out for signs of scorching.

3. Once the apples have cooked down, they are ready to be sauced. Remove the cinnamon stick and press the apple pulp through a wire sieve or a food mill.

4. Return the purée to the pot and reheat over medium-low heat. Add maple syrup and lemon juice. Cook the sauce down for a thicker consistency, about 1 hour.

5. Meanwhile, review canning basics on page 146 and prepare a hot water bath with four 1-pint (500 mL) jars and lids according to step 2 on page 147.

6. Working with one jar at a time, remove jar from hot water and place a wide-mouth funnel into the top. Using a ladle, fill jar with hot applesauce, leaving ½ inch (1 cm) headspace. Seal the jar. Repeat with remaining jars.

7. Process for 20 minutes in a hot water bath according to steps 4 and 5 on page 147.

6 pounds (2.7 kg) apples (mixed varieties, such as Cortland, Honeycrisp and Melba)

1 cup (250 mL) fresh-pressed apple cider (not hard cider) or apple juice

1 cinnamon stick

2 tablespoons (30 mL) pure maple syrup

1 tablespoon (15 mL) lemon juice

STORAGE
Applesauce will keep on a pantry shelf for up to 1 year. Remove rings and label the jars with the date.

PEACHES PRESERVED IN HONEY SYRUP

In making my mother's recipe for canned peaches my own, I've swapped the traditional sugar for mild honey syrup that pairs well with the peaches. I also like to tuck a bit of spice in the jar to infuse the syrup over the months on the pantry shelves. A little goes a long way. I'm also pro peel. Peeling isn't hard work, but it's an extra step, and one I don't deem necessary. I try to source organic fruit and I use a natural fruit and veggie soak to remove pesticides (check out www.naturecleanliving.com for one product). If you prefer not to eat the skins, simply slip them off once you have served up a bowl. The canning process loosens them right up.

Look for freestone peaches and be sure fruit is ripe before you begin.

MAKES 6 (1-PINT/500 ML) JARS

1 cup (250 mL) honey

3 quarts (3 L) firm yet ripe peaches

½ lemon

Aromatics of choice (optional; see "Suggested Flavor Parings")

SUGGESTED FLAVOR PAIRINGS

Add any one (not all!) of the following aromatics or spirits to each pint jar to infuse the peaches.

- ½ vanilla pod
- 5 whole cloves
- 1 fresh lavender sprig
- ½ cinnamon stick
- ¼ tonka bean
- slice of fresh ginger
- 2 star anise
- ¼ cup (60 mL) brandy or bourbon

1. Review canning basics on page 146 and prepare a hot water bath with six 1-pint (500 mL) jars and lids according to step 2 on page 147.

2. In a medium pot, heat honey with 3½ cups (875 mL) water and bring syrup to a boil. Reduce heat and keep hot. Slice a peach in half and remove the pit. Rub lemon half on a tray or large platter and arrange peach halves cut side down to prevent the exposed flesh from browning. Repeat with remaining peaches.

3. Working with one jar at a time, remove jar from hot water. Pack peach halves, cavity side down, into jar. Gently press down on them to fit 5 or 6 halves into each jar. Tuck your aromatic into the jar. Ladle hot honey syrup over peaches, leaving ½ inch (1 cm) headspace. Lightly tap jar on a tea towel to help dislodge any large air bubbles. Wipe rim with a clean damp cloth and seal jar. Repeat with remaining jars.

4. Process for 25 minutes in hot water bath according to steps 4 and 5 on page 147. Let stand, undisturbed, for 48 hours.

STORAGE

Preserves will keep on a pantry shelf for up to 1 year. Remove rings and label the jars with the date.

BLUEBERRY CARDAMOM BUTTER

Marisa McClellan, one of my canning friends and the author of several preserving cookbooks, introduced me to the method of slow cooker fruit butter. It's a lifesaver for busy moms who are constantly called out of the kitchen. A U-pick up the road from where we live offers up the most stunning blueberries, and in the early fall they are at their sweetest. It would be a crime not to preserve them for winter, and so this simple summer fruit butter is my canning choice. Cardamom brings a mild floral quality to the blueberries, and the lemon juice adds necessary acidity while complementing the spice.

MAKES 7 (HALF-PINT/250 ML) JARS

1. Submerge blueberries in cool water and skim off any stems or leaves that rise to the top. Drain well. Add berries to a food processor and blend until puréed like a smoothie. You should have about 10 cups (2.4 L) of purée.

2. Transfer blueberry purée to a slow cooker and set the timer for 8 hours with the temperature on low. Cover, but leave the lid open a crack to allow the steam to escape. At first the blueberry purée will congeal like Jell-O, due to the natural pectin; this is normal.

3. Cook the butter for 6 to 8 hours, stirring once an hour or so. Cooking time will vary with different slow cooker brands. The butter will slowly reduce and thicken somewhat. In the final hour of cooking, add the sugar, lemon juice and cardamom. Remove lid, stir well and turn heat to high. Stay close by for this part, as you need to stir the butter every 15 minutes.

4. Meanwhile, review canning basics on page 146 and prepare a hot water bath with 7 half-pint (250 mL) jars and lids according to step 2 on page 147.

5. Once blueberry butter is the consistency of applesauce, it is ready to can. If you want a very smooth spread, purée it again with an immersion blender. If not, your butter is ready for processing. Don't worry if it looks slightly runny, as blueberries contain plenty of natural pectin and the butter will thicken up when it cools. Working with one jar at a time, remove jar from hot water and place a wide-mouth funnel into the top. Using a ladle, fill jar with butter. Wipe rim with a clean, damp cloth. Seal the jar. Repeat with remaining jars.

6. Process for 10 minutes in hot water bath according to steps 4 and 5 on page 147.

4 quarts (4 L) blueberries

2½ cups (625 mL) raw cane sugar

3 tablespoons (45 mL) freshly squeezed lemon juice

½ teaspoon (2 mL) freshly ground cardamom

KITCHEN TIP

You can use a blender, Vitamix or food processor to purée your blueberries.

STORAGE

Butter will keep on a pantry shelf for up to 1 year. Remove rings and label the jars with the date.

MAKE-AHEAD CURRANT SCONES

Perhaps it is my British heritage weighing in on the subject, but I staunchly believe everyone needs a reliable scone recipe in their back pocket, preferably one that can be made ahead, frozen and then baked with minimal effort on a Sunday morning. This is my recipe for such occasions, as well as for my annual jam swap, when the taste testers come out in throngs. I've been known to stash a batch of these currant scones in the freezer to facilitate a smooth (and tasty) breakfast in bed served up by Danny and the kids. Genius? Pretty close.

MAKES 16 MEDIUM SCONES

1 cup (250 mL) whole wheat flour

1 cup (250 mL) all-purpose flour

1 tablespoon (15 mL) baking powder

¾ teaspoon (4 mL) fine sea salt

½ cup (125 mL) unsalted butter, cold

½ cup (125 mL) dried currants

1 large egg

3 tablespoons (45 mL) pure maple syrup

¾ cup (175 mL) table (18%) cream, chilled

1. Combine whole wheat flour, all-purpose flour, baking powder and salt in a medium bowl. Whisk to blend. Grate butter on a box grater into flour mixture, and toss gently with your fingers to combine. Mix in currants.

2. In a small bowl, beat egg with a fork until frothy. Pour in maple syrup and cream; beat again. Pour liquid into dry ingredients and lightly mix together with the fork just until the dough comes together.

3. Turn dough out onto a lightly floured counter and use your hands to bring it together. Press it into a disk that is 8 inches (20 cm) across and about ¾ inch (2 cm) thick. Cut dough into 8 wedges, and then cut each wedge in half.

4. Arrange scones on a parchment-lined baking sheet and freeze until solid.

5. Preheat oven to 375°F (190°C). Arrange scones on a parchment-lined baking sheet and brush with a little more cream or milk. Bake for 22 to 25 minutes or until light golden. Serve warm, preferably with homemade jam.

VARIATION
Add a tablespoon (15 mL) of fresh orange or lemon zest for a fragrant scone.

STORAGE
The unbaked scones will keep in an airtight container or bag in the freezer for up to 2 months. Bake directly from frozen.

ZUCCHINI CORNBREAD

In the fall the garden is producing zucchini at a terrific rate, and we are always looking for new uses for the prolific squash. Cornbread is a staple around our table, especially when paired with autumn soups and stews. This tender version is flecked with green zucchini, yielding a moist cornbread with crispy edges. It is particularly tasty when enjoyed warm from the oven and spread with blueberry butter (page 159).

SERVES 8

1. Preheat oven to 375°F (190°C). Line a loaf pan with parchment paper.

2. Whisk together cornmeal, flour, sugar and salt in a medium bowl. Sift in baking powder and baking soda. Whisk to combine very well.

3. Crack eggs into another medium bowl and beat well. Pour in milk and cream; mix to combine.

4. Trim ends from zucchini and finely grate the squash. Using your hands, gather up the shredded zucchini and squeeze out the excess liquid. Place the grated zucchini in a measuring cup; you should have about ½ cup (125 mL).

5. Add dry ingredients to egg mixture and stir to combine. Fold in grated zucchini, followed by melted butter. Mix just until combined. Scrape batter into prepared pan.

6. Bake cornbread for 40 to 45 minutes or until a toothpick inserted into the center comes out clean. Cool for 10 minutes in the pan, then lift out and cool completely on a rack.

1½ cups (375 mL) fine cornmeal

½ cup (125 mL) all-purpose flour

1 tablespoon (15 mL) raw cane sugar

1 teaspoon (5 mL) sea salt

1 tablespoon (15 mL) baking powder

½ teaspoon (2 mL) baking soda

3 large eggs

¾ cup (175 mL) 2% milk

¼ cup (60 mL) heavy (35%) cream

1 medium zucchini (around 6 ounces/175 g), washed

¼ cup (60 mL) unsalted butter, melted

STORAGE

This cornbread will keep in an airtight container for up to 1 day or in the freezer for up to 8 weeks.

8
ORCHARD OUTINGS

Endive, Apple and Almond Salad with Apple-Almond Dressing • Cream of Pumpkin Soup • Maple-Sriracha Toasted Pumpkin Seeds • Balsamic-Glazed Scallops with Apple, Leek and Swiss Chard • Cranberry Pear Mincemeat • Apple Cinnamon Layer Cake • Sour Cream Pear Pie with Cornmeal Pecan Streusel • Hot Spiced Apple Cider

Years before I ever ducked under the low-slung branches of an apple tree and followed the ruts made from tractor wheels between the rows, I was smitten with orchards. In my childhood summers, fruit trucks drove up the infamously long Highway 97 to Canada's Far North, the Yukon, to bring us the harvest from the Okanagan Valley in British Columbia. We purchased sun-kissed peaches, plums and cherries in the summer, and in autumn, blush pears and vividly colored apples. I would imagine the hillsides that produced this abundance and the gentle climate with enough warm days to grow this food. I decided I would be married in an orchard.

Upon moving to Quebec's countryside, I finally set foot in an orchard, and those excursions were every bit as romantic as I had imagined as a young girl. On my days off from the restaurant, Danny and I would slip away to a local farm and wander, hand in hand, through the groves of pears and apples. He'd lean his back against a trunk and I'd nestle in close. The clouds would drift by overhead and the trees rustle in friendly camaraderie as we kissed the afternoon away.

We would eventually be married in an apple orchard, just as I had dreamed so many years before. It was a late spring that year; the apple trees shimmered in green, but withheld their blossoms for warmer days. Although the sun shone, it was a cool day, but we felt only the warmth of our young love and the thrill of the moment we had been anticipating for years. My dad walked me down the freshly mown aisle of pale green grass, while my sister-in-law, Laura, played a violin solo from a movement of Vivaldi's "Four Seasons." In a simple ceremony before family and friends, we were wed.

A few years later we returned with a few friends, a baby in a wrap and a bottle of strong apple cider. We brought a streusel-topped pear pie (page 180) and a wedge of cheese, and perched on the low-slung branches to chat. Conversation was woven between mouthfuls of cheddar-topped pie. Noah had his first suck on a sweet Cortland, his wind-kissed cheeks nearly as red as the blush apple tightly grasped in his hands.

Nowadays when we return in the fall, the children outnumber the adults, skipping down the lanes between the rows of Empires and McIntoshes, following the grooves from heavy wagon wheels. They skillfully climb the tallest ladders, searching for the orchard's largest apple, and wave from behind the foliage. When they grow tired of apple picking, they play tag, running until they throw themselves under a tree to rest. By then, our crate is heaped high with fruit and our tummies are growling.

We've brought a picnic spread, supplemented with local apple cider from the farm, and feast on cups of pumpkin soup (page 170) and torn baguette until the sun sinks low, setting fire to the orange maples on the hills in the distance.

On the way home we stop at a pumpkin patch, and the children weave in between the squash, choosing two for decoration. Danny loads up the trunk with the smaller sugar pumpkins, my choice for roasting and turning into soup and pies. On our way out, we treat ourselves to a small paper bag of blistering hot apple beignets from the farm stand—the perfect sweet finish to our orchard outing.

APPLE VARIETIES AND THEIR USES

Should you be so fortunate as to find yourself in an apple orchard, you may be surprised at the selection of varieties. Vintage and modern, old favorites and new, the options are as varied as their uses. Here's a quick breakdown to help you remember what to sauce and what to slice.

PIE APPLES

These apples hold their shape when baked and are ideal for slicing thinly into pancakes, drying for apple chips or packing between pastry for the perfect apple pie.

Varieties: Braeburn, Cox's Orange Pippin, Granny Smith, Jonathan, Golden Russet (dries particularly well)

COOKING APPLES

If you're looking to make classic applesauce or purée, these are your best bet. Cook them down even further for one of our favorite spreads, apple butter, or combine them with winter squash for an ideal fall soup (page 170).

Varieties: Cortland, Empire, Fuji, Lobo, McIntosh, Spartan, Winesap

MUNCHING APPLES

Straight from the tree is the best way to enjoy these apples. Everyone has their particular favorite, but several are known for their fine munching qualities.

Varieties: Cox's Orange Pippin, Honeycrisp, Empire, Gala, Golden Delicious, Golden Russet, Granny Smith, Jonathan, Lady, Lobo, McIntosh, Spartan

SALAD APPLES

Some apple varieties are less likely to discolor than others and are ideal for salads.

Varieties: Cortland, Russet (my preference for salads and sandwiches), Granny Smith

CIDER APPLES

If you enjoy juicing your apples or making homemade cider, choose apples that are known for the quality of their juice.

Varieties: Cortland, Crispin, Empire, Granny Smith, McIntosh, Melba, Winesap

Ideally, store apples in a paper bag in a cool, dark place and away from other vegetables. And it's true what they say: "One bad apple rots the whole bunch." Apples give off ethylene gas, and so just one bruised or rotting apple will give off enough to swiftly ripen and, soon after, rot the others.

ENDIVE, APPLE AND ALMOND SALAD WITH APPLE-ALMOND DRESSING

Radicchio and endive are two of my preferred autumn salad greens, probably because they pair so well with apples, and these days, I want Russets in every salad, if you please. They are my favorite fall munching apple and first pick for slicing into sandwiches, desserts and salads like this one. This dish is a simple collection of ingredients, but the apple cider and ground almond dressing truly elevate it into something memorable. The dressing can be made a few days in advance, but prep the salad only minutes before you serve it and be sure to toss it at the table.

Fresh-pressed apple cider is unfiltered raw apple juice (nonalcoholic) that can be found in the refrigerated section of your whole foods store.

SERVES 6

1. **MAKE THE DRESSING** In a blender, cream together almonds, apple cider, sherry vinegar and honey. With the blender running, drizzle in the olive oil. Season dressing with salt and transfer to a jar. Cover and chill.

2. **MAKE THE SALAD** Peel off the outer leaves of the endives and discard. Coarsely chop the bulbs down to the core and place in a large salad bowl. Repeat with radicchio, tossing it with the endive.

3. Core apple, slice it into 1/4-inch (5 mm) rounds, then dice and add to the salad. Add almonds. Toss salad with 3 tablespoons (45 mL) of the Apple-Almond Dressing. Garnish with Parmesan and serve immediately.

For the apple-almond dressing
1/4 cup (60 mL) blanched almonds, toasted

2 tablespoons (30 mL) fresh-pressed apple cider

1 tablespoon (15 mL) sherry vinegar

1 tablespoon (15 mL) honey, warmed until runny

3 tablespoons (45 mL) olive oil

1/4 teaspoon (1 mL) salt

For the salad
6 large Belgian endives

1/2 head radicchio

1 Russet apple, washed

1/2 cup (125 mL) slivered almonds, toasted

1/4 cup (60 mL) shaved Parmesan cheese

STORAGE
Salad dressing will keep in the refrigerator for up to 3 days.

CREAM OF PUMPKIN SOUP

I tend to love my squash soups on the spicy side, laced with fresh ginger and balanced out with a dab of coconut cream, but that is not the path to take when I am trying to get my children to have seconds, or even firsts. Nope, they prefer things on the sweeter side, so this soup pairs pumpkin with sweet onion and apples, and a touch of maple syrup to seal the deal. A swirl of cream enriches it further, and before long we are scraping the bottom of the pot. For an extra kick, Danny and I sprinkle Maple-Sriracha Toasted Pumpkin Seeds (page 172) into our soup, but the kids are happy dunking slices of crusty baguette.

SERVES 6

1 tablespoon (15 mL) olive oil

1 small sweet onion, chopped

1 pound (500 g) chopped peeled pumpkin (about ½ small pie pumpkin or 4 cups/1 L)

1 garlic clove, chopped

1 large sweet apple, such as Honeycrisp or Gala

2 cups (500 mL) vegetable stock

1 bay leaf

¼ cup (60 mL) heavy (35%) cream, plus more for garnish

1 tablespoon + 1 teaspoon (20 mL) pure maple syrup

1 teaspoon (5 mL) salt

Sour cream, for garnish

Maple-Sriracha Toasted Pumpkin Seeds (page 172), for garnish

1. In a Dutch oven or deep cast-iron skillet, heat olive oil over medium heat until shimmering. Add onion and sauté for about 3 minutes, stirring frequently. Add pumpkin and garlic; sauté for 1 minute. Add apples and sauté for another 2 minutes.

2. Add stock. The liquid should just barely cover the mixture. Add bay leaf. Simmer over medium-low to low heat until the squash and apples are very tender, 12 to 15 minutes, depending on the size of the pumpkin pieces. Discard the bay leaf.

3. Carefully transfer mixture to a blender or food processor and purée. Add cream, maple syrup and salt. Blend again until combined. Pour into bowls and garnish with more cream, a dollop of sour cream and toasted pumpkin seeds.

KITCHEN TIP
Choose pie pumpkins for this recipe. They are the smaller ones, and are much more flavorful.

STORAGE
This soup will keep in an airtight container in the refrigerator for up to 2 days.

MAPLE-SRIRACHA TOASTED PUMPKIN SEEDS

I like an abundance of pumpkins around in the fall for decoration, flanking the front door and spilling off the porch, but it's not long before my boys are begging to carve them into funny faces. I yield to their pleading, only because I'm secretly craving a handful of toasted seeds. So Mateo spreads brown paper on the floor of the kitchen while Noah fetches a bowl and two spoons. I remove the tough stem and they dip their arms deep into the pumpkins to scoop up all the seeds.

Pumpkin seeds are some of the most nutritious seeds available—and to think some people just throw them away! And did you know that one pie pumpkin will nearly always yield exactly 1 cup (250 mL) of seeds? An unusual yet highly addicting fall snack, these sweet and spicy maple-Sriracha pepitas will have you frequently reaching for a handful. Fortunately, they are simple to make. Leave out the Sriracha if you are making them just for the children—unless, of course, your children like some heat.

MAKES 2 CUPS (500 ML)

2 cups (500 mL) fresh pumpkin seeds, unwashed

1 tablespoon (15 mL) pure maple syrup

1 teaspoon (5 mL) garlic salt

1 teaspoon (5 mL) Sriracha

1. Preheat oven to 325°F (160°C). Toss pumpkin seeds with maple syrup, garlic salt and Sriracha. Mix thoroughly.

2. Spread pumpkin seeds evenly on a lightly greased rimmed baking sheet. Roast for 45 to 50 minutes or until light golden. You do not need to stir them.

3. Cool the seeds completely on the baking sheet, then snack happily.

STORAGE
These pepitas will keep in an airtight container for up to 3 days or in the freezer for up to 8 weeks. Crisp them up again in a 350°F (180°C) oven for 5 minutes or so.

BALSAMIC-GLAZED SCALLOPS WITH APPLE, LEEK AND SWISS CHARD

If scallops don't come to mind when you think of fast food, consider again. They cook with a mere flash in the pan and yield a sense of pride when you serve them up seared golden on the edges and creamy in the center. The only ones worth eating feel firm and smell fresh but tend to be pricy, so we save them for a special evening when we've put the kids to bed and plan a quiet dinner for two. This is our favorite fall recipe for scallops, highlighting mild leeks, sweet apples and slightly bitter chard. It's a complete meal, especially when paired with a pint of local hard cider.

SERVES 2

1. Remove the small muscle from the side of each scallop and set scallops aside.

2. Wash the leek and remove several of the outer layers; reserve them for a soup or stock. Slice the inner leek in half lengthwise and lay cut side down on your cutting board. Chop leek into 1/2-inch (1 cm) pieces. In a large sauté pan, heat 2 teaspoons (10 mL) each butter and oil over medium heat. When the butter is bubbling, add the leek. Cook for 5 minutes, stirring occasionally.

3. Meanwhile, cut apple into quarters and remove the core. Slice each quarter into 1/4-inch (5 mm) slices. Add the apple to the pan and sauté for 1 minute. Add apple cider. Partially cover the pan and cook for 7 minutes or until both leek and apple are soft and all the liquid has evaporated away.

4. Meanwhile, slice Swiss chard into thick ribbons. When the leek and apple are ready, push the mixture to the side of the pan and add 1 teaspoon (5 mL) of the butter. Add the chard and toss it in the melted butter, then mix it with the apples and leeks. Season with 1/2 teaspoon (2 mL) salt. Cook for 2 minutes, tossing often. Sprinkle with 1 tablespoon (15 mL) of the balsamic vinegar and give it one final stir. Remove from heat and keep warm.

5. In a 10-inch (25 cm) skillet, heat 1 tablespoon (15 mL) each butter and oil over high heat. Generously salt scallops on both sides. When the butter is bubbling, reduce heat to medium-high and use a pair of tongs to place the scallops in the pan. Sear scallops for about 3 minutes or until a golden crust forms on the bottom. Gently turn the scallops and cook for another 3 minutes.

6. Divide apple-chard mixture between 2 shallow bowls and top each with 3 scallops. Return the scallop pan to the heat and add the remaining 2 tablespoons (30 mL) balsamic vinegar. Bring it to a ferocious boil, then drop in the remaining 1 tablespoon (15 mL) butter. Swirl just until the butter melts, then pour the glaze over the scallops. Serve at once.

6 large fresh sea scallops (not previously frozen), patted dry

1 leek

3 tablespoons (45 mL) salted butter

1 tablespoon + 2 teaspoons (25 mL) olive oil

1 Honeycrisp apple

1/2 cup (125 mL) fresh-pressed apple cider (unfiltered, raw apple juice)

1 medium bunch Swiss chard, stems and thick ribs removed

Sea salt

3 tablespoons (45 mL) balsamic vinegar

CRANBERRY PEAR MINCEMEAT

I believe if more people knew that making homemade mincemeat was as easy as tipping ingredients into a pot, stirring every so often and then transferring it all to a jar, mince desserts would be making more of an appearance on holiday dessert tables. My version of the festive British favorite is chock-full of tart cranberries, sweet pears, freshly ground spices and a touch of maple syrup. It's bursting with flavor and downright decadent. I like to make it when the local pears are at their sweetest and the first cranberries are harvested. Those two share a shelf at the market, then a brief car ride home, to be later married together with a splash of whiskey and preserved in my pantry until Christmas.

Little jars of mincemeat make delightful holiday gifts, although mine never get that far. Come December my mince is always turned into a hundred or so tartlets, which, I can assure you, seldom last to see Santa come down the chimney.

MAKES 5 (HALF-PINT/250 ML) JARS

1 cup (250 mL) fresh-pressed apple cider (unfiltered, raw apple juice)

1 cup (250 mL) dark turbinado sugar

2 medium Bartlett or Anjou pears (unpeeled)

2 cups (500 mL) whole cranberries, ideally fresh but frozen work, too

1½ cups (375 mL) unsweetened dried cranberries

1½ cups (375 mL) dried currants

2 teaspoons (10 mL) freshly ground cinnamon

1 teaspoon (5 mL) ground cloves

½ teaspoon (2 mL) grated fresh ginger (or 1 teaspoon/5 mL dried)

¼ cup (60 mL) Sortilège (Canadian maple whiskey; may substitute whiskey, brandy or port)

⅓ cup (75 mL) pure maple syrup

1 teaspoon (5 mL) pure vanilla extract

1. In a large saucepan, warm apple cider and sugar over low heat, stirring to dissolve the sugar. Quarter, core and grate the pears. Add pear and whole cranberries to the cider. Tip in the dried cranberries, currants, cinnamon, cloves and ginger. Stir well.

2. Simmer over medium-low heat for about 20 minutes, stirring often, until mixture starts to darken and most of the liquid has been absorbed.

3. Remove from heat and add the whiskey, maple syrup and vanilla. Stir thoroughly to incorporate everything and crush the whole cranberries slightly. At this point you can transfer the mincemeat into clean jars and store in the refrigerator for several weeks or in the freezer for up to 3 months. To can the mincemeat, proceed with the recipe.

4. Review canning basics on page 146 and prepare a hot water bath with 5 half-pint (250 mL) jars and lids according to step 2 on page 147.

5. Working with one jar at a time, remove jar from hot water and place a wide-mouth funnel into the top. Using a ladle, fill jar with mincemeat, leaving ½ inch (1 cm) of headspace. Use a small spatula or plastic bubble remover to remove air pockets. Seal jar. Repeat with remaining jars.

6. Process for 15 minutes in hot water bath according to steps 4 and 5 on page 147.

STORAGE
Mincemeat will keep on pantry shelves for up to 1 year. Remove rings and label the jars with the date.

VARIATIONS
You may use cranberry or filtered apple juice in place of the fresh cider. If desired, add ½ cup (125 mL) chopped walnuts to the mincemeat before making tarts. Use my Basic All-Butter Pie Crust (page 293) for best results.

APPLE CINNAMON LAYER CAKE

How often do you come across a cake that is better on the second (or even third) day? This naturally sweetened cake is just that. It is bursting with apples, which keep it moist while the honey and cinnamon have a chance to meld together. Frequently requested on birthdays, this cake is filled and topped with a modest amount of cream cheese frosting flavored with apple butter and a touch of maple syrup. The blend requires its own time to mellow and transforms into a creamy, apple-sweet frosting. While the refrigerator time is important, this layer cake should be served at room temperature to properly showcase its flavors. If you don't have homemade apple butter on hand, find jars in the organics section of your grocery store or at your natural foods store.

SERVES 10 TO 12

1. **MAKE THE CAKE**   Preheat oven to 325°F (160°C). Grease two 8-inch (20 cm) round cake pans and line the bottoms with a round of parchment paper.

2. In a small saucepan, warm the coconut oil until it is runny, then pour it into a large bowl. Add maple syrup, honey and vanilla; whisk together vigorously. Add eggs, one at a time, beating well after each addition.

3. In another bowl, sift together flour, cinnamon, baking soda, baking powder and salt. Slowly add the dry ingredients to the wet mixture, stirring just until smooth. Do not overmix. Gently fold in apples just enough to coat them with batter.

4. Divide batter between the prepared pans and bake for 45 to 50 minutes or until a toothpick inserted in the center comes out clean. Cake will turn quite dark on the top because of the honey. Cool cakes in the pans on racks for 10 minutes, then loosen around the edges of the pan with a small knife. Invert cakes onto racks, peel off the parchment and cool completely.

5. **MAKE THE FROSTING WHILE CAKES COOL**   In the bowl of a stand mixer fitted with the whisk attachment, beat cream cheese and butter until light and fluffy. Add maple syrup and beat again, scraping down the sides of the bowl. Add apple butter and salt. Beat until smooth.

6. Place one cake round on a cake stand or serving plate and top it with half of the frosting. Place the second cake on top and press down gently. Spread remaining frosting on the top of the cake and smooth frosting to finish.

STORAGE
This cake will keep well, wrapped in plastic wrap and refrigerated, for up to 4 days or in the freezer for up to 8 weeks. Bring up to room temperature before serving.

For the cake

1 cup (250 mL) coconut oil

½ cup (125 mL) pure maple syrup, at room temperature

¾ cup (175 mL) liquid honey

1 teaspoon (5 mL) pure vanilla extract

3 medium eggs, at room temperature

2¼ cups (550 mL) unbleached all-purpose flour

1½ teaspoons (7 mL) cinnamon

1 teaspoon (5 mL) baking soda

1 teaspoon (5 mL) baking powder

1 teaspoon (5 mL) salt

3 cups (750 mL) peeled and chopped pie apples, such as Granny Smith or Russet

For the frosting

8 ounces (250 g) cream cheese, at room temperature

½ cup (125 mL) unsalted butter, at room temperature

3 tablespoons (45 mL) pure maple syrup

¼ cup (60 mL) apple butter, at room temperature

Pinch of salt

SOUR CREAM PEAR PIE WITH CORNMEAL PECAN STREUSEL

As much as the apple pie is the darling of the fall season, pears deserve their due, especially when delicately spiced and tucked into a rustic pie such as this one. Bucking tradition, this pie boasts a crunchy cornmeal pecan streusel topping that is simple to pull together and offers a nice contrast of texture against the creamy fruit filling. I probably don't have to tell you, but this harvest pie is best enjoyed with a scoop of vanilla ice cream.

SERVES 8

½ recipe Basic All-Butter Pie Crust (page 293), rolled out and fitted into a 9-inch (23 cm) pie plate, crimped and chilled

For the streusel

½ cup (125 mL) pecans

½ cup (125 mL) raw cane sugar

¼ cup (60 mL) fine cornmeal

¼ cup (60 mL) all-purpose flour

¾ teaspoon (4 mL) cinnamon

¼ teaspoon (1 mL) ground cardamom

6 tablespoons (90 mL) cold unsalted butter, cut into small pieces

For the filling

8 firm medium Bartlett or Anjou pears

½ cup (125 mL) sour cream

½ cup (125 mL) raw cane sugar

3 tablespoons (45 mL) all-purpose flour

1½ teaspoons (7 mL) cinnamon

½ teaspoon (2 mL) ground cardamom

1. MAKE THE STREUSEL   Combine pecans, cane sugar, cornmeal, flour, cinnamon and cardamom in a food processor. Pulse about 10 times or until nuts are chopped. Add butter cubes and process until small clumps form, about 20 seconds. Transfer to a bowl, cover and refrigerate. (Streusel may be prepared 1 day ahead.)

2. Preheat oven to 375°F (190°C).

3. MAKE THE FILLING   Core pears and cut into ½-inch (1 cm) pieces. You should have about 6 cups (1.5 L).

4. In a large bowl, toss pears with sour cream to coat. In a small bowl, mix sugar, flour, cinnamon and cardamom. Sprinkle mixture over pears and use a sturdy spatula to combine.

5. Transfer pear filling to prepared crust, heaping it high. Evenly sprinkle pecan streusel over the pears. Place the pie on a baking sheet to catch any drips.

6. Bake pie until pears are tender and streusel is golden, about 1 hour and 10 minutes. Transfer to a rack and cool.

VARIATION
Mascarpone may be substituted for sour cream with delicious results.

KITCHEN TIP
Double the amount of streusel and freeze extra for a second pie.

STORAGE
This pie will keep, covered and refrigerated, for up to 3 days.

HOT SPICED APPLE CIDER

Fragrant and sweet, this rustic beverage is our absolute favorite drink to pass around to friends on a cool fall afternoon. The scents of the lemongrass, ginger and other aromatics are so transporting, you'll forget winter is just around the corner. Fresh apple cider is sometimes called "cold pressed" or "fresh pressed" and is an unfiltered, unsweetened pure apple juice. It is unpasteurized, and recognizable by its murky brown color. While we don't press our own apples yet, we readily enjoy drinking and cooking with this natural juice. Most orchards sell their own version or you can find it in the refrigerated area of the organics section in your grocery store.

SERVES 4 TO 6

1 cinnamon stick

1 star anise

4 whole cloves

4 or 5 black peppercorns

4 cups (1 L) fresh-pressed apple cider (unfiltered, raw apple juice)

¼ cup (60 mL) raw cane sugar

½-inch (1 cm) slice peeled fresh ginger

1 stalk lemongrass, bruised (or 1 lemon, sliced)

1. In a large saucepan, toast cinnamon, star anise, cloves and peppercorns over medium heat for 2 to 3 minutes, stirring occasionally to prevent them from burning. The heat brings out their aromatics.

2. Add cider, sugar, ginger and lemongrass. Bring to a boil over high heat, stirring occasionally to dissolve the sugar.

3. Reduce heat and simmer, partially covered, for 30 minutes. Strain into mugs and serve hot.

KITCHEN TIP
Need a natural cold remedy? When the winter blues have me in their grips, I often brew up a batch of this cider to help combat cold symptoms. Simply replace the sugar with a few tablespoons of honey and double the amount of fresh ginger.

STORAGE
This cider will keep in the refrigerator for up to 5 days. Reheat before serving.

HOMESTEADING

A Plea for Eating in Season

In the fall we munch Honeycrisp apples by the bushel and slice into pumpkins and scoop out the seeds to toast for a snack. We haven't purchased asparagus in months, and the only berries around are served up in smoothies from gems we have frozen. This is what it looks like to practice seasonal eating: choosing to enjoy (or preserve) produce only during the months it is grown and harvested. A pint of freshly picked, sun-ripened raspberries that perfumes your kitchen with its fragrance is the only argument really needed for eating seasonally, but here are a few other good reasons.

- Produce is ripened naturally (as opposed to picked prematurely so it can be shipped long distances), and harvested when perfect, so its unparalleled freshness provides us with a boost of extra nutrition.

- Too many veggies are jet-lagged from those long trips from South America to your neighborhood grocery store—and more seriously, too much fossil fuel is being consumed to get them there.

- You may not see your purchases making an impact on a global scale, but your requests for regional, farm-grown food might change the future of a neighboring farm.

- Costs are down for fruits and vegetables in season. You may not realize it, but you pay a premium for food that has traveled a long way.

- Most kids can tell you that pumpkins turn up in the fall, but how many can pinpoint the asparagus season?

- Waiting for those first leaves of baby spinach and green garlic in spring only builds your appreciation for them, and if you withhold from buying hard, bland melon all year, you will easily fall in love all over again with that sweet July cantaloupe.

As a general rule, eat root vegetables, citrus and hearty greens in the fall and winter; eat salads, berries and tomatoes in the summer. It's a little more complicated than that, but you get the idea.

SOURCING LOCAL FOODS AS A FAMILY

Choosing local foods as a family fosters a greater appreciation for it, and with our little ones, we need them as interested in fresh fruits and vegetables as possible.

I choose our outings based on fond memories from early childhood: harvesting potatoes, picking up a bucket of honey from a bee farm or stopping for fresh eggs at the neighbors'. I scarcely remember a grocery store trip, perhaps because the farm excursions were much more fun. Now, whether we are purchasing a side of beef or a crate of apples, we take our children to the source of our food, and talk about the trip before and after. It's always good dinner conversation to imagine a day in the life of a farmer. The opportunity to touch the food as it comes out of the ground or off a tree is a learning one for children. Those memories will trigger lots of enjoyment and associations at the table.

Here are a few ideas for sourcing locally grown foods as a family.

- Start in your own backyard. A kitchen garden or a local community garden are two excellent options to provide you with an abundance of carrots, potatoes and onions in the fall, as well as a rich learning experience.

- Community Supported Agriculture. CSA is a "subscription" service of fruits and veggies, purchased directly from the farm on a regular basis, and sometimes even delivered to your front door.

- Farmers' markets and city open-air markets support local growers and spotlight what is in season. Most such markets have a rich family culture, and an outing can be more of an event than a regular shopping trip. Most provinces, territories and states have a website dedicated to helping you locate farmers' markets in your area. Try Local Harvest (www.localharvest.org) for more information.

- Find a local U-pick farm or orchard. Ask around at your local market or try the Pick Your Own website (www.pickyourown.org). It's a good resource, not only for finding farms but for offering recipes and tips for what to do with your haul. Here are some tips for your U-pick excursion:

  - Bushes have thorns, produce can stain and fields can get muddy. Dress appropriately, and remember to bring hats for all family members.

  - Decide how you'll use the produce before picking. It's easy to over-pick, so be prepared to have freezer or refrigerator space when you get tired of eating berries, apples or other produce.

  - Call the farm before you visit—picking conditions can vary from day to day, and the farmer will let you know the best time to arrive and the conditions to expect.

  - Bring the camera and pack a picnic!

- Another option for sourcing local food is the produce stands located right on the farms themselves. Driving down quiet country roads, it's hard not to pass at least a handful of signs boasting such riches as honey, farm-fresh eggs or grass-fed beef. If you have an area nearby that is registered agricultural land, there is a good chance the farmers are willing to sell small amounts directly to consumers.

- Farm stands are not the only way to source local in small cities and large towns. Support local small businesses. Artisanal breads, cheeses, baked goods, preserves and so on are just some of the goodies that will be found in many communities.

9
COMFORT FOODS

Crispy Cornmeal Pancakes with Honey-Orange Syrup • Clara's Clam Chowder • Tartiflette with Oka • One-Bowl Carrot-Spice Oatmeal Muffins • Mushroom, Bacon and Broccoli Rabe Fall Pizza • Chicken Leek Shepherd's Pie • Chocolate Beet Sheet Cake • Mexican Hot Cocoa

Without warning, temperatures drop in the fall, leaving us scrambling on those frosty mornings to remember where we stashed the hats and mittens. After-school snacks include mugs of Mexican Hot Cocoa (page 207) and still-warm One-Bowl Carrot-Spice Oatmeal Muffins (page 197), which warm the fingers and tummies of boys who braved one last treacherous bike ride on the iced-over lane. The cocoa is rich and dark, and they sip (and occasionally slurp) it from the sidelines of a chessboard, where a fierce yet silent battle rages between brothers. We set our clocks back an hour and adjust to eating dinner at dusk, often illuminated by candles just because. I ladle comforting clam chowder (page 194) into bowls and take requests for family favorites such as Chicken Leek Shepherd's Pie (page 201).

On weekends, we gather in the kitchen. The children anxiously await the first snowflakes of the year, and to distract them, I invite them to cook and bake with me. Never has there been a better time to tie on aprons and revive our spirits with a lineup of comfort foods. I have the time to spend teaching. The garden has been harvested and the pantry is stocked with home preserves. We begin with a requisite pancake breakfast, pouring chubby cornmeal pancake figures into the cast-iron pan and watching bubbles form around the edges. A precarious flip by six-year-old Mateo is accompanied by giggles all around, and then he transfers the awkwardly shaped yet adorable pancake to the plate and breakfast is served. Crispy Cornmeal Pancakes with Honey-Orange Syrup (page 193) are a family favorite.

In the late afternoon, when the sun is slanting behind the maples, we gather around the farm table and I set out toppings for pizza and open a jar of roasted tomato sauce (page 288). I bring the wooden bowl of Honey Whole Wheat Pizza Dough (page 292) from where it has been rising in the oven and we shape it into rounds. Even the youngest helps, making her own small pie with intense focus.

When should kids start cooking? For me the answer is a simple one: immediately. At least, bring them in the kitchen with you as soon as possible. Let them feel the pulse of the home at this central spot from an early age, and when it comes time to get cooking—really cooking, with knives, ingredients and heat—they will have already picked up a wealth of skills intuitively. Cooking with your children may not always be a piece of cake, but the benefits far outweigh the challenges. They can learn practical skills, such as counting and measuring, along with social skills like following instructions, patience and working together—all while fostering creativity.

For years, I've been insisting that teaching kids about food can begin in the grocery store or the garden, but the real magic happens when they're alongside me in the kitchen. A bleak and blustery fall day calls for comfort food, with recipes simple enough for children. It is an ideal opportunity to teach your little ones that cooking can be more than a chore—it can be fun.

This chapter collects our make-together favorites for breakfast, lunch, snack time and family dinner.

TIPS ON THRIVING WITH CHILDREN IN THE KITCHEN

Laying a foundation for a healthy attitude to food starts long before children are old enough to independently prepare a simple meal. That confidence and know-how are far more likely to come later if you are willing to invest the time in teaching them when they are young and impressionable.

Begin teaching in the grocery store. Teach your toddlers the names of the fruits and vegetables, and talk to your older children about cost comparisons and simple money management. Include all your children in some decision making. For example, ask them, "Should we cook spaghetti or fusilli with our sauce tonight?" Don't let your children make demands about your purchases, but do help them feel that you're taking their tastes into consideration.

Brush up on safety rules. Set kitchen guidelines early and never waver. Ensure knives, small appliances and potential toxins are put away out of reach.

Equip your crew. I use a sturdy stool, a child's apron or two and a few tools that are small and fit nicely in their hands.

Pick the right recipe. Choose a recipe with simple steps that children can do themselves—and that yields delicious results that will leave them excited to cook and bake again. One-Bowl Carrot-Spice Oatmeal Muffins (page 197) is a good starting point.

Talk, smell and taste together. Children are sponges for information. Explain what you are making in simple terms. Talk about each ingredient, where it comes from and what makes it special. Guide them through the task at hand in a way they can easily understand. Also, have your child smell ingredients as well as touch and taste when applicable. It will help them become familiar with a whole new world of flavors.

Relax and enjoy the time together. The ideal time to cook with your kids is not on soccer night or just before you are rushing them out the door to dance class. Cook together on the weekend, when everyone is a bit more relaxed and there is no time crunch to getting dinner on the table. Also, start your prep earlier than normal to allow for the necessary safety lessons and supervision.

End with cleanup. Now is the perfect time to teach kids to see a task through from beginning to end, and to teach them that cleanup can be a fun part of cooking, too! Have them rinse the dishes, unload the dishwasher or clear the trash or compost.

And don't forget: Praise is invaluable, as is plenty of patience on your part.

Sparking your child's curiosity in food can help lead to a lifelong interest in healthful eating, cooking or even farming. It's never too early or too late to begin. Lastly, it's important to remember that all children are different. Interest levels and attention spans vary vastly; you'll know just how much to attempt with your child.

CRISPY CORNMEAL PANCAKES WITH HONEY-ORANGE SYRUP

Even though we were three teenagers and a tween in the house when I was growing up, my mother never stashed boxed toaster waffles in the freezer or chalky pancake mix in the pantry. From as far back as I can remember, griddlecakes of all sorts began with our own eggs and stone-ground wheat flour. I would stand at the stove and lazily pour small circles of batter into the wide cast-iron pan to make silver dollar pancakes, which we would devour by the dozens. Now my boys push wooden stools up to the counter and help to measure the ingredients and beat the batter. Nothing much has changed over the years, only now I'm making bunny and snowman shapes instead of silver dollars.

Fluffier than most pancakes, thanks to the addition of buttermilk and a generous amount of butter, these corn cakes disappear fast when drenched with Honey-Orange Syrup. When I was growing up, we scooped local honey from a big bucket into a small cast-iron pot and set it on the woodstove to melt for our pancakes. I've kept the pot of honey around over the years, only now I zest and juice an orange into it for a glistening, citrus-infused syrup that spreads over our pancakes like a beam of sunshine in the morning. Happiness is a stack of these tender, golden pancakes covered in syrup.

MAKES 9 (6-INCH/15 CM) PANCAKES AND 1 CUP (250 ML) SYRUP

1. **MAKE THE HONEY-ORANGE SYRUP** In a small pot, whisk together honey and the freshly squeezed orange juice over medium heat. Continue stirring until mixture comes to a boil and the orange juice is completely incorporated. Remove from heat and stir in orange zest. Allow syrup to cool slightly before serving. It will thicken as it cools. Transfer to a jug for serving or a glass jar for keeping. (Syrup may be made up to 1 week ahead.)

2. **MAKE THE PANCAKES** In a large bowl, whisk together whole wheat flour, all-purpose flour, cornmeal and baking soda. In a large cast-iron skillet (the same one that you will use for cooking the pancakes), melt the butter. Add honey and stir with a heat-resistant spatula until honey is dissolved and the two ingredients are incorporated. Set aside to cool slightly.

3. Measure buttermilk into a large glass measuring cup. Crack in eggs and beat with a fork. Add liquid to flour mixture and stir to combine. Add melted butter mixture and beat batter very well.

4. Reheat the skillet over medium heat and lightly brush with oil. Pour batter into the middle of the pan and cook until small bubbles start to form and edges are brown and crisp. Flip pancake and cook for another minute or so. Wrap pancakes in a clean tea towel to keep warm. Repeat with remaining batter. Serve pancakes hot with Honey-Orange Syrup.

For the honey-orange syrup
1 cup (250 mL) organic golden honey

Zest and juice of 1 large orange (use a microplane for zesting)

For the pancakes
½ cup (125 mL) whole wheat flour

½ cup (125 mL) all-purpose flour

½ cup (125 mL) fine cornmeal

1 teaspoon (5 mL) baking soda

¼ cup (60 mL) salted butter

3 tablespoons (45 mL) honey

1 cup (400 mL) buttermilk

2 large eggs

Vegetable oil, for frying

STORAGE
Honey-Orange Syrup will keep in an airtight container in the refrigerator for up to 1 week.

VARIATION
Along with the orange juice, add 1 tablespoon (15 mL) Grand Marnier to the honey syrup. Serve to grown-ups.

CLARA'S CLAM CHOWDER

A family camping trip on the coast of Maine instilled in us a permanent hankering for clam chowder, preferably the creamy version. We figure that if we can't set up a little home away from home on Popham Beach, then at least we can occasionally recreate the chowder from the town of Bath.

   Elegant without being overly rich, this filling soup is a delightful nod to beautiful autumn vegetables and will leave you feeling satisfied and comforted. It's a particular favorite of young Clara, who gets right in her bowl with her fingers and fishes for the clams. Make a double batch if you can; its flavor improves on the second day.

SERVES 4

2 slices bacon, chopped

1 small leek, white part only, washed

1 rib celery, diced

1 garlic clove, chopped

1 bay leaf

1 pound (500 g) potatoes, peeled, diced and rinsed

½ teaspoon (2 mL) freshly ground black pepper

½ teaspoon (2 mL) salt, or to taste

2 cups (500 mL) clam juice

1 cup (250 mL) chopped canned clams

½ cup (125 mL) table (18%) cream

½ cup (125 mL) whole milk

2 tablespoons (30 mL) chopped fresh Italian parsley, plus more for garnish

1. In a medium pot, cook bacon over medium heat for about 5 minutes or until it starts to brown. Meanwhile, cut leek in half lengthwise, then cut each half lengthwise again to give you 4 strips. Chop each strip into ½-inch (1 cm) pieces.

2. Add leeks, celery, garlic and bay leaf to the bacon and stir well, scraping the bottom of the pot to get all the bacon bits up. Add the potatoes, pepper and salt; stir to combine. Cook for 2 minutes, stirring often. Vegetables will wilt and start to become translucent.

3. Pour in clam juice and bring to a simmer. Simmer soup for 10 minutes, stirring occasionally, or until potatoes are cooked through but not falling apart. Remove from heat.

4. Stir in chopped clams, cream, milk and parsley. Return soup to medium-low heat and cook for about 5 minutes, but do not let it boil. Taste and adjust seasoning if necessary. Ladle into bowls and garnish with additional parsley.

STORAGE
This chowder will keep in the refrigerator for up to 2 days.

TARTIFLETTE WITH OKA

Tartiflette is comfort food for grown-ups, and when we indulge, it's an occasion. We put the children to sleep, open a bottle of chilled white wine and settle down for a date night in. It's a decadent recipe that showcases the creamy and earthy fall potatoes, newly harvested from the garden. It's rich enough to be a meal on its own, rounded out with a crisp salad. We live just a short distance away from where Oka cheese is made, and we're seldom without a round or two on hand. Feel free to swap in the traditional Reblochon cheese if Oka is not available.

SERVES 4 AS A SIDE, 2 AS A MAIN

1. Preheat oven to 350°F (180°C). Lightly butter a round 2-quart (2 L) casserole (a cast-iron skillet would work too).

2. Place potatoes in a medium pot and cover with cold water. Bring to a boil and add 1 teaspoon (5 mL) of the salt. Cook the potatoes until tender but still somewhat firm in the center, about 15 minutes. Drain, cool slightly, and cut into smaller cubes.

3. In a large skillet over medium-high heat, lightly brown the bacon. Drain off excess fat, leaving about 1 tablespoon (15 mL). Add onion and cook for 2 minutes. Deglaze the skillet with white wine and boil for 1 minute or until the wine is reduced by half.

4. Tip in the cubed potatoes. Sprinkle with nutmeg, pepper and remaining ¼ teaspoon (1 mL) salt. Mix well. Pour into the prepared casserole dish. Drizzle with cream. Remove the rind from the bottom of the cheese and lightly scratch the top rind. Place the cheese, rind side up, on top of the potatoes.

5. Bake for 40 to 45 minutes, until the cheese is melted and the potatoes are cooked through. Serve immediately.

2 pounds (1 kg) yellow-fleshed potatoes, scrubbed and cut into large pieces

1¼ teaspoons (6 mL) salt, divided

5 ounces (150 g) thick-cut bacon, chopped into ½-inch (1 cm) pieces

1 small onion, thinly sliced

⅓ cup (75 mL) white wine

Pinch of nutmeg

¼ teaspoon (1 mL) freshly ground black pepper

¾ cup (175 mL) heavy (35%) cream

1 wheel (8 ounces/250 g) Oka cheese

ONE-BOWL CARROT-SPICE OATMEAL MUFFINS

The beauty of this recipe is its versatility, as it can happily accommodate almost any substitutions you like, and believe me, with the picky eaters around my table, I've tried quite a few variations. Oatmeal is one of the constants in the recipe and provides, in my opinion, necessary texture. Other than that, try grated zucchini in place of the carrot. Leave out the cranberries and toss in raisins or chocolate chips in their place. Go nuts with chopped pecans, walnuts or sunflower seeds; you'll only further add to the flavor and great texture of this popular snack.

The oats need to soak in the milk for 1 hour, so take that into consideration before getting started.

MAKES 12 MEDIUM OR 24 MINI MUFFINS

1. Combine milk, vinegar and oats in a large bowl and let stand for 1 hour.

2. Preheat oven to 375°F (190°C). Line a 12-cup muffin pan or 24-cup mini muffin pan with cupcake papers.

3. Crack the egg into the oat mixture; add sugar and beat with a whisk to combine. Whisk in melted butter.

4. Sift flour, baking powder, baking soda, salt, cinnamon and nutmeg into the bowl. Gently fold into batter, taking care not to overmix.

5. Sprinkle grated carrot and cranberries into the bowl and combine muffin batter gently but thoroughly. Use a large ice cream scoop or 1/3-cup (75 mL) measuring cup to scoop batter into muffin tins.

6. Bake until light brown and tops spring back when gently touched, 12 to 14 minutes. Cool in pans for a few minutes, then transfer muffins to a rack to cool completely.

1 cup (250 mL) milk, at room temperature

1 teaspoon (5 mL) white vinegar

1 cup (250 mL) old-fashioned rolled oats

1 large egg, at room temperature

1/4 cup (60 mL) raw cane sugar

1/2 cup (125 mL) unsalted butter, melted and cooled slightly

1 cup + 2 tablespoons (280 mL) all-purpose flour

1 teaspoon (5 mL) baking powder

1/2 teaspoon (2 mL) baking soda

1/2 teaspoon (2 mL) salt

1/2 teaspoon (2 mL) freshly ground cinnamon

1/4 teaspoon (1 mL) freshly grated nutmeg

3/4 cup (175 mL) grated carrots

1/2 cup (125 mL) dried cranberries

STORAGE
These muffins will keep in an airtight container for up to 3 days or in the freezer for up to 3 months.

MUSHROOM, BACON AND BROCCOLI RABE FALL PIZZA

In Quebec the standard all-dressed pizza is the Tout Garni: green peppers, button mushrooms and pepperoni. It's tolerable when you're helping friends move apartments and stop for a lunch break, but hardly ideal for a wholesome family dinner. My version is a nod to the local classic, in a pairing that balances salty, umami and bitter for a memorable bite. Homemade whole wheat dough and a sweet tomato sauce further elevate the pizza and ensure the delivery boy never knocks on your door.

SERVES 6

10 slices thick-cut bacon

1 large head broccoli rabe (rapini)

3 teaspoons (15 mL) olive oil, divided

8 ounces (250 g) chanterelle or cremini mushrooms

Cornmeal, for sprinkling on pans

1 recipe Honey Whole Wheat Pizza Dough (page 292)

1 cup (250 mL) Roasted Tomato Pizza Sauce (page 288)

3 cups (750 mL) grated mozzarella cheese

1. Cut bacon into 1/4-inch (1 cm) cubes and fry until crispy. Cool bacon on a paper towel and reserve the grease for general kitchen cooking such as flour tortillas (page 294).

2. Trim broccoli rabe heads, leaving a good 3 inches (8 cm) of stalk and the leaves. Toss with 2 teaspoons (10 mL) of the olive oil. Wipe mushrooms with a damp cloth and trim the stems if needed. Slice in half or quarters, depending on their size.

3. Position oven racks on the lower and middle levels and preheat oven to 450°F (230°C). Brush two rimmed baking sheets with the remaining 1 teaspoon (5 mL) olive oil and sprinkle with cornmeal.

4. Divide dough in half and on a lightly floured surface, roll each portion into a large rectangle, about 14 × 10 inches (35 × 25 cm). Working with one pizza at a time, lift the dough onto the prepared pan and press out with your fingertips to ensure the dough is even thickness. Don't worry about filling the pan or getting a perfect shape. Repeat with remaining piece of dough.

5. Divide sauce between the pizzas and spread around evenly, leaving a slight border. Top with bacon, mushrooms and rapini. Sprinkle pizzas with cheese.

6. Bake, rotating the pans at least once to ensure even browning of the bottom crust, for 15 minutes or until the cheese is golden and bubbly and the underside of the crust is light brown. Slice and serve at once.

CHICKEN LEEK SHEPHERD'S PIE

The oven-to-table method for feeding the family is one that I embrace wholeheartedly. It cuts down on dishes and is the best way to present a family-friendly casserole like this twist on a traditional shepherd's pie. No one would guess that this cold-weather comfort food is actually leftovers in disguise. It makes good use of the trimmings of a roast chicken and its mashed potato cohort. Winter leeks, homemade chicken stock and a splash of cream round out the all-star cast of ingredients, and the result is a dinner our little ones often request.

SERVES 6

1. Preheat oven to 350°F (180°C).

2. In a medium stovetop-to-oven casserole, melt butter over medium-high heat. Add chopped leeks; cook for 5 minutes, stirring often. Sprinkle with flour. Stir to coat the leeks in flour, scraping up any browning bits on the bottom of the pan. Slowly add chicken stock, stirring, and then cream. Reduce heat to medium-low and simmer for 5 minutes, stirring frequently. Sauce will thicken slightly.

3. Stir in parsley, salt, pepper and shredded chicken. Remove from heat. Sprinkle corn kernels over the chicken and top with a layer of mashed potatoes. At this point, the pie can be cooled, covered and refrigerated for up to 2 days before baking and serving.

4. Bake for 30 to 40 minutes, until the potatoes are light brown and the dish is hot in the center. Serve hot.

1 tablespoon (15 mL) salted butter

1½ cups (375 mL) chopped leeks, white and pale green parts only, well washed

1 tablespoon (15 mL) all-purpose flour

¾ cup (175 mL) chicken stock (page 286)

¼ cup (60 mL) heavy (35%) cream

1 tablespoon (15 mL) chopped fresh parsley (or 1 teaspoon/5 mL dried)

½ teaspoon (2 mL) salt

½ teaspoon (2 mL) black pepper

3 cups (750 mL) shredded cooked chicken or turkey

1 cup (250 mL) frozen or drained canned corn kernels

3 cups (750 mL) leftover mashed potatoes

STORAGE

This pot pie will keep in the refrigerator for up to 2 days or in the freezer, well-wrapped in plastic, for up to 3 months.

MAKE A MENU PLAN

When the leaves change color on our maples, it's time to adopt a fall routine. Gone are the carefree days of summer, where snacks replace meals; instead, I write up a menu plan that helps me get into a Monday-to-Friday dinner groove. Like any good habit, it takes time to implement, but the long-term benefits are well worth any effort put into making it a standard practice.

Writing a weekly menu plan is a good way to save money and help get organized for weeknight meals on busy school and work days. Follow the steps below and you won't have to compromise on bringing the family around the table for good, wholesome food.

1. Grab a notebook and a pen and list the days of the week.

2. Fill in any known meals, such as "Dinner at Grandpa's."

3. Brainstorm dinner ideas for the other days. Take into consideration what produce is in season or on sale that week at your local market.

4. Plan for using leftovers for at least one of the days, thus getting two meals from the effort of preparing one. Double a recipe and freeze half for another week when you don't have time to cook, or incorporate the leftovers from one meal into another, such as roast chicken today becoming chicken shepherd's pie tomorrow (page 201). See chapter 12, "Batch Cooking," for plenty of ideas.

5. Once you have decided on your meals, do a quick pantry and freezer check. Make a list of any ingredients you'll need to round out the dishes on your menu.

6. Post the menu plan in plain sight so you remember to stick to it. It also serves as a reminder if you need to thaw anything from the freezer.

7. Shop only for what you need and then enjoy a full week of knowing that there won't be a single day where you're scrambling for a dinner idea.

KIDS CAN
learn to pack a school lunch

In September, my boys head back to school, swinging their lunch boxes and tripping down the leaf-strewn lane to catch the bus.

Getting children involved with making their school lunches is a creative way to interest them in food and, in the long run, make healthier food choices on their own.

As you include your kids in the morning lunch routine, you'll find they will surprise you with their adeptness and enthusiasm. Maybe not at the beginning, but it will come. Once your children are proficient lunch-makers, it will take one more thing off of your to-do list in the morning.

- Have children select a different fruit and vegetable each week. Giving them a little choosing power can help expand on what they're used to. They can participate in washing, chopping and portioning the produce, too.

- Bake granola bars with your children, then cut, wrap and freeze in individual portions for lunches. (Try Orangette Chocolate Oat Bars, page 103.)

- Boil half a dozen eggs for an easy protein option and let your children peel them.

- Offer a few options for sandwiches or wraps and have your children make them in the morning before school.

- At the beginning of the week, set out an assortment of dried fruit, seeds and salty snacks and have your kids create their own trail mix. Portion into small resealable bags.

- Make a big batch of smoothies with your children's favorite ingredients, then portion into freezer cups and freeze. Place in the lunch box instead of individual store-bought yogurt.

- Make a batch of Carrot-Spice Oatmeal Muffins (page 197) and let your children customize the add-ins.

- Once in a while, have your kids fix breakfast for lunch: pancakes, waffles or jam-filled scones are just as good served up cold with a thermos of cold milk. (Try Crispy Cornmeal Pancakes, page 193.)

- Ask each child to list a handful of recipes they love, then work together to learn how to make them. The more you empower kids to be little cooks, the more they actually want to make and enjoy the food.

CHOCOLATE BEET SHEET CAKE

When I was a girl, there was a chocolate cake recipe in my mother's handwritten cookbook that I would mix up as often as I was allowed. Years later, I realized that I continued to bake it merely out of nostalgia, as it really wasn't all that great. And so the hunt was on for chocolate cake I could get just as attached to but that also tasted fabulous. Around the same time, I began occasionally adding puréed vegetables to my baking and cooking to get a few extra vitamins into my children's diets. Eliminating processed sugars was also a priority. This recipe is a result of melding that chocolate sheet cake from the past with the natural ingredients I use in my kitchen today. It has become a favorite in our home, frequently requested at birthdays and for dessert after Sunday dinner. Perhaps my children will continue to bake it when they are grown up, although hopefully for its full, rich flavor as much as for the sentiment of home it evokes.

SERVES 10 TO 12

3 medium beets, roasted or boiled, peeled

1 cup (250 mL) all-purpose flour

1 cup (250 mL) whole wheat flour

½ cup (125 mL) cocoa powder

2 teaspoons (10 mL) baking soda

½ teaspoon (2 mL) sea salt

2 medium eggs

1 cup (250 mL) unsalted butter, melted

1 cup (250 mL) honey

⅔ cup (150 mL) pure maple syrup

⅓ cup (75 mL) strong coffee, cooled

¼ cup (60 mL) buttermilk

1. Preheat oven to 350°F (180°C). Oil a 13- × 9-inch (3 L) baking pan.

2. Purée the cooked beets in a food processor and then measure them; you should have 1 cup (250 mL) of beet purée. Transfer purée to a fine-mesh sieve and drain off any excess moisture while you prepare the batter.

3. In a medium bowl, sift together all-purpose flour, whole wheat flour, cocoa, baking soda and salt. Crack eggs into a large bowl and whisk until frothy. Pour in the melted butter and beat until incorporated. Add honey and maple syrup, then beat until mixture is smooth and glossy. Add coffee and the beet purée; combine well.

4. Gently whisk the dry ingredients into the wet ingredients. Pour in buttermilk; whisk just to eliminate lumps, but do not overmix. Scrape batter into the prepared pan and spread evenly with a spatula.

5. Bake for 25 to 35 minutes, until a wooden toothpick inserted near the center comes out clean. Cool in the pan on a rack for about 10 minutes. Slice into squares and serve warm or at room temperature.

KITCHEN TIP
Cook the beets up to 3 days ahead of time and this cake will come together fairly quickly. You can boil, steam or roast your beets whole, then peel and purée them. To roast, wrap oiled beets in foil and roast in a 400°F (200°C) oven until they can be pierced with a fork. Peel while still warm. Alternatively, buy whole cooked beets in the prepared salads section of most supermarkets.

STORAGE
Well wrapped in plastic, this cake will keep for up to 4 days at room temperature or in the freezer for up to 8 weeks.

MEXICAN HOT COCOA

When I was growing up in the Yukon, winter arrived early. Once a year we invited everyone we knew for a sledding party that began after breakfast and lasted into the night, when the northern lights flickered overhead. When my friends and I would come in out of the cold to peel off our socks and warm our toes, my mother always offered cups of spiced hot cocoa from an orange Le Creuset pot on the back of our woodstove.

A childhood favorite of mine, this decadent drink eliminates the need for any powdered imitation. The aroma wafting from the cinnamon entices you for a mug, and the chili powder–infused cocoa warms you from the inside out. Top it with a homemade marshmallow or a dollop of softly whipped cream and snuggle under a quilt to wait out winter.

SERVES 4

1. In a small pot, combine cocoa powder, sugar, cinnamon, chili powder and ½ cup (125 mL) of the milk. Whisk well to eliminate any lumps. Whisk in the remaining 2½ cups (625 mL) milk and the vanilla.

2. Gently bring to a simmer over medium heat, stirring occasionally. Turn off heat, cover and let steep while you warm 4 mugs by filling them with hot water.

3. Taste the cocoa and adjust the flavoring if desired—more sugar for a sweeter drink, more chipotle chili powder for a stronger kick of heat.

4. Empty the water from the mugs and divide the Mexican hot cocoa among them. Garnish with a dollop of whipped cream or a homemade marshmallow and serve at once.

¼ cup (60 mL) cocoa powder

3 tablespoons (45 mL) raw cane sugar

½ teaspoon (2 mL) ground cinnamon

2 dashes chipotle chili powder

3 cups (750 mL) 2% milk

1 teaspoon (5 mL) pure Mexican vanilla extract

Softly whipped cream or Maple Marshmallows (page 104), for garnish

CINNAMON SHORTBREAD
BARS ~WITH
dark chocolate
GANACHE

WINTER

10

HOLIDAY GATHERINGS

Kale, Pomegranate and Pine Nut Salad • Quebec Tourtière • Butter Roasted Turkey • Cranberry Clementine Relish • Honey Ginger Sweet Potato Purée • Whole Wheat Chocolate Chunk Cookies with Orange Zest • Cinnamon Shortbread Bars with Dark Chocolate Ganache • Ice Cider Caramel Corn • Rolled Spiced Gingerbread • Rich Holiday Eggnog

Family, friends and food make up much of our Christmas fête in Montreal. There's a slow stream of guests who duck under the twinkling porch lights, stamp the snow off their boots and step in from the cold. From the hot-spiced apple cider and shortbread squares at my cookie swap in early December to the ice cider caramel corn and chilled bubbly in the wee hours of the morning on New Year's Day, we celebrate a month of bringing people together over food and drink.

On the snowy Saturdays leading up to Christmas we immerse ourselves in baking projects to holiday music. Cinnamon, cloves and ginger are sifted into the rolled gingerbread dough that is mixed up by the double batch and baked, tray after tray, until cut-outs of all shapes and sizes line the countertops (page 232). The cookies are decorated with silver dragées and sculpted into houses with chimneys and a tiny cinnamon-stick woodpile, but they're mostly consumed plain and simple, one gingerbread boy at a time.

A few weeks later it's my annual holiday cookie exchange, and for the last hour, girls have tumbled through the door, laden with tins and Tupperware. Diaper bags slap against their hips as they unwrap the layers off their youngest, who run to play with Clara. I relieve them of their baking and hand them a glass of homemade eggnog (page 236), which wins new converts every year. I've also made coffee and we nibble a stunning array of cookies while furiously talking all at once in a vain attempt to catch up. We admire the cookie-laden table and finally get down to the business of swapping. As usual, a snowstorm has blown in, and I set a few extra plates for those who wish to stay for dinner.

We are scattered all over North America, but once a year our fellow university grads come home to Montreal for Christmas and we gather for drinks, dinner and an evening of reconnecting. These days someone always introduces a new baby or announces a pregnancy. We're intentional with our time, and there is much more emphasis on connecting rather than fussing over food. We stay up far too late, but it's the holidays—it's what you do.

Before we know it, the calendar shows it is the twenty-fourth. There is only one option for the Christmas Eve menu in Quebec: it must be the province's favorite pork pie, tourtière (page 219). I serve mine with a platter of garlic-roasted mushrooms and an enormous wooden bowl of well-dressed kale salad with toasted pine nuts and glistening pomegranate seeds (page 216). We have family from out of town sleeping over, and somehow I get talked into staying up for a game of Agricola and a round of spiced (and spiked) eggnog.

Then it's Christmas morning, and the cats wake up first, demanding their breakfast, and then stretching lazily on the carpet next to the brown-paper-wrapped presents under the twig tree. I'm up early to pop a tray of muffins or scones into the oven, which I serve with homemade jam and *café à volonté*, of course. Eggs, sausages and wild blueberry pancakes with heaps of Quebec maple syrup all come later on, when we join up with cousins and siblings across town for a late brunch.

We're still finding our way with Christmas dinner traditions, and I suppose it will be so for some time to come, as is the case with blended families composed of members young and old, near and far. Some years we are fifty-strong at the home of one set of in-laws, for a hot turkey dinner with all the fixings, followed by an ample sweets table. Other years, we host another side of the family around our table, simply adorned with candles, fir boughs and pine cones. I roast a traditional turkey (page 220) and serve it with a tart cranberry sauce (page 224) and a gingery sweet potato purée (page 225). Family members contribute salads and desserts, making the meal a group effort. We exchange small gifts before the meal, but we're most grateful for having everyone together in good health.

In the slow days after Christmas, Danny, the children and I drift back and forth between the bright lights of Montreal and our snow-buried homestead. It's our special time to soak up a little culture at the cafés, museums and occasionally the ballet, as well as revel in simple childhood joys like playing in the snow and getting creative on family art day at home. Tucked in between holly-jolly parties are an equal number of down days, when we dress in layers and traipse out behind the house to go sledding or ice skating—or cozy up indoors and organize our own chess tournament with the boys.

Occasionally we invite friends over to hit the ice or the slopes, and I keep things simple: Mexican hot cocoa (page 207) for all, with a plate of shortbread squares (page 229). Guests may stay to dinner if they like, and I pull a casserole of butternut squash mac and cheese (page 265) from the freezer, which bakes up beautifully for a warm and comforting winter meal.

We've hosted a fête on New Year's Eve for as long as I can remember; it's much simpler to invite a group of friends over than plan to go out. No hefty babysitter fee, no cover charge, no late-night winter driving—just a good time in the comfort of our own home. Of course, it's also a great excuse to play board games, set out some simple party food, chill a bottle of champagne in the snowbank and set off fireworks into the night. The trick is to keep it simple and enlist plenty of helping hands instead of attempting an elaborate event on your own strength.

Days before our party, I prepare my famous Ice Cider Caramel Corn (page 230). An entire bottle of ice cider goes into each batch and lends a tangy sweetness to the addicting snack. I set out the last of the Christmas cookies (assuming they made it this far) and assemble a cheese tray with crackers and winter fruits. Around nine we ring in the New Year with the children with much whooping and balloon popping. The kids' uncle Michael sets off a round of fireworks in a snowbank in the backyard, and the children watch from the patio door, their faces pressed up against the glass. I wrap my arms around Mateo and feel his heart flip-flopping in his chest as the loud ones reverberate against the glass.

We wash the residue of candy canes from their sticky faces and tuck the children into their beds. As soon as they have drifted off into dreamland, we pop the first bottle of bubbly. This is much better than waiting until midnight, because we have a chance to enjoy it, and as the host, I don't have to worry about sending anyone home inebriated. We snack on caramel corn and cookies and reflect on the past year.

Perhaps the best holiday gatherings are the sleepy, snowed-in day where we linger in pajamas, spoon up turkey noodle soup and play Scrabble by candlelight. It's a day to regroup as a family and remember that having each other is the best gift of all.

KALE, POMEGRANATE AND PINE NUT SALAD

Enjoying a winter salad when I was young required a trip out in the cold to fetch the kale. Once out in the twinkling expanse of our snow-covered garden, with its gentle lumps here and there, I thought no one would ever guess there was life underneath. I would kick away the snow with my boots and dig with my woolen mittens until the bright green stalks came into view. It was our daily salad and much-needed boost of vitamin C during the long Yukon winters. My mother always made her kale salads with a sweet poppy seed dressing, and to this day it is my favorite way to eat kale. Use the best black pepper you can find.

SERVES 8

For the vinaigrette

½ small garlic clove, crushed

1 tablespoon (15 mL) pure maple syrup

1 tablespoon (15 mL) cider vinegar

1 teaspoon (5 mL) poppy seeds

½ teaspoon (2 mL) sea salt

½ teaspoon (2 mL) freshly ground black pepper or pepper blend

¼ teaspoon (1 mL) Dijon mustard

2 tablespoons (30 mL) olive oil

For the salad

1 large bunch kale

2 cups (500 mL) pomegranate seeds

½ cup (125 mL) pine nuts

1. **MAKE THE DRESSING**   In a small jar, combine garlic, maple syrup, vinegar, poppy seeds, salt, pepper and Dijon. Cover and shake well. Add olive oil. Cover, shake again and reserve.

2. **MAKE THE SALAD**   Cut away woody stalks and tough center ribs from kale greens. Wash and dry the kale. Slice it into thin ribbons. Dump the shredded kale into a large salad bowl. Give the vinaigrette a vigorous shake and pour over the kale. Toss well and let marinate for about 15 minutes, giving it a toss every once in a while to help break down the fibers.

3. Add pomegranate seeds and pine nuts. Toss again and taste for seasoning. Add a little more salt if desired. Serve at once.

VARIATION

Crumble ¼ cup (60 mL) blue cheese over the salad for a truly extravagant dish.

STORAGE

This salad dressing will keep in a jar in the refrigerator for up to 4 days.

QUEBEC TOURTIÈRE

Essentially, tourtière is a meat pie: lightly spiced ground pork (but can include beef, veal or game) layered between flaky pastry, and served with green ketchup or chutney. A total comfort food, tourtière has a place of honor on Christmas Eve tables in French-speaking Canada and needs no accompaniment save a tossed salad or bowl of steamed peas. Tourtière can be enjoyed warm or cold, for brunch, lunch or dinner, and also makes scrumptious little hand pies, if you have time for that sort of thing.

MAKES 2 (9-INCH/23 CM) TOURTIÈRES

1. In a large, heavy pot such as a Dutch oven, combine ground pork with 2 cups (500 mL) cold water. Mixture should be slightly soupy. Over medium heat, bring pork to a simmer, stirring frequently.

2. Add onion, celery, savory, pepper, nutmeg, cloves and bay leaves. Cook the filling, covered, over medium-low heat for 1¼ hours, stirring often. Add a little more water if the filling dries out completely.

3. Stir in oats and salt; cook for an additional 2 to 3 minutes. Discard bay leaves and cool the filling completely.

4. Preheat oven to 425°F (220°C). Line two 9-inch (23 cm) pie plates with rolled pastry. Divide filling between the pie shells and spread it out evenly. Brush around the rim of the pastry with the beaten egg. Place top crusts on both pies and press gently around the edges to seal. Trim pastry, crimp edges and cut 3 or 4 steam vents in top crust. Brush tops with beaten egg.

5. Bake tourtières for 15 minutes, then reduce heat to 375°F (190°C) and bake for another 25 minutes or until the crust is golden. Serve hot, accompanied by Fall Fruit Chutney (page 150).

3 pounds (1.5 kg) ground pork (ideally organic and local)

1 cup (250 mL) finely chopped onion

1 cup (250 mL) finely chopped celery

1½ teaspoons (7 mL) dried savory, crushed

1 teaspoon (5 mL) freshly ground black pepper

½ teaspoon (2 mL) nutmeg or mace

½ teaspoon (2 mL) ground cloves

2 bay leaves

½ cup (125 mL) quick-cooking rolled oats

1½ teaspoons (7 mL) salt

Double recipe Basic All-Butter Pie Crust (page 293) or other pastry for two 9-inch (23 cm) double-crust pies

1 egg, beaten, for glaze

KITCHEN TIP

Unbaked pies can be frozen; do not brush tops with egg. Wrap them well in plastic wrap and freeze. To bake, unwrap and brush the top with a little beaten egg. Place frozen pie in a preheated 375°F (190°C) oven. Bake until golden and heated through, 50 to 60 minutes. Baked pies can be cooled, wrapped well in plastic wrap and frozen. Remove tourtière from the freezer a few hours before serving, if possible. Wrap in foil to keep it moist, and warm in a 300°F (150°C) oven until heated through, 25 to 30 minutes.

STORAGE

Baked tourtière will keep in the refrigerator for up to 4 days. Frozen tourtière will keep in the freezer for up to 3 months.

BUTTER ROASTED TURKEY

Roast turkey does not make a frequent appearance on the Monday-to-Friday meal plan, but there's no need to feel daunted by a task that, in all honesty, is straightforward. I'm a sworn believer in a simple method that has come from years of practice and yielded great results every time, both for myself and for my blog readers. I don't bother to brine or baste the turkey. I don't stuff it and I don't truss it. I keep my cooking time shorter than most, but lengthen the resting period. The result is a perfectly golden, moist turkey that is relatively hassle-free.

Be sure to read through the method completely and read the accompanying notes before the big day.

1 fresh or thawed frozen turkey
About 2 teaspoons (10 mL) sea salt
½ cup (125 mL; 1 stick) unsalted butter, at room temperature

Note: If you purchased a pre-brined turkey, skip to step 3. Begin by removing any packaging, string or trussing and reserving neck and giblets. Remove wing tips.

1. The day before you plan to roast the turkey, remove it from any packaging and snip free any string or trussing. Remove neck and giblets from the body cavity, reserving for stock if desired. With a sharp knife, remove the wing tips (up to the first joint) and add those to the stock pot, too.

2. Pat the bird dry with paper towel. Place turkey on a sturdy tray or pan and season it all over with sea salt. Leave uncovered in the fridge overnight. This will allow the bird's skin to dry out, making it crispier. In addition, the salt will add flavor to the meat without the hassle of a brine bath.

3. Two hours before roasting, remove the turkey from the fridge and rub softened butter all over the bird. Coating the skin with butter will help to keep the meat moist, add flavor and ensure the skin turns a perfect golden brown.

4. Place turkey breast up on a rack in a large, shallow roasting pan with a little space all around the turkey. Elevating the turkey allows for the heat to get all around and permits the skin to crisp properly. Leave the turkey on the counter and allow it to come to room temperature. This takes about 1½ to 2 hours, depending on the size of the bird. Bringing the meat up to room temperature (about 70°F/21°C) will both cut down on the cooking time and ensure the bird cooks evenly.

5. Position oven rack on lowest level (remove remaining rack) and preheat oven to 400°F (200°C).

6. Roast turkey for 20 minutes. Reduce heat to 350°F (180°C) and roast for the remainder of the cooking time, as given below. If the top is browning too quickly, loosely cover the turkey with foil.

Here are my approximate cooking times
8 pounds (3.5 kg)—$1^3/4$ hours
10 pounds (4.5 kg)—2 hours
12 pounds (5.4 kg)—$2^1/2$ hours
15 pounds (6.5 kg)—$2^3/4$ hours
17 pounds (7.7 kg)—3 hours
20 pounds (9 kg)—$3^1/2$ hours

For larger birds, add about 12 minutes per pound (500 g) to the cooking time.

Oven temperatures can vary, so even if the turkey has been in the oven for the given time, you should still check for doneness. A meat thermometer should register 170°F (75°C) when inserted into the thickest part of the thigh (but not touching the bone).

7. After pulling the bird from the oven, it is time for the all-important step: resting. This time gives the cooking juices a chance to be reabsorbed into the meat instead of leaking out as soon as the turkey is sliced into. Transfer the turkey to a tray that will collect any accumulating juices (not all will be reabsorbed) and loosely tent the bird with foil. Rest for *at least* 30 minutes or up to an hour. Meanwhile, make your gravy and reheat side dishes in the oven, then carve the turkey and serve. Be sure your gravy is blistering hot and it won't matter if the turkey is merely warm.

TIMING NOTES
Timing a roast turkey is key, as no one wants an underdone or overdone bird. I count backwards from when I plan to serve dinner, and it works like a charm every time: Dinnertime minus a 30-minute resting period minus an approximate 3-hour roasting time minus 2 hours to bring it up to room temperature = the moment I remove the bird from the refrigerator.

SIZING NOTES
Cooking for a crowd? Plan on 1½ pounds (750 g) of turkey per person. For example, a 12-pound (5.4 kg) bird will serve 8 people and still leave you with leftovers. Too much turkey math for you? The Turkey Farmers of Canada website (www.tastyturkey.ca) has a fantastic "Whole Bird Calculator" complete with thawing times.

HOW TO REHEAT ROASTED TURKEY OR LEFTOVERS

This kitchen trick is nothing I can take credit for, but is a tried-and-true method used by my mother-in-law, Dorothy, every Thanksgiving and Christmas. Roasting the turkey and getting the carving out of the way ahead of time is a huge time-saver, especially when you are feeding up to fifty people like she does on a major holiday. It also frees up the oven for side dishes and means that the gravy can be made in advance with the turkey drippings.

If you are considering roasting a turkey ahead of time, or simply want to reheat leftovers, this method is for you. Reheating time will vary depending on how many pounds of turkey you are warming. Check it frequently and watch that it doesn't go longer than needed.

1. Carve the turkey and slice into portions.

2. Line an ovenproof dish with iceberg lettuce.

3. Layer sliced turkey over the lettuce.

4. Drizzle turkey with a little turkey or chicken stock.

5. Top the turkey with additional iceberg lettuce.

6. Cover dish tightly with foil and chill until needed.

7. Preheat oven to 350°F (180°C).

8. Bake for 20 minutes with foil and lettuce intact.

9. Check if the turkey is heated through.

10. If hot enough, transfer turkey to a platter and discard the lettuce. Serve at once.

CRANBERRY CLEMENTINE RELISH

I lost a favorite pot during the initial turkey feast I cooked in our first home. An unattended cranberry sauce cooked down into a molten sticky mess, then into charcoal that billowed smoke. The pot never stood a chance, but the experience *did* teach me to buy an extra bag of cranberries and stash one in the freezer for emergencies.

My favorite cranberry sauce comes together in just a few minutes and can be made up to a week in advance. It's sweet and tangy, slightly reminiscent of chutney, but stays true to the flavors of classic cranberry sauce. Just don't burn it.

MAKES 2 CUPS (500 ML)

3 cups (750 mL) fresh or
  frozen whole cranberries
  (a 12-ounce/340 g bag)
½ cup (125 mL) raw cane sugar
4 clementines, scrubbed
1 teaspoon (5 mL) cider vinegar

1. In a medium saucepan, combine cranberries and sugar. Zest one of the clementines over the sugar. Peel the fruit and coarsely chop the segments, removing seeds as you go. Add all the pulp and juice to the pot. Juice the remaining 3 clementines and strain the juice into the pot. Add ½ cup (125 mL) water.

2. Over medium heat, bring the mixture to a low boil. Cook for 5 minutes, until the cranberries have popped and the liquid begins to evaporate and get sticky. Reduce heat to medium-low. Add cider vinegar. Cook the relish gently for 5 more minutes, stirring occasionally.

3. Transfer the sauce to a pint (500 mL) jar to cool.

STORAGE
This sauce will keep in an airtight container in the refrigerator for up to 7 days or in the freezer for up to 3 months.

HONEY GINGER SWEET POTATO PURÉE

Danny declares that this vegetable side has outshone the main dish more than once. Perhaps because its velvety texture and sweet-spicy combination is so hard to resist. It's equally delicious reheated on the second day, which makes it an excellent do-ahead option for holidays or Sunday dinner. I've been known to top it with toasted pecans, and large coconut flakes are also delicious sprinkled over as garnish.

SERVES 4 TO 6

1. Preheat oven to 375°F (190°C) and line a rimmed baking sheet with foil. Place sweet potatoes in center of the pan, drizzle with olive oil and season with salt. Fold up foil to enclose potatoes and seal edges. Be sure no air can escape.

2. Bake until potatoes feel soft when pressed from outside the foil, about 1 hour and 45 minutes. Turn off oven and allow potatoes to finish cooking with residual heat, about 15 minutes.

3. Meanwhile, melt butter in a small saucepan. Stir in honey and ginger and leave to infuse for those final 15 minutes.

4. Peel skins from potatoes and place flesh in a large bowl. Using a potato masher, mash potatoes. Alternatively, purée potatoes in a food processor. Fold in ginger and honey butter. Season purée with salt and pepper. Serve hot.

2½ pounds (1.125 kg) sweet potatoes (about 3 large)
2 tablespoons (30 mL) olive oil
Sea salt
¼ cup (60 mL) salted butter
1 tablespoon (15 mL) honey
1 teaspoon (5 mL) grated fresh ginger
Black pepper

STORAGE
This dish will keep in the refrigerator, covered, for up to 24 hours. One hour before serving, remove plastic wrap and reheat in a 325°F (160°C) oven until the sides are bubbling and the center is piping-hot.

WHOLE WHEAT CHOCOLATE CHUNK COOKIES WITH ORANGE ZEST

I'm not organized in every aspect of housekeeping or homesteading, but I do pride myself on always having a batch of cookie dough in the freezer. This recipe is a favorite, equally so for its relation to the beloved classic and its unique orange nutty flavor. These cookies are happiness; large and soft, slightly raised, chewy on the outside and tender in the middle. Perfect for a school lunch treat or a baking project with your preschooler.

MAKES 48 COOKIES

3 cups (750 mL) whole wheat bread flour

1¼ teaspoons (6 mL) baking powder

1 teaspoon (5 mL) baking soda

1 teaspoon (5 mL) salt

1 cup (250 mL) unsalted butter, cut into ½-inch (1 cm) cubes

1 cup (250 mL) raw cane sugar

½ cup (125 mL) honey

2 large eggs

1 teaspoon (5 mL) pure vanilla extract

1 large orange, scrubbed

8 ounces (250 g) bittersweet chocolate, coarsely chopped into ¼- and ½-inch (5 mm and 1 cm) pieces

1. Position oven racks in upper third and lower third of oven and preheat oven to 350°F (180°C).

2. Whisk together flour, baking powder, baking soda and salt; set aside.

3. In the bowl of a stand mixer fitted with the paddle attachment, cream butter with sugar until fluffy, about 3 minutes. Add honey and mix to combine.

4. Add eggs, one at a time, beating well after each addition. Stop the mixer and scrape down the sides of the bowl. Add the vanilla; mix well. Using a microplane, zest the orange over the bowl to get the oils with the zest.

5. Add flour mixture and mix to combine. Add chopped chocolate and give it one final stir.

6. Using a 1½-tablespoon (20 mL) ice cream scoop, scoop half of the cookie dough into balls and place 12 balls 2 inches (5 cm) apart on each of two baking sheets. Bake cookies, rotating baking sheets once halfway through the baking time, for 9 to 11 minutes or until light brown around the edges but still soft in the center. Transfer to racks to cool completely.

7. When baking sheets are cool, portion out the remaining 24 cookies and refrigerate or freeze on baking sheets for later enjoyment.

STORAGE
These cookies will keep in an airtight container for up to 4 days or in the freezer for up to 3 months. The raw cookie dough balls will keep in the refrigerator for up to 4 days or in the freezer for up to 6 months. To bake frozen cookie dough balls, place on a baking sheet and bake directly from frozen in a 350°F (180°C) oven for 12 to 13 minutes.

CINNAMON SHORTBREAD
BARS ~ WITH
dark chocolate
GANACHE

CINNAMON SHORTBREAD BARS WITH DARK CHOCOLATE GANACHE

Rolled shortbread dipped in dark chocolate has long been a holiday favorite of mine, but in recent years it has been a luxury I have had to do without, as it is too time consuming. These bars are my adaptation of the beloved shortbread and chocolate pairing—except there is no rolling and cutting, no tempering of the chocolate and positively *no* dipping. Instead, I give you a straightforward two-layer bar that triggers all the fond memories with its soft, crumbly shortbread base and rich, dark chocolate ganache topping. Laced with spice, these bars typify what holiday baking should be: simple, sensational and completely irresistible.

You may want to bake a double batch and leave them plain to keep around for when friends unexpectedly drop in for tea.

MAKES 32 SMALL BARS

1. Preheat oven to 350°F (180°C). Line a 9-inch (2.5 L) square baking pan with parchment paper, leaving an overhang on two opposite sides.

2. Beat together butter and sugar until fluffy, about 3 minutes, scraping down the sides of the bowl as needed. Add flour, cinnamon and a pinch of salt, and stir until evenly combined. Press shortbread into the bottom of the prepared pan and use the bottom of a glass to ensure it is firmly packed.

3. Bake for 23 minutes or until the edges begin to turn golden brown. Cool in the pan on a rack.

4. Chop chocolate and place in a medium heatproof bowl. In a small saucepan, warm cream with a pinch of salt over medium heat until it just begins to form steam and boil. Pour hot cream over the chopped chocolate and stir gently with a heatproof spatula until chocolate is melted and mixture is smooth. Let the ganache set for about 10 minutes to thicken slightly.

5. Spoon the ganache onto the cooled cinnamon shortbread base and spread evenly with the spatula. Cover with plastic wrap and chill the bars for at least 4 hours or overnight. Loosen the sides of the shortbread with a sharp knife. Using the sides of parchment paper, lift the slab out of the pan and place on a cutting board. Cut into 32 squares.

¾ cup (175 mL) unsalted butter, at room temperature

½ cup (125 mL) raw cane sugar

1½ cups (375 mL) all-purpose flour

1 teaspoon (5 mL) cinnamon

¼ teaspoon (1 mL) salt, divided

4 ounces (175 g) best-quality bittersweet chocolate

⅔ cup (150 mL) heavy (35%) cream

STORAGE

These bars will keep in an airtight container in the refrigerator for up to 1 week or in the freezer for up to 8 weeks.

ICE CIDER CARAMEL CORN

With nearly an entire bottle of ice cider in the coating, this caramel corn is definitely not intended for the kids' table—they won't appreciate it—but it is very suitable for impressing your friends. Because it freezes so well, I like to portion a batch into jars or cellophane bags and keep them stashed in my chest freezer for an *à la minute* holiday hostess gift.

MAKES 18 CUPS (4.5 L)

18 heaping cups (4.5 L) popped popcorn (about 1 cup/250 mL kernels)

1¼ cups (300 mL) ice cider

1 cup (250 mL) raw cane sugar

¾ cup (175 mL) heavy (35%) cream

½ cup (125 mL) unsalted butter

⅓ cup (75 mL) dark agave syrup

¼ teaspoon (1 mL) salt

¼ teaspoon (1 mL) baking soda

KITCHEN TIP

Don't have a candy thermometer? Fill a small cup or bowl with ice water and drop ½ teaspoon (2 mL) of boiling caramel into it every so often. Caramel is ready when it forms a small ball between your fingers.

STORAGE

This caramel corn will keep in an airtight container for up to 2 weeks or in the freezer for up to 6 months.

1. Position oven racks in upper and lower third of oven and preheat oven to 275°F (140°C). Line two rimmed baking sheets with parchment paper. Divide popcorn between two large bowls and have two sturdy heatproof spatulas on hand.

2. In a 3-quart (3 L) heavy pot, bring ice cider to a boil over high heat. Boil for 8 to 10 minutes, until it is darker in color and somewhat syrupy. Remove from heat and pour into a liquid measuring cup, scraping the dregs from the pan with a heatproof spatula. It should measure ¼ cup (60 mL). Set aside.

3. In the same pot, combine sugar, cream, butter, agave and salt. Bring to a boil over medium heat, and boil rapidly for 3 minutes, stirring occasionally. Remove from heat and stir in the reduced ice cider. Return to medium-high heat and boil the syrup for another 4 to 5 minutes or until it reaches the soft-ball stage (240°F/116°C).

4. Remove from heat and add baking soda. Stir the foamy blond-colored caramel vigorously. Pour the ice cider caramel over the bowls of popcorn and toss like a salad with heatproof spatulas to coat evenly. If you have room, combine both bowls into one larger one and stir very well to ensure all the popcorn is evenly coated.

5. Divide popcorn between the prepared baking sheets and spread in a (mostly) single layer. Bake for 1 hour. Every 15 minutes, remove one pan at a time from the oven. Take the four corners of the paper and shake the caramel corn into the center, then redistribute it around the pan in a single layer.

6. After 1 hour of baking, turn off oven, prop the door open slightly and cool caramel corn for 10 minutes in the oven. Break apart the caramel corn if you like.

ROLLED SPICED GINGERBREAD

Make sure your ground spices are less than a year old to ensure you can enjoy cookies with the fullest flavor. This gingerbread improves with age, so don't hesitate to fill a tin and keep it around for teatime.

MAKES 6 DOZEN (3-INCH/8 CM) COOKIES

2 cups (500 mL) all-purpose flour

1½ cups (375 mL) whole wheat flour

2 teaspoons (10 mL) baking powder

½ teaspoon (2 mL) salt

¼ teaspoon (1 mL) baking soda

2 teaspoons (10 mL) cinnamon

2 teaspoons (10 mL) ground ginger

¼ teaspoon (1 mL) ground cloves

¼ teaspoon (1 mL) ground allspice

½ cup (125 mL) raw cane sugar

¼ cup (60 mL) coconut oil

¼ cup (60 mL) unsalted butter

1 cup (250 mL) dark molasses

1 large egg

STORAGE

These gingerbread cookies will keep in an airtight container at room temperature for up to 1 week or in the freezer for up to 3 months.

1. In a medium bowl, whisk together all-purpose flour, whole wheat flour, baking powder, salt, baking soda, cinnamon, ginger, cloves and allspice.

2. In a large bowl, cream together sugar, coconut oil and butter until smooth. Add molasses and beat well. Beat in egg and mix until the batter is smooth.

3. Add the dry ingredients and mix until a stiff dough forms. Turn out onto a clean counter and form into two balls. Flatten each ball into a disk and wrap in plastic wrap. Chill for at least 2 hours or up to 3 days.

4. Preheat oven to 375°F (190°C). Remove dough from refrigerator about 30 minutes before rolling.

5. Roll out the dough between two large pieces of parchment paper to prevent it from sticking to the counter and the roller. You can also skip the paper and use liberal amounts of all-purpose flour, but the first method yields a more tender cookie. Cut the cookies out with floured cookie cutters and transfer to a rimmed baking sheet.

6. Bake gingerbread for 8 minutes for a softer cookie and about 11 minutes for a cookie with more snap to it. Cool cookies completely on a rack before decorating.

HOMESTEADING

Homemade Edible Holiday Gifts

I don't sew or quilt, and I only knit sporadically, so edible treats are the kind of handmade gifts that I know how to do well. If you are a procrastinator, I strongly advise against heading out of the house to shop, for you will only endure painfully long lineups, grumpy salesclerks, crowded parking lots and—if you live in a cold climate as I do—icy roads. Instead, choose an item or two from this list, wrap on an apron and create a delicious homemade food gift.

HOMEMADE EDIBLE HOLIDAY GIFT IDEAS

- Ice Cider Caramel Corn (page 230)
- Cinnamon Shortbread Bars with Dark Chocolate Ganache (page 229)
- Whole Wheat Chocolate Chunk Cookies with Orange Zest (page 226)
- Cranberry Pear Mincemeat (page 176)
- Cinnamon Applesauce (page 155)
- Maple Walnut Granola (page 11)
- Maple Pecan Butter Tarts (page 19)
- Maple Marshmallows (page 104)

MORE CREATIVE EDIBLE GIFT IDEAS

- chocolate-dipped dried fruit
- homemade crackers
- flavored salts
- drink mixes
- spiced nuts
- homemade candy

HOMEMADE INFUSED OIL

Infused oils add flavor to salad dressings, marinades and vegetable dishes. I usually make mine with rosemary because I've got a big healthy plant of it, but you can use most any fresh herb. Sage, thyme, oregano and tarragon would all be top choices for me, besides rosemary.

Here is the basic method for homemade infused oil. Estimate 4 or 5 generous stems of herbs for each cup (250 mL) of olive oil.

- Sterilize bottles or jars (see page 147).
- Wash herbs and pat dry.
- Warm olive oil in a pot.
- Stuff herbs into bottles.
- Top up bottles with warm oil.
- Cool oil, and then top bottles with cork or screw cap.
- Label and include instructions to remove herbs after a week.

PACKAGING AN EDIBLE GIFT

Stock up on items for pretty packaging well before the holidays, as it's much easier to dress up a jam jar or bag of cookies if you already have what you need on hand for presenting the gift. For decorating and packaging an edible gift:

- Bags—clear cellophane or brown paper decorated with children's art
- Jars—any size or shape will do
- Bottles—good for oils and vinegars
- Tins—all shapes and sizes; antiques are particularly charming
- Dishes—a pretty mug, an ice cream bowl, an espresso cup
- Small boxes—you can cover them in Christmas paper
- Baskets
- Wax paper and ribbon
- Baking pans, mini loaf pans or small pie plates
- Now round up a little ribbon or burlap garden twine and get the kids set up with stiff paper and markers to make and decorate labels for your homemade gifts.

KIDS CAN
make, bake and decorate

For a child, few holiday events can match the sheer joy of baking Christmas cookies together as a family. It fosters creativity, instills confidence and is good old-fashioned fun. In the weeks leading up to Christmas, we make a little time for after-school cookie baking. It gives my boys something to look forward to and doesn't even feel overwhelming amidst all the other holiday activities.

The key is to break everything down into manageable steps.

Step 1: Choose a recipe. Every family has their favorite; ours is Rolled Spiced Gingerbread (page 232), a healthier version of the traditional holiday cookie. Rolled shortbread or sugar cookies are popular options for decorated cookies.

Step 2: Gather the ingredients. Have everything ready to go at the beginning of the week to ensure the project goes smoothly. Besides ingredients to make the cookies, pick up a few decorations and tins to package some cookies as gifts. Also, gather aprons, rolling pins, cookie cutters—and a camera to capture the fun.

Step 3: Mix the dough. Rolled cookie dough is always best after it has chilled, so the night before, measure and mix according to the recipe you have chosen. Wrap the ball of dough tightly in plastic wrap and refrigerate overnight.

Step 4: Roll, cut and bake. Remove the dough you made the previous day from the refrigerator a half hour before you begin. The dough will be easier to roll when it's at room temperature and there will be less cracking of the shapes. Roll the dough between two large pieces of parchment paper to prevent it from sticking to the counter and the roller. Dip cutters in flour before cutting out each shape to avoid sticking.

Once shapes are baked, cool them completely and store in an airtight container until you are ready to decorate.

Step 5: Decorate and create. Before starting this step with your children, prepare a batch of your favorite icing and set out the decorations. If you use food coloring (I do once or twice a year), it's fun to let the children add it and watch the transformation. Give free rein to their creativity and accept that it may get messy. Don't forget: you're making memories.

Last tip? Give your children freedom to sample and taste. Christmas comes but once a year!

RICH HOLIDAY EGGNOG

This bourbon-spiked, nutmeg-laced eggnog never fails to win people over at my holiday parties. Why eggnog got such a bad rap, I'll never know, but those versions must not have been made with whole cream and pure maple syrup. This seasonal beverage packs a punch, so serve it over a full glass of ice, preferably with a cookie on the side.

SERVES 10

3 egg yolks

½ cup (125 mL) pure maple syrup

2 cups (500 mL) whole milk

1¼ cups (300 mL) heavy (35%) cream

1 cup (250 mL) bourbon

¼ cup (60 mL) rum of your preference

1 teaspoon (5 mL) pure vanilla extract

Pinch of salt

Whipped cream and nutmeg, for garnish

STORAGE

Eggnog will keep in the refrigerator for up to 2 days. Shake well before pouring.

1. In a large bowl, whisk egg yolks with maple syrup until creamy.

2. Pour in milk, cream, bourbon and rum; stir to combine. Stir in vanilla and salt.

3. Transfer eggnog to a clean pitcher, cover and chill well, ideally overnight.

4. Stir vigorously before pouring. Serve on the rocks with a dollop of soft whipped cream and a sprinkling of nutmeg if desired.

11

SUNDAY DINNERS

Nova Scotia Seafood Chowder • Rosy Grapefruit and Pomegranate Spritzers • Fennel-Celery Salad with Meyer Lemon and Walnuts • Slow Cooker Cider Ham • Crispy Rosemary Roast Potatoes • Brussels Sprouts with Honey and Hazelnuts • Citrus Cheesecake • Toasted Oat and Cocoa Smoothies

During the winter months, Sunday dinner enjoyed at midday is a tradition in our home, a leisurely meal where I pour gravy, swirl wine and spoon custard over preserved fruit. For once, there is no rush to be somewhere, and we are connecting as a family before a new week begins.

My love of Sunday dinner ignited one chilly day after church, at a young age, when friends of my parents invited my family to share a meal. We didn't get invited out often, perhaps because we numbered six and each of us sported a healthy appetite. It was terribly exciting to go somewhere new instead of making the long trip home for an undoubtedly nourishing but most unexciting bowl of cabbage soup. I must have been six or seven at the time, because I recall being about eye level with the feast spread on a crisp white tablecloth. There was roast and gravy, carved and poured at the table, and white tureens heaped with steaming mashed potatoes and bright green peas, a delicacy for us as my parents seldom purchased frozen vegetables.

I was on my best behavior, instilled by my British father: only speaking when spoken to and laying my cloth napkin across the flounces of my dress. I don't remember a snippet of conversation, so engrossed was I in my china plate of Sunday dinner. Would I be offered a second soft white roll? Indeed I would, thank you very much. Our hosts were gracious, soft-spoken and ever so generous. When the meal was cleared, our host Debbie set out delicate crystal dessert bowls and spooned homemade fruit preserves into them. The whipped cream–topped cherries and peaches were passed around the table, a grand finale to an elegant feast.

For a long time afterward, I wanted to be just like Debbie: set a fine table and carve a roast at the head of it. I wanted to preserve my own stone fruits and confidently serve them simply adorned for a perfect dessert in the heart of winter. I wanted to take in families—the ones with gangly teens and messy babies—and provide an atmosphere of hospitality. I wanted to serve up heaps and heaps of soft rolls with sweet butter and never reproach the child who reached for a second or third.

It's taken nearly thirty years, but I've finally accomplished my goal, and Sunday dinner is now a highlight of our week. As it turns out, it's a mighty practical time to entertain guests or just enjoy an unhurried family dinner. We have our main meal of the day around one in the afternoon, in true British "Sunday roast" fashion. There are a number of reasons why this works best for us at our current stage in life. Consider weeknight dinners during the school months: they are bookended with homework and often hurried so that baths can be taken and stories read before an early bedtime hour. Our Saturdays are often a blur of activities and errands in the morning, followed by a social event in the afternoon and into the evening.

That leaves Sunday for slowing down, savoring a meal together and connecting with each other and close friends. As we have small children and they droop as the day wears on, a midday meal ensures we can include them and expect proper manners. It also frees up the evening to unhurriedly prepare for the week ahead and maintain the usual bedtimes. When we're hurtling through life at a terrific rate, Sunday dinner provides an opportunity to sit down as a family, civilized-like, at least once on the weekend.

Another bonus? I feel better when I eat a main meal in the day and a lighter one later in the evening. On Sunday nights we'll fix just a small snack for supper and still go to bed feeling satisfied. A cold roast beef sandwich or a bowl of leftover chowder is usually sufficient. A favorite snack of the children's (and mine) would have to be Toasted Oat and Cocoa Smoothies (page 254).

But the day isn't just for family. Sunday dinner is an occasion to catch up with friends in our home. It's nothing unusual for us to invite a couple of friends back to our place after church and pull several extra chairs around our table as we share our spread. The focus is connecting, and the heart is hospitality, so there is no need to worry about impressing.

Even if you are cooking for a small crowd, Sunday dinner is an ideal way to get a jump start on meals for the week ahead. I love cooking for leftovers, and whenever I cook a roast I will make extra for school lunches. Vegetables, whether roasted or steamed, I prepare in double for frittatas, salads and soups, and I will frequently shake up a double amount of salad dressing to last through the week. Every little bit of advanced prep helps, so stock up on groceries and double your recipes.

There's something elegant about a well-rounded meal in the middle of the day, but Sunday dinner doesn't have to mean hours and hours of cooking. On Friday I'll pencil out a menu and shop for items I need. Then I prepare a part of the meal on Saturday: the dessert, a salad dressing and a vegetable side. I chill a bottle of wine and set the table, too. Much of what makes the meal so special is sitting down to a well-dressed table, so I take time to fold cloth napkins, prepare a simple, seasonal centerpiece and polish the glasses. On Sunday, I cook a roast with potatoes or something along those lines, and reheat the vegetable side. Then I open the wine and toss the salad just before we sit down. It doesn't have to be any more complicated than that.

I've come to rely on the five S's when I don't have much time to plan. They are easy to remember:

1. **SPRITZER.** A splash of juice topped with sparkling water is easy enough to pour guests as they arrive (Rosy Grapefruit and Pomegranate Spritzers, page 244). If you wish to have more of a cocktail, keep a bottle of rosé or Prosecco chilled and add it to the spritzer just before serving.

2. **SOUP.** Soup is always a good choice because it offers warmth from the winter chill, and it's easy to double the recipe and serve a crowd. Most soups can be prepared in advance (Roasted Carrot, Parsnip and Thyme Soup, page 268) and are even better enjoyed on the second day.

3. **SLOW COOKER.** No, it's not just for weeknight suppers, but it can turn out a juicy cider ham (page 247), pot roast or chicken dinner, too.

4. **SIDES.** Many side dishes can be made a day ahead and reheated, like Honey Ginger Sweet Potato Purée (page 225) or Maple Cider Baked Beans (page 12).

5. **SWEETS.** It is my firm belief that Sunday dinner needs a sweet finish. It could be as simple as a plate of shortbread squares (page 229), a jar of peach preserves (page 156) or classic Citrus Cheesecake (page 252).

I always plan the dessert last, in case my guests offer to make a contribution to the meal. Then I kindly accept and ask them to bring a dessert, making it clear that anything they bring—homemade or purchased—is most welcomed.

After dessert, we will bundle up and head outside for a walk, if the weather permits. On particularly blustery days, we will stay in and stay cozy, while the boys play a game of chess. Our youngest, Clara, has her own small set; she squats on the floor to meticulously stand each piece upright and then swiftly mows them down with a laugh and a toss of her pigtails.

Essentially, we are making slow family food a priority, one week at a time. Sunday dinner is a tradition that carves out a healthy family food culture to last for generations.

NOVA SCOTIA SEAFOOD CHOWDER

On my first visit to the Maritimes, we arrived to find the city of Halifax shrouded in fog and damp sea air. Ravenous, our family of five turned up on my sister's doorstep at dinnertime and were rewarded with the hauntingly delicious aroma of seafood chowder. Miranda simmered a stock, poached several pounds of "chowder mix"—seafood easily sourced at any grocery—and served it up in deep bowls. We inhaled the fragrant steam and dipped our spoons into what was the best chowder I had ever tasted. She poured a crisp white wine and passed crusty bread to signal the start of a meal I will always look back on as simple, elegant and deserving of being routinely reproduced for loved ones.

You can buy fish stock at most fishmongers; look in the frozen foods section. If not, premium canned fish stock is delicious, too.

SERVES 6

2 medium red potatoes, scrubbed

3 cups (750 mL) fish stock

Pinch of saffron threads

2 tablespoons (30 mL) olive oil

2 medium onions, finely chopped

1 fennel bulb, trimmed and diced

1 can (8 ounces/284 mL) diced tomatoes

3 garlic cloves, minced

2 bay leaves

Zest of 1 orange

2 tablespoons (30 mL) chopped fresh thyme

1 teaspoon (5 mL) salt

1 pound (500 g) mixed skinless fish fillets such as haddock and salmon

8 ounces (250 g) raw shrimp, peeled and deveined

¼ cup (60 mL) heavy (35%) cream

Freshly ground black pepper

1. Dice potatoes, place them in a bowl and cover with stock to keep them from turning brown. Soak saffron in 2 tablespoons (30 mL) hot water.

2. Heat olive oil in a 3-quart (3 L) pot over medium heat. Add onions and fennel; cook until soft, about 5 minutes, stirring occasionally. Stir in the potatoes and stock, saffron liquid, tomatoes, garlic, bay leaves, orange zest, thyme and salt. Bring to a simmer. Cook for 10 to 12 minutes or until potatoes are tender.

3. Meanwhile, chop fish into 1-inch (2. 5 cm) pieces. (At this point you can hold the mixture until just before serving.)

4. Add fish. Reduce heat to medium-low and simmer for 1 to 2 minutes. Add shrimp and simmer for 2 more minutes.

5. Pour in cream. Season with salt and pepper. Stir gently to distribute the embellishments. Taste and adjust seasoning and serve at once.

STORAGE

This chowder will keep in the refrigerator for up to 24 hours.

ROSY GRAPEFRUIT AND POMEGRANATE SPRITZERS

As we are a no-soda household, we have a Tupperware jug that does brisk business, serving up juices, lemonade and flavored water. On special occasions, such as Sunday dinner, we'll serve up a fruity spritzer in jam jars for glasses and hand out straws around the table for fun. I never tire of the sweet and tart winter beverage options, and this pomegranate-grapefruit combination is one of my favorites. Freshly squeezed grapefruit juice makes for an exceptional sip and is well worth the effort.

SERVES 6

3 cups (750 mL) red grapefruit juice

2 cups (500 mL) pomegranate juice

2 cups (500 mL) sparkling water or seltzer

1 red grapefruit, scrubbed and sliced

1. In a large pitcher or jar, combine grapefruit juice, pomegranate juice and 1 cup (250 mL) ice. Top up with sparkling water and stir well.

2. Pour into glasses and garnish with a slice of grapefruit. Serve at once.

VARIATION
Add a splash of rosé wine, Prosecco, gin or Campari to the glasses—just not all four at once!

FENNEL-CELERY SALAD WITH MEYER LEMON AND WALNUTS

Our winters run long and cold, and somewhere in the middle I grow weary of the usual local ingredients. Fortunately, Meyer lemons make an appearance in stores sometime after Christmas, as bright as the sunshine I am missing so much. They are not local, but I can't resist a handful of the organic variety. Because they are so precious, I like to use them in their entirety, minus the seeds, and this crunchy winter salad is a perfect example.

I like to serve it piled high on small plates of smoked salmon, add a crust of baguette and call it an appetizer. The tart-sweet Meyer lemon is essential to the salad's allure, but in a pinch, you can substitute the zest and juice of a standard lemon.

SERVES 4

1. Cut Meyer lemon in half from top to bottom. Lay one half cut side down and slice as thinly as possible. Discard seeds.

2. Juice the remaining lemon half into a bowl. Add olive oil, salt and pepper. Whisk the dressing with a fork and then add the sliced lemons. Set aside to marinate while you prepare the salad.

3. Thinly slice fennel crosswise and place in a medium salad bowl. Slice the celery. Chop walnuts. Add celery and walnuts to the fennel.

4. Pour in the lemon dressing and toss the salad thoroughly. Taste for seasoning and add more salt if needed. Serve at once.

1 Meyer lemon, scrubbed

2 tablespoons (30 mL) extra-virgin olive oil

½ teaspoon (2 mL) sea salt

¼ teaspoon (1 mL) black pepper

1 fennel bulb, trimmed

5 inner tender ribs celery

¾ cup (175 mL) walnuts, toasted

VARIATION
Add a few forkfuls of Quick Pickled Gingered Baby Carrots (page 95) for a salad with a little extra pop!

SLOW COOKER CIDER HAM

A ham really is one of the simplest ways to feed a crowd, and this recipe is among the easiest. If you categorize slow cooker meals under "gray and unappetizing," think again. This ham presents beautifully, and is fork-tender thanks to a long and gentle cook time.

We pair it with Maple Cider Baked Beans (page 12) and crunchy Fennel-Celery Salad (page 245) for a cold-weather Sunday dinner. Use the leftover ham as a head start on weekday meals.

SERVES 8 TO 10

1. Pour cider into a 6-quart (6 L) slow cooker. In a small bowl, combine maple syrup, Dijon, ginger and pepper. Zest the orange into the bowl and mix marinade ingredients together.

2. Rub marinade all over the ham, using every bit of it, and place the ham in the slow cooker. You may need to trim the ham to make it fit. Just add the trimmings to the slow cooker as well.

3. Peel the orange and coarsely chop the pulp, discarding any seeds. Add the orange around the sides of the ham and tuck the cinnamon stick in also.

4. Cover the slow cooker and cook on low for 8 hours or on high for 4 hours.

5. To serve, transfer ham to a platter. Cover to keep warm. Strain liquid from the slow cooker into a gravy pitcher and serve with the ham.

1¼ cups (300 mL) fresh-pressed apple cider (unfiltered, raw apple juice)

¼ cup (60 mL) pure maple syrup

2 tablespoons (30 mL) smooth or grainy Dijon mustard

¼ teaspoon (1 mL) ground ginger

¼ teaspoon (1 mL) black pepper

1 orange, scrubbed

1 best-quality bone-in smoked ham (6 to 7 pounds/2.7 to 3.15 kg)

1 cinnamon stick

KITCHEN TIP

Save the ham bone for a stock or split pea soup.

STORAGE

This ham will keep in an airtight container in the refrigerator for up to 3 days.

CRISPY ROSEMARY ROAST POTATOES

Done just right, crispy roasted potatoes are a perfect side for Sunday dinner, and can accompany any sort of roast. They can also double as hash browns alongside eggs and bacon for brunch, should you prefer to sleep in. My version, one of the most popular recipes on *Simple Bites*, uses cornmeal to coat the potatoes. This crunchy addition, combined with a high cooking temperature, ensures an utterly crispy potato with a moist, fluffy interior. A cast-iron pan yields the best results.

SERVES 6

1. Position a rack on the lowest level of the oven and preheat oven to 425°F (220°C).

2. Cut each potato in half, then in half again, until you have 4 evenly sized chunks per potato. Place in a medium pot with 1 teaspoon (5 mL) of the salt, cover with cold water and set over high heat. Bring potatoes to a boil, then reduce heat slightly and boil for 2 minutes.

3. In a large bowl, mix together cornmeal, remaining 1 teaspoon (5 mL) salt and pepper. Drain potatoes, then transfer to the bowl with the cornmeal and toss gently to coat.

4. In a 12-inch (30 cm) cast-iron pan or heavy skillet, heat olive oil over high heat. When small bubbles begin to rise (but before oil is smoking) and oil is *very* hot, add rosemary and garlic. Stir carefully with tongs for a minute to infuse the oil.

5. Carefully add cornmeal-crusted potatoes all at once to the hot oil and arrange them with your tongs so that they are evenly distributed around the pan. Place the skillet in the oven and roast for 15 minutes. Carefully remove pan from oven and turn each potato so the crispy side faces up. Roast for another 20 to 25 minutes or until golden all over.

6. Using a slotted spoon, transfer potatoes to a serving platter. Sprinkle with chopped fresh rosemary and a sprinkling of sea salt if desired. Serve at once.

2 pounds (1 kg) red potatoes (about 6 or 7 medium), peeled
2 teaspoons (10 mL) salt, divided
2 tablespoons (30 mL) cornmeal
½ teaspoon (2 mL) black pepper
¾ cup (175 mL) olive oil
Leaves from 2 sprigs fresh rosemary, minced, plus more chopped for garnish
8 garlic cloves, peeled

KITCHEN TIP
Don't toss the oil from the pan. Instead, let cool, then strain through a coffee filter or fine sieve and reserve for roasting vegetables.

BRUSSELS SPROUTS WITH HONEY AND HAZELNUTS

During the gray days of winter, I get excited to cook Brussels sprouts and eat them over and over. Danny is equally enthusiastic about these cruciferous vegetables. However, our children are not yet converted. That's okay—more for us.

In this recipe, honey complements the slight bitterness of the sprouts, and twice-toasted hazelnuts add an essential crunch. It's important not to overcook the sprouts, as they can become bitter and will lose much of their nutritional value. They should stay a vibrant green and retain a little of their bite.

SERVES 4

¼ cup (60 mL) whole raw hazelnuts

4 teaspoons (20 mL) olive oil, divided

2 tablespoons (30 mL) liquid honey, divided

¾ teaspoon (4 mL) sea salt

1 pound (500 g) Brussels sprouts

1 tablespoon (15 mL) butter

1 grapefruit, scrubbed

Freshly ground black pepper

KITCHEN TIP
Look for bright green sprouts that are firm and dense. Choose sprouts of similar size so they cook evenly, and go for the smaller heads (about 1¼ inches/3 cm across) as they are usually more tender.

1. Preheat oven to 350°F (180°C).

2. Toast hazelnuts on a baking sheet in the oven for 8 minutes. Pour them into a clean tea towel and wrap them up. Vigorously rub the hazelnuts through the towel to remove the skins. Don't worry if they don't all come off.

3. In a small microwaveable bowl, whisk together 1 teaspoon (5 mL) of the olive oil and 1 teaspoon (5 mL) of the honey. Warm for 15 seconds or so in the microwave and stir to combine. Add nuts to the mixture and toss to coat. Sprinkle with a generous pinch of sea salt. Return the nuts to the baking sheet and toast in the oven for another 12 to 15 minutes or until they are light brown. Turn the pan of hot hazelnuts onto a cutting board and let them cool. Coarsely chop.

4. Trim the bottoms of the Brussels sprouts. Peel off the outer leaves and discard. Slice sprouts in half top to bottom.

5. In a large sauté pan over medium-high heat, melt butter together with the remaining 3 teaspoons (15 mL) olive oil. Add sprouts and cook, stirring frequently, just until they turn a vibrant green, with browned bits, 6 to 8 minutes.

6. Reduce heat to low and drizzle sprouts with the remaining honey. Using a microplane, zest the grapefruit into the pan. Season Brussels sprouts with salt and pepper and stir to combine thoroughly. Transfer to a serving bowl. Sprinkle with honey-roasted hazelnuts and serve hot.

CITRUS CHEESECAKE

Washing dishes at the local gourmet joint isn't such a bad job for a teen if you secure their beloved cheesecake recipe in the bargain. My adapted version of this cake has graced the sweets table at countless baby showers, church luncheons, graduation celebrations and birthday parties. No matter the event, it is always a suitable dessert, and no matter the company, no one can resist a slice.

As the seasons change, I vary the flavors of the cheesecake, as well as the accompanying toppings. In spring I use Meyer lemons and spoon rhubarb compote over the top of each slice. Summer calls for plenty of lime zest in the batter and a jug of blueberry syrup for drizzling. When the snow flies, I seek out blood oranges to flavor the cheesecake and garnish the top with a festive ring of pomegranate seeds or slices of clementines for the holiday season. Rest assured, however, that this cheesecake requires no embellishment; it's also lovely on its own.

Plan to make the dessert the day before serving it, as it benefits from an overnight chill.

SERVES 8 TO 12

For the crust

1¼ cups (300 mL) graham cracker crumbs

2 tablespoons (30 mL) raw cane sugar

¼ cup (60 mL) unsalted butter, melted

For the filling

3 packages (8 ounces/250 g each) cream cheese, at room temperature

¾ cup (175 mL) raw cane sugar

⅓ cup (75 mL) sour cream

Zest and juice of 1 lemon, scrubbed

Zest and juice of 1 orange, scrubbed

5 large eggs, at room temperature

For the topping

1½ cups (375 mL) sour cream

¼ cup (60 mL) raw cane sugar

1 lemon, scrubbed

1. Preheat oven to 350°F (180°C).

2. MAKE THE CRUST   In a small bowl, combine graham cracker crumbs and sugar. Add melted butter and mix with a spatula until butter is evenly distributed. Dump into a 9-inch (23 cm) springform pan. Shake the pan to distribute the damp crumbs evenly, and then pack down well. Bake crust for 8 to 10 minutes or until slightly golden. Cool.

3. MAKE THE FILLING   In the bowl of a stand mixer fitted with the paddle attachment, beat together cream cheese and sugar until smooth. Add sour cream, citrus zest and citrus juice. Mix well. Add eggs, one at a time, mixing after each addition but not too vigorously. Pour filling over crumb crust.

4. Bake for 50 to 60 minutes. The cheesecake will have puffed significantly and the middle will still be slightly jiggly. Cool on a rack for 15 minutes. The cake will sink as it cools.

5. MAKE THE TOPPING   Combine sour cream and sugar in a small bowl. Zest the lemon into the bowl. Add 2 tablespoons (30 mL) lemon juice. Stir well.

6. Pour lemon topping over the warm cheesecake and let stand for half an hour at room temperature. Cover cheesecake with plastic wrap and refrigerate for at least 6 hours or overnight.

7. Run a knife around the edge of the pan and lift off the sides of the pan. If desired, slip a sharp knife under the crust and slide the cheesecake off the base and onto a cake stand or serving platter. Garnish cheesecake with sliced clementines, pomegranate seeds, a spoonful of blueberry butter (page 159) or preserved peaches (page 156).

KITCHEN TIP

To get a pretty and tidy slice, cut the cheesecake with a hot knife. Run a sharp knife under hot water, give it a quick wipe with a clean tea towel and then slice the cheesecake. Repeat for each cut.

STORAGE

This cheesecake will keep, wrapped and in the refrigerator, for up to 4 days.

TOASTED OAT AND COCOA SMOOTHIES

Sunday-evening eats are quick and hassle-free, often featuring eggs, leftovers or blender creations. This smoothie, a result of using up the odd leftover bits of pumpkin purée, became a fast favorite after the children dubbed it "chocolate milkshake." It's an unconventional milkshake, that's for sure, but one that the whole family will enjoy. For a dairy-free version, substitute almond milk for the milk in the recipe; the results are equally popular.

SERVES 2

¼ cup (60 mL) quick-cooking rolled oats

4 teaspoons (20 mL) cocoa powder

¼ teaspoon (1 mL) pumpkin pie spice or cinnamon

1½ cups (375 mL) milk

¼ cup (60 mL) pure pumpkin purée

½ frozen banana

1 tablespoon (15 mL) pure maple syrup

¼ teaspoon (1 mL) pure vanilla extract

1. Preheat broiler. Combine oats, cocoa powder and pumpkin pie spice in a pie plate. Toast under the broiler for 1 minute, then give it a shake to redistribute the ingredients, and toast for 1 more minute. The cocoa will darken a shade and the oats will turn light golden and smell fragrant. Cool completely.

2. In a blender, combine milk, pumpkin purée, banana, maple syrup and vanilla. Blend until combined. Add toasted oat mixture and blend until smooth and frothy. Pour into glasses and serve at once with a straw.

KITCHEN TIP

Freeze extra pumpkin purée in ice cube trays for future quick smoothies.

ENTERTAINING HACKS
FOR JAM JARS

A few winters back, Danny and I hosted a sit-down dinner on Christmas Day for fourteen family members. I had ordered the leg of lamb, counted to be sure we had enough chairs and assembled a simple rustic centerpiece with pine boughs and pomegranates. Everything was coming together smoothly when I realized I didn't have enough matching drinking glasses. Heck, I didn't even have that many glasses, period.

Fortunately, I keep a sizable stash of jam jars around for preserves and was able to round up the required number of half-pint jars. As it turned out, they matched the country-chic feel of my table with its linen tablecloth and pine boughs.

Mason jars are exceedingly versatile, and it's a good idea to keep a dozen or so stashed in a closet for simple entertaining hacks. Here are a few of my favorite uses for jars of all sizes.

Drinks. Serve up cocktails, party punch or water in jars as I did that Christmas. It makes for an easy cleanup, as everything goes in the dishwasher, no handwashing or polishing required.

Flowers. Arrange a simple bouquet in a mason jar as a centerpiece. Better yet, fill several jars with blooms and run them down the entire center of the table.

Candles. Nestle tea lights in the bottom of a collection of vintage jars and cluster them together for another variation on the table centerpiece. You can use sand, rock salt or bath salts to hold them in place.

Condiments. Skip the ketchup bottle or the sticky mustard pot and spoon condiments into small jelly jars to serve at the table. They may be prepared in advance and kept in the refrigerator with a lid.

Cutlery canister. Wrap the guests' silverware in a cloth napkin and tuck it into a mason jar at each place setting. Alternatively, set out wide-mouth quart jars to hold the appropriate utensils at the start of a buffet line.

Dessert. From peach trifle (page 129) to sticky maple pudding (page 20), desserts served in jars will forever be appreciated. I've made everything from elaborate molten chocolate cakes to simple ice cream scoops served with caramel sauce. Wide-mouth half-pint jars work the best for me.

Edible gifts. For party favors or hostess gifts, the jam jar can hold anything from caramel corn (page 230) to a stack of cookies. Or, you know, jam.

KIDS CAN
learn about
unprocessed foods

We want our children to grow up to be healthy eaters, aware of the way their food is produced and how their food choices affect the planet. Most important, we want them to connect the dots between health, whole food and happiness.

Choosing to "eat unprocessed" narrows your food choices down to real, whole foods. The ingredients listed on the foods you buy should be recognizable, and the contents of your basket should change with the seasons. And yes, you guessed it, there is a lot of cooking involved.

If you are looking to make a commitment to eating more whole foods, I have a few tried-and-true tips for approaching this lifestyle with children.

1. TALK IT OUT. Communication is essential, especially with little ones who may be missing their jar of processed, sugary peanut butter or their chicken nuggets. Explain in simple terms that processed foods contain empty calories and additives that our bodies can't thrive on. If your children are older, watch an eye-opening food documentary such as *Food, Inc.* together as a family and discuss it afterward.

2. FOCUS ON WHAT YOU CAN EAT, RATHER THAN ON WHAT YOU CAN'T. There's always a healthier homemade version of kids' favorite foods, whether mac and cheese (page 265), hot chocolate (page 207) or cookies (page 226). Begin a list of whole foods that your family enjoys, keep it heavy on the fruits and vegetables, and add to it every time you discover a new favorite.

3. USE THE "UNPROCESSED" CHALLENGE AS AN OPPORTUNITY TO TRY NEW INGREDIENTS AND GET OUT OF A COOKING RUT. Even with a background in professional cooking and a large cookbook collection, I can easily slip into a rut of making the same old eight or ten dinners in a month. Making a plan to eliminate processed foods is the perfect kick in the pants to *really* change things up. Your kids can help choose new dinners as well as snacks and drinks. My kids love the Toasted Oat and Cocoa Smoothie (page 254) for an afternoon snack.

4. MAKE A MENU PLAN (PAGE 202). A menu plan will help you stock your pantry with whole ingredients, determine a few meal options and focus your commitment to unprocessed foods. It's a vital step in succeeding with this way of feeding the family, especially for busy parents with myriad other projects on the go.

5. INVITE THE KIDS INTO THE KITCHEN WITH YOU (PAGE 190). Allowing children to help prepare the food gives them a sense of ownership and pride. They will be more willing to try a new dish or ingredient when they have had a hand in cooking it.

6. GET TO KNOW YOUR SEASONAL FRUITS, VEGETABLES AND FRESH HERBS. Let the kids pick produce at the market—one fruit and one vegetable each—and include them in the preparation of their food item. Kale chips, sweet potato fries and squash macaroni and cheese (page 265) are all good examples of kid-friendly foods that highlight vegetables, and Chocolate Beet Sheet Cake (page 204) will never fail to impress them.

7. START SMALL. Don't impose more on your children than you think they are comfortable with. Each month in our house we challenge ourselves to a week of "hard-core" unprocessed eating, and let the rest of the month be "soft core." We go out for ice cream or poutine— in moderation, of course. Some households can implement a restrictive diet practically overnight and still thrive; ours just isn't one of them. Find the balance that works for your family, and most important—have fun!

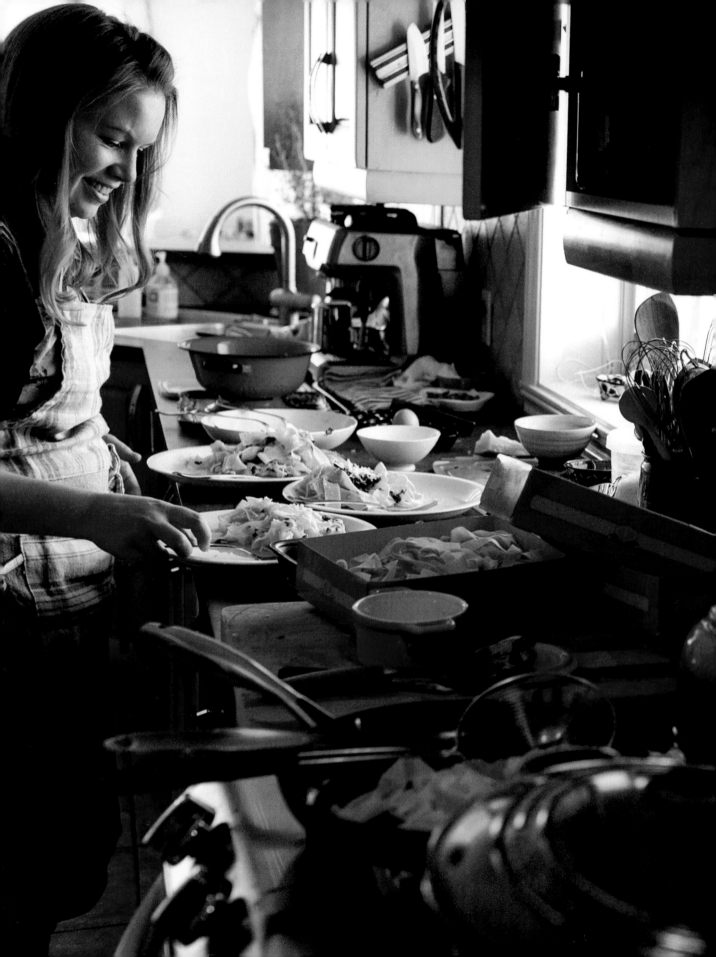

12
BATCH COOKING

Maple Pumpkin Chili • Cheesy Butternut Squash Penne • French Onion Soup •
Big-Batch Bolognese • Roasted Carrot, Parsnip and Thyme Soup • Mild Marinara Sauce •
Tender Baked Meatballs • Everyday Mexican Beans

A job at a nondescript Italian bistro helped me pay my way through culinary school. After an hour-long commute, my bus would drop me off in front of a strip mall, and I'd let myself in the back door. It wasn't the sort of convivial Italian restaurant, with hanging salamis and slabs of prosciutto, where nonnas rolled meatballs at a table in the back. Nope, it was a corner-cutting, penny-pinching, sad state of a bistro, with boxes and boxes of frozen filled pasta delivered at night and served up the next day in enormous hotel pans, smothered in sauce and dusted with chalky Parmesan cheese.

Wages were appallingly low—barely enough to cover my monthly bus pass, loft rent and a few groceries. But with only experience, not papers, to show for myself, my ruddy-faced boss wouldn't pay a penny more. It was this situation that propelled me to enroll in culinary school to get certification and find a better job. At the bistro, I perfected the skill of working efficiently. Each evening I prepared tray after tray of meatballs, vats of marinara sauce and buckets of Bolognese, a kind of cooking boot camp with a vengeance. Once the sauces were simmering, I moved on to soups: vegetable noodle, ribollita and that beloved Italian classic, minestrone. Later, there were salads to prepare and stash in the walk-in for the next day's lunch, and finally, desserts.

It was a torturous job, but one that I could perform while in a state of exhaustion. I took away a handful of recipes from the Italian bistro that I adapted to become our family favorites, but the best takeaway was the discipline of batch cooking I acquired behind the stoves and the speed to execute the dishes.

Nowadays, I rely on my freezer for dinner at least once a week, counting on a stockpile of soups, stews and main dishes for backup plans on days when I just can't keep up. During the coldest month of winter, when I've been out and about maneuvering the snowy roads and enduring traffic, I'm comforted with the knowledge that at least dinner is taken care of and we'll have time for homework with the boys. Time and time again, batch cooking comes to the rescue.

Freezer cooking can be a huge asset to kitchen prep time. No matter how busy the day gets, it's important for our family to finish the day around the table for a nourishing dinner. Making extra and freezing it is my time-saving practice to make that happen. If the thought of a frozen entree doesn't sound appealing, let me remind you that many family-friendly meals freeze and reheat extremely well, and hearty winter dishes top the list of freezer cooking fare.

Chances are you already practice batch cooking in some form or another. Maybe you double a pie crust recipe and freeze half, or you crisp more bacon than you need and tuck some away for sandwiches later in the week. It makes perfect sense to go through the motions only once, dirty the dishes only once, and then reap the benefits of your work on another day when you are strapped for time.

Dinner, advanced

Batch cooking doesn't only mean a stack of lasagnas piled high in the freezer or quadrupling a recipe of chocolate chip cookie dough. My freezer includes jars of chopped herbs in oil, pre-marinated meats, pesto and a Costco-size block of Parmesan grated in the food processor and frozen for quick uses later. This prepped food offers a springboard to dinner and the opportunity for a meal with substance.

Not only do you get to predetermine the taste and quality of your meals, but you also get the handy convenience that comes with having parts of meals ready to go: boil some linguine from your pantry, make a salad and toss the hot pasta with thawed pesto and a sprinkle of pre-grated Parmesan.

Saving the season

Batch cooking allows us to enjoy seasonal produce year-round. Such is the case with my Roasted Tomato Pizza Sauce (page 288), made and frozen or canned in the peak of summer and enjoyed on dark winter nights. Filling our pantry and our freezer allows us to enjoy healthy organic produce months after the summer has faded. The recipes in this chapter focus on produce that is easily available in winter—and lean on hearty comfort foods like meatballs, chili and soups to warm the tummy.

Preparedness

If you're itching to get away on that girls' weekend retreat, stocking the freezer for weekend meals will get you one step closer to escaping. Are you hosting a family reunion or do you have a surgery scheduled? Rest assured in knowing that you have a stash of meals reserved for the occasion.

Meals for others

One of my favorite benefits of batch cooking is that it helps you spread some love to others in the form of a home-cooked meal. My friends and I like to heap presents on first-time mothers, but we also give the baby showers a delicious spin by each contributing a frozen, home-cooked meal for the mommy-to-be's freezer. Often this is a greater blessing than the matching blankets and baby bibs. It certainly was when I first brought my children home from the hospital.

I've long been an advocate of preparing heat-and-serve meals for others with dishes that are nourishing, travel well and freeze well. What is the best thing to bring a family dealing with illness, a friend on bed rest or the new couple who moved in next door? Cookies, muffins and other treats are wonderful, but in most situations, what people really need are nourishing main meals, because snacks can only go so far. A nourishing root vegetable soup (page 268) or a comforting dish of meatballs (page 273) are the dishes that will benefit your recipient the most.

Storage

I prefer to store many things in glass jars instead of plastic so I can easily see what is inside. Glass is also BPA-free. I use mason jars, Weck jars (www.weckjars.com) and recycled jars from the kitchen.

Tips for freezing soups, stocks, sauces and chilies in jars:

- Cool overnight in the fridge.
- Leave 2 inches (5 cm) of headspace to allow for expansion.
- Freeze with lids off.
- Place on a flat surface in freezer.
- Add lids when stock is solid and label with the date.
- Try to use straight-sided jars and not the jars with shoulders, which tend to break more easily.

Equipment for batch cooking

You can't double or triple a recipe if you don't have the right equipment to properly execute the dish. Read through each recipe before you begin and check that your pots, pans, mixers and blenders are large enough to accommodate what you want to cook.

MAPLE PUMPKIN CHILI

This recipe came about from a pot of overly spicy chili that my children could not eat. Back on the stove it went, with a helping of pumpkin purée and a splash of maple syrup. These two ingredients balanced out the fiery chipotle and all was well again. We prevented a loss and gained a new family favorite. Pumpkin is high in vitamin A, and this nourishing chili is a good way to include this vegetable in your child's diet. It's even better on the second day, when the flavors have had a chance to meld, so keep that in mind when you plan your menu.

SERVES 6

1 tablespoon (15 mL) olive oil

3 mild Italian sausages (about ⅔ pound/350 g)

1 pound (500 g) lean ground beef

1 large onion, finely chopped

1 small fennel bulb, cored and finely chopped

2 large garlic cloves, minced

2 teaspoons (10 mL) ground cumin

1 teaspoon (5 mL) dried oregano

½ teaspoon (2 mL) chipotle chili powder

½ teaspoon (2 mL) freshly ground black pepper

2 cups (500 mL) beef stock

1 cup (250 mL) pure pumpkin purée

1 can (14 ounces/398 mL) crushed tomatoes

1 can (14 ounces/398 mL) kidney beans, drained and rinsed

2 tablespoons (30 mL) pure maple syrup

1½ teaspoons (7 mL) salt

1. Heat olive oil over medium-high heat in a large, heavy pot. Slit sausage casings and remove the filling. Discard the casings. Add sausage meat and ground beef to the pot. Cook the meats until they are lightly browned, about 5 minutes, using a wooden spoon to break up the ground meats into smaller pieces.

2. Stir in onion and fennel; cook for 2 minutes.

3. Add garlic, cumin, oregano, chili powder and black pepper; stir to combine. Add beef stock, pumpkin purée, tomatoes, kidney beans and maple syrup. Stir well as you bring the chili up to a low boil.

4. Simmer for 1 hour over low heat, stirring occasionally. Season with salt. Serve hot.

VARIATION
Replace the fennel with celery if desired.

STORAGE
This chili will keep in an airtight container in the refrigerator for up to 3 days or in the freezer for up to 6 months. Freeze in jars, leaving 1 inch (2.5 cm) of headspace, or in sturdy reusable containers. Thaw overnight in the refrigerator, then reheat in a pot.

CHEESY BUTTERNUT SQUASH PENNE

Macaroni and cheese is a mainstay around any family table and this one elicits whoops from my three penne gobblers. I'm equally enthusiastic about the dish because it is made with organic whole wheat pasta and uses an entire butternut squash, a vegetable my boys would otherwise not touch with a ten-foot pole. A little bacon doesn't hurt either. The squash acts as a thickener for the cheese sauce, eliminating the step of making a roux. The casserole freezes magnificently, so go ahead and make two while you're at it.

SERVES 6

1. Position racks in the middle and lower third of the oven and preheat oven to 400°F (200°C).

2. Cut squash in half lengthwise and scoop out the seeds. Wrap both halves individually in foil. Place on a baking sheet and roast in the middle of the oven for about 1 hour, until they feel soft when squeezed through the foil.

3. Meanwhile, line a rimmed baking sheet with foil and spread bacon on the sheet. Bake below the squash until crispy, about 15 minutes. Transfer bacon to a paper towel to drain. Crumble and set aside.

4. Bring a large pot of water to a boil and season with 1 teaspoon (5 mL) of the salt. Add penne and cook according to package directions. Drain pasta and spread out on a baking sheet to cool.

5. Pour cream into the same pot. Scoop the hot squash flesh out of the skins with a spoon and add to the cream. Scrape both squash halves clean.

6. Over low heat, whisk cream and squash until incorporated. The sauce will be a little lumpy. Add remaining 1 teaspoon (5 mL) salt, pepper and 1½ cups (375 mL) of the grated cheese. Cook, whisking constantly, until the cheese melts and is stringy.

7. Add the pasta and stir to coat. Transfer to a freezer-to-oven casserole. Sprinkle with remaining ½ cup (125 mL) cheese and the crumbled bacon. (At this point you can cool the pasta completely, then wrap in plastic wrap and freeze, or you can continue on to bake.)

8. To finish, bake the casserole, uncovered, for 15 to 20 minutes. Serve at once.

1 small butternut squash
(about 1¼ pounds/625 g)

5 slices bacon

2 teaspoons (10 mL) sea salt, divided

1 pound (500 g) whole wheat
penne rigate

1 cup (250 mL) half-and-half (10%)
cream

¼ teaspoon (1 mL) black pepper

2 cups (500 mL) grated mild or
medium cheddar cheese, divided

STORAGE

This casserole will keep, well wrapped and refrigerated, for up to 4 days or in the freezer for up to 3 months. To reheat from frozen, place the frozen casserole in a 375°F (190°C) oven and bake for 45 to 50 minutes or until heated through.

FRENCH ONION SOUP

French onion soup should not be rushed. Well, the onion-chopping part, yes. Use a food processor or blitz through them with a knife as fast as you can. Once they are in the pot, however, brew a pot of tea and read a cookbook while the onions slowly caramelize and take on that dark brown color. In this Canadian version of the French classic, enhanced by maple syrup and garnished with aged cheddar cheese, the flavor is so robust it makes a satisfying supper on a cold winter night.

If you have an opened bottle of white wine around, this soup benefits from a generous splash or two added with the stock. It makes a big batch, but the onion soup base freezes well, making for a delightful midweek dinner in the future.

SERVES 8

3 tablespoons (45 mL) olive oil

3½ pounds (1.6 kg) sweet onions, such as Vidalia (about 4 large), thinly sliced

2 garlic cloves, minced

2 tablespoons (30 mL) pure maple syrup

2 cups (500 mL) chicken stock

2 teaspoons (10 mL) fresh thyme leaves

1 small sprig fresh rosemary

2 teaspoons (10 mL) salt

1 teaspoon (5 mL) black pepper

8 slices whole wheat baguette, toasted and buttered

2 cups (500 mL) grated aged cheddar or your favorite melting cheese

Small sprigs fresh thyme, for garnish

1. Heat oil in a heavy pot over medium-high heat. Add onions and cook, stirring frequently, for about 10 minutes or until they have completely wilted and start to caramelize. Reduce heat to medium-low and cook onions slowly, stirring occasionally, for another 20 minutes.

2. Add garlic and cook for a minute or so, then stir in maple syrup. Add 3 cups (750 mL) water, the stock, thyme and rosemary. Bring soup to a boil, then reduce heat and simmer for 20 minutes. Season with salt and pepper.

3. Meanwhile, preheat broiler.

4. Divide hot soup among 6 large or 8 smaller ovenproof bowls or ramekins set on a rimmed baking sheet. Top with toasted baguette slices and cover generously with cheese. Broil for 2 to 3 minutes or until cheese is melted and light brown. Garnish with a sprig of fresh thyme and serve at once.

STORAGE

Soup base keeps in an airtight container in the refrigerator for up to 3 days. To freeze, at the end of step 2, cool soup completely. Review tips for freezing in jars, page 261. Transfer cooled soup to 1-quart (1 L) jars or reusable containers, cover and freeze for up to 3 months. Thaw overnight in refrigerator, then proceed with recipe.

BIG-BATCH BOLOGNESE

My husband, Danny, was practically raised on spaghetti Bolognese, and so it was one of the dishes that made it into our regular repertoire from the beginning. Because it freezes and reheats so well, the sauce is an ideal candidate for batch cooking. A jar from the fridge or freezer has saved many a dinner over the years, and I expect to be making many more pots in the years to come. In the summer, I load the sauce with fresh basil and oregano, but this winter version is heavy on the garlic instead. Grated mushrooms melt into the sauce, hidden from suspicious children, leaving behind only their delicious umami flavor. This is a rich sauce, meant to be assembled with care and then simmered slowly to develop deep flavor. It's even better on the second day.

MAKES 16 CUPS (3.8 L)

1. In a large, heavy pot, heat oil over medium heat. Add onion and cook for about 2 minutes, stirring occasionally, until the onion softens. Add celery and cook for another 2 minutes, stirring occasionally.

2. Increase heat to medium-high and add ground beef. Brown the meat for about 10 minutes, stirring it occasionally and breaking it apart with a sturdy wooden spoon or spatula. Beef should be well crumbled with no pink remaining.

3. Meanwhile, grate mushrooms on the large holes of a box grater. Add mushrooms, garlic, oregano and pepper to the pot. Mix well and cook for 2 minutes.

4. Empty in the cans of crushed tomatoes and the balsamic vinegar. Stir thoroughly, getting right to the bottom. Reduce heat to low, add the bay leaves and simmer the sauce for 90 minutes. Stir occasionally, scraping the bottom of the pot.

5. Discard bay leaves. Stir in salt, then taste and adjust seasoning if desired. Serve at once over pasta or cool completely if storing.

3 tablespoons (45 mL) olive oil

2 cups (500 mL) chopped red onion (1 large)

2 cups (500 mL) diced celery

3 pounds (1.5 kg) lean ground beef

8 ounces (250 g) cremini mushrooms

4 large garlic cloves, minced

2 teaspoons (10 mL) dried oregano

1 teaspoon (5 mL) freshly ground black pepper

4 cans (28 ounces/796 mL each) crushed tomatoes

1 tablespoon (15 mL) balsamic vinegar

2 bay leaves

2 teaspoons (10 mL) sea salt, or more to taste

VARIATION

I've long embraced the laid-back approach to pasta sauce, in which a collection of fridge ingredients can be combined and simmered to perfection. Put your own spin on this recipe. Add a splash of red wine or a smattering of root vegetables, or cook the onion in bacon fat.

KITCHEN TIP

Add Parmesan cheese rinds and let them simmer with the Bolognese. It saves them a trip to the garbage and further enhances the flavor of the sauce.

STORAGE

This sauce will keep in an airtight container in the refrigerator for up to 5 days or in the freezer for up to 6 months. Freeze in jars, leaving 1 inch (2.5 cm) of headspace, or in sturdy reusable containers. Thaw overnight in the refrigerator, then reheat in a pot.

ROASTED CARROT, PARSNIP AND THYME SOUP

I was never much of a fan of cooked carrots, a dislike that goes as far back as I can remember. As a child, I much preferred my carrots pulled straight from the earth and wiped clean on the autumn grass. Fortunately I discovered the delights of roasting this root vegetable, and now my ideal soup begins with pairing carrots and parsnips, caramelizing them in the oven before simmering them into a sweet and rich soup enhanced with fresh thyme and bulked up with new potatoes. You'll be glad the recipe makes enough for leftovers.

MAKES 16 CUPS (3.8 L)

1 pound (500 g) young carrots, peeled and sliced into ½-inch (1 cm) coins

1 pound (500 g) parsnips, peeled and sliced into ¾-inch (2 cm) coins

2 tablespoons (30 mL) extra-virgin olive oil, divided

1 tablespoon (15 mL) fresh thyme leaves

1 teaspoon (5 mL) salt, divided,

½ teaspoon (2 mL) black pepper

1 small onion, sliced

8 ounces (250 g) potatoes, peeled and cut into 1½-inch (4 cm) chunks

4 cups (1 L) chicken or vegetable stock

1. Preheat oven to 400°F (200°C).

2. Toss carrots and parsnips in 1 tablespoon (15 mL) of the olive oil. Add thyme, ½ teaspoon (2 mL) of the salt and the pepper; toss again. Spread in an even layer on a rimmed baking sheet and roast for 30 minutes or until vegetables are softened.

3. Meanwhile, in a large, heavy pot, heat remaining 1 tablespoon (15 mL) oil over medium-high heat. Add onion and cook, stirring often, for about 2 minutes. Add potatoes, stock and 2 cups (500 mL) water. Bring to a boil, then reduce heat to medium and simmer, partially covered, for 8 minutes or until the potatoes are medium-tender.

4. Add roasted vegetables to the soup. Partially cover and bring to a boil, then remove lid and simmer for 15 minutes. Remove from heat and let soup stand a few minutes to cool slightly.

5. Blend soup in batches until smooth. Add salt to taste—don't be shy, as the seasoning dramatically changes the taste. Add a few tablespoons of cream, if desired, for an extra-rich taste. Serve hot.

STORAGE

This soup will keep in an airtight container in the refrigerator for up to 3 days. To freeze, cool soup to room temperature, then transfer to 1-quart (1 L) wide-mouth jars or reusable containers. Leave 1 inch (2.5 cm) of headspace to allow for expansion. Freeze for up to 3 months. Thaw soup overnight in the refrigerator. Transfer to a medium pot and bring to a simmer over medium heat, whisking well.

MILD MARINARA SAUCE

Quick to make and versatile, this is one sauce you'll want to simmer up in your largest pot and freeze for enhancing dishes for months ahead. It's handy to have around for recipes like chicken parmesan or baked meatballs (page 273). I love to spoon it over baked cauliflower or layer it with ricotta and flat noodles for a vegetarian lasagna. The marinara simmers for a good long time to develop flavor, so make it on a day when you are not rushed.

MAKES 12 CUPS (2.8 L)

6 cans (28 ounces/796 mL each) diced or whole tomatoes

½ cup (125 mL) extra-virgin olive oil

8 large garlic cloves, finely chopped

2 teaspoons (10 mL) salt

1 teaspoon (5 mL) dried oregano

1 teaspoon (5 mL) dried basil

½ teaspoon (2 mL) red pepper flakes (optional)

1. Purée or blend the canned tomatoes with their juices until smooth.

2. Heat a large, heavy pot over medium heat and add olive oil. Heat oil for 1 minute, then add garlic. Stir continuously for an additional 1 minute, taking care not to let the garlic brown.

3. Stir about ½ cup (125 mL) of the tomato purée into the garlic. Cook for about 1 minute; the olive oil will take on a golden color. Caramelizing the tomato in the garlic oil will give the sauce a boost of flavor.

4. Add remaining tomato purée, salt, oregano, basil and red pepper flakes, if using. Stir well. Simmer over medium-low heat for at least 4 hours, stirring occasionally. The sauce will thicken. Continue cooking if you want an even thicker sauce.

5. Taste and adjust salt if desired. Serve at once or cool completely if storing.

STORAGE

This sauce will keep in an airtight container in the refrigerator for up to 5 days or in the freezer for up to 6 months. Freeze in jars, leaving 1 inch (2.5 cm) of headspace, or in sturdy reusable containers. Thaw overnight in the refrigerator, then reheat in a pot.

TENDER BAKED MEATBALLS

It seems I am always making meatballs to feed a crowd, perhaps because my eldest, Noah, has been requesting them for his birthday dinner since he was three. Mounds of spaghetti topped with these tender meatballs are as much of a tradition as blowing out the candles on the birthday cake. This is not a laborious recipe, thanks to the help of a food processor and baking the meatballs instead of browning them in batches in a skillet. Get the children up to the counter to help with the rolling and watch things really speed along.

MAKES 30 MEATBALLS

1. Preheat oven to 425°F (220°C).

2. Peel onion and cut into quarters. Peel garlic.

3. In a food processor, combine onion, garlic and parsley. Blitz for about 15 seconds, until everything is chopped but not puréed. Add milk, eggs, salt and pepper. Pulse 10 times to combine the mixture.

4. Place ground beef, veal and pork in a large bowl. Pour in the parsley slurry, Parmesan and panko. Using your hands, work the meatball mixture very gently, incorporating all the ingredients together with as little handling as possible. This is key for keeping the meatballs tender.

5. Roll the meat into 30 balls, each roughly the size of a small peach. Place them on a tray or a sheet of wax paper until all are shaped. Wash your hands well.

6. Pour olive oil into a large roasting pan or divide between two ovenproof skillets. Place the pan in the oven for 2 minutes to heat the olive oil. Remove pan from oven and carefully tip in the meatballs. Distribute them quickly, using a pair of tongs, and slide the pan back into the oven as quickly as you can. This will help the meatballs to get a partial sear on the bottom, that delicious brown crust so prized in a meatball.

7. Bake for 20 minutes, then reduce heat to 350°F (180°C). Slide out the oven rack a little and carefully tip the marinara sauce over all the meatballs. Stir gently to distribute the meatballs and sauce evenly around the pan. Bake for 30 more minutes. Serve at once over pasta, or cool completely if storing.

¼ sweet onion

2 garlic cloves

1 cup (250 mL) loosely packed fresh parsley leaves

¼ cup (60 mL) milk

4 eggs

1½ teaspoons (7 mL) salt

¼ teaspoon (1 mL) freshly ground black pepper

1 pound (500 g) each ground beef, veal and pork

½ cup (125 mL) grated Parmesan cheese

⅔ cup (150 mL) panko crumbs

¼ cup (60 mL) olive oil

6 to 8 cups (1.5 to 2 L) Mild Marinara Sauce (page 270)

STORAGE

These meatballs will keep in an airtight container in the refrigerator for up to 3 days or in the freezer for up to 6 months. Freeze in 3 batches of 10 meatballs each, together with marinara sauce, in sturdy reusable containers. Thaw overnight in the refrigerator, then reheat in a pot.

EVERYDAY MEXICAN BEANS

My sister Haidi married Nick from New Mexico and inherited a handful of recipes passed down from his Mexican grandmother, who simmered a pot of these pinto beans and rolled a fresh batch of tortillas every morning. Haidi often makes a double batch to make the time spent worthwhile and because these beans are so versatile. I have to agree. Adding a smoked ham hock makes the best beans, but I have made them with several slices of bacon, or even a spoonful of bacon fat, or a generous pour of olive oil for a vegetarian option. Whatever you choose, beans taste better and are more easily digested when cooked with a little fat.

One of our favorite suppers is simply this—a scoop of beans beside a couple of warm corn tortillas layered with grated cheese, topped with a spoonful of salsa. Adding a few slices of avocado and a dollop of sour cream are all one could ask for. These also often make an appearance as refried beans: mashed and heated up in a skillet. Combined with grated cheese, they make tasty bean burritos (page 100).

MAKES 8 CUPS (2 L)

4 cups (1 L) dried pinto beans

4 garlic cloves

1 teaspoon (5 mL) dried oregano

1 can (14 ounces/398 mL) tomato sauce

2 rounded tablespoons (40 mL) raw cane sugar

1 smoked ham hock (nitrate-free if possible)

Sea salt

1. Spread the beans on a tray and pick over them to remove any stones, then rinse the beans under cool water. In a medium pot, cover the beans with an inch (2.5 cm) of water. Let soak overnight.

2. The next morning, drain beans and cover with fresh water. Bring to a boil over medium heat. As they boil, skim off the scum that rises to the surface.

3. Partially crush garlic with the side of a knife or your palm and add it to the beans. Add oregano, tomato sauce, sugar and the ham hock. Do not salt the beans now, as it will cause them to be tough. Return to a boil, reduce heat to low, cover and simmer for at least 2 hours. The liquid will be reduced to the top of the beans and the beans should be tender. Remove ham hock.

4. Season with sea salt. Cool completely and transfer to two 1-quart (1 L) jars or reusable containers.

STORAGE

Beans will keep in an airtight container in the refrigerator for up to 5 days or in the freezer for up to 6 months. Freeze in 1-quart (1 L) jars, leaving 1 inch (2.5 cm) of headspace, or in sturdy reusable containers. Thaw overnight in the refrigerator, then reheat in a pot.

HOMESTEADING

Good Freezer Maintenance

Batch cooking's best friend is the chest freezer, but if that should happen to fail, all your efforts could be for naught. Fortunately there are plenty of ways to avoid a meltdown inside your deep-freeze. Here are my best tips for good freezer maintenance.

- Operate a new freezer for 24 hours before adding any food in order to let your freezer stabilize.

- Do not pack your freezer with too much tepid food over a 24-hour period. Whenever possible, thoroughly chill food in the refrigerator, then wrap well and transfer to the freezer.

- Keep your freezer level. There is a motor with a compressor running in there to keep things cold. Motors and other moving metal parts need oil to lubricate them, otherwise they heat up and fail prematurely. Keeping the freezer level ensures that oil will properly drain back to the oil pan and keep the compressor humming for years to come.

- Do not put your freezer in a tightly enclosed space. It won't take long before the temperature in the cramped quarters starts to increase. The heat from the room is going to creep back into your freezer, making it work even harder to keep things cold.

- Avoid loading up your freezer to the brim. The cold air needs room to circulate around the sides and top of the food to work optimally.

- On the flip side, the freezer works most efficiently if it is *mostly* full. So if you have a lot of empty space in the deep-freeze, fill some milk cartons three-quarters full of water and put them in the freezer (but not all at once!). When you need the space, you can simply defrost the ice and use the water for houseplants.

- Only if you absolutely have to, use an extension cord specifically made for appliances. These cords are designed for the full rated power draw of your appliance and will not cause your compressor to "brown out" or be a fire hazard. These cords are worth the money to protect your investment.

- Store glass jars in the freezer in a wooden or cardboard box. In the rare case that a jar should shatter, the glass is contained and you don't have to worry about shards getting lost amidst your other foods.

- Clean and de-ice once a year. This will help your freezer run more efficiently and will also help you to organize what is in there and maximize your space. A brand-new mop helps to easily scrub the bottom of a chest freezer and reach into the far corners.

- Stay organized. Use plastic baskets to store foods by type and put a label on each. Keep small adhesive labels and a permanent marker on hand to mark individual containers clearly. Use clear containers whenever possible so you can find things quickly.

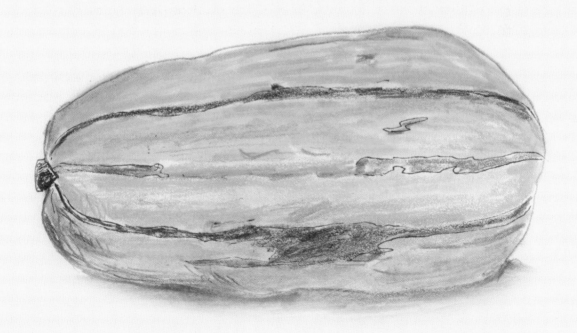

KIDS CAN
benefit from a chore
chart in the kitchen

I have learned much from my mother over the years, and creating a motivational sibling chore chart for easy household chores ranks among the best. It's nothing fancy, just a grid on a paper with tasks running top to bottom down one side and the days of the week listed across the top. But this visual schedule sparked incentive in my children like nothing else.

While it's been great to have household jobs completed fairly squabble-free, I'm most appreciative of the scheduled time in the kitchen we have had together thanks to the chore chart. Helping with meals—breakfast, school lunch (see page 203) and dinner—is included in the listed tasks. When I am spending an afternoon batch cooking, the children's helping hands are valuable for tasks like rolling meatballs, washing greens and grating cheese.

Here are a few reasons why the chore chart works for our family.

- **Simple jobs.** None of the tasks on the chart are daunting, and most can be completed in less than five minutes, independently.

- **Equal tasks.** My boys are between six and nine. Everything is about "fairness," so the chart has them alternate tasks each day. They have equal opportunities for the "fun" jobs, such as collecting eggs, and the less desirable tasks, such as emptying the dishwasher.

- **Include fun stuff, too.** Along with such typical jobs as "Set the Table" and "Empty the Compost," I make space in the chart for play, which the children love having assigned. I include both "Outdoor Play" and "Quiet Play," as I want to make time each day for fresh air and sunshine as well as creative play with arts and crafts.

- **Assign jobs when boredom hits.** Only when the boys are skimming around the house, causing trouble, do I enforce "job time" on them. I try never to interrupt them when they are playing nicely. They've learned that if they don't keep themselves busy, I'll put them to work!

- **Complaining gets an extra job.** Of course there are moments when one or the other drags their feet at a task. If the grumbling gets too loud, I'll assign one more job to the complainer.

- **Rewards.** Screen time in our home is not given freely, but by zipping through their homework or chores, the boys can earn time for computer games, Wii or Netflix.

- **Praise them excessively.** A simple kind word, such as "good job" or "that was really helpful of you," goes a long way to getting your kids to buy in and self-start the tasks.

The chore chart has a twofold benefit. First, your children learn independence. Second, everyone is more relaxed in day-to-day life because the household is working as a team, with each person performing his or her respective tasks.

13

PANTRY STAPLES

Dark Chicken Stock • Roasted Tomato Pizza Sauce • Honey Whole Wheat Pizza Dough • Basic All-Butter Pie Crust • Soft Wheat Flour Tortillas • Everyday Sandwich Bread • Buttermilk Oat Hamburger Buns • Homestead Homemade Yogurt

I come from an "unprocessed" background in food, meaning we didn't buy any packaged foods and stayed away from anything with additives or preservatives. In our rural setting, we grew and raised most of our provisions, and sought out local sources for others. We purchased organic grains, legumes and other basics at a health food store and avoided supermarkets for the most part. My mother taught us the art of simple home cuisine, which laid the foundation for my love of whole foods.

The strong, unprocessed food culture that my siblings and I were immersed in as children has had a lasting influence on our current food choices. It is this obvious connection that has encouraged me to avoid processed foods in our home as much as possible and create a healthy food culture for my family. Notice I said *as much as possible*. I don't pretend that there isn't an occasional box of cold cereal shaken into bowls on a Saturday morning. We're not nearly as hard-core as my mother was, and that is fine. It's important to remember that every little bit counts, and starting slowly is better than not starting at all.

My homestead upbringing instilled in me a lifelong love of cooking from scratch. Now, as a mother of three, I still choose many homemade pantry staples over grocery store convenience, desirous of the unbeatable flavors and natural foods of my youth. I may no longer own a flock of goats and turn their milk into cheese, but I can still simmer my own bone broth, jar homemade yogurt and slice soft sandwich bread that didn't come from the grocery store. In my pantry there are no mixes or little packaged foods. Pie crusts are made from scratch, pizza sauce is simmered for hours and not dumped from a can, and family favorites such as tortillas are lovingly made by hand.

Making my own food staples, instead of relying on the supermarket to feed my family, is a conscious choice. It helps that homemade staples are my love language. Few tasks yield as much satisfaction for me as turning out homemade versions of basic food items. Hamburger buns rise into golden domes and fill the house with the smell of a bakery. Homemade yogurt is a fun science experiment every time and spoons up thick and creamy into bowls. Dark chicken stock simmers all day and yields a rich broth that I use to enhance soups, sauces and all sorts of main dishes.

Shall I continue? How we love having our own pizza dough and soft flour tortillas as the base of countless family meals. And pie crust from scratch? Well, that is a must. This chapter only begins to scratch (sorry) the surface of pantry staples. The recipes here are but an introduction to the enjoyment of creating basic foods in your own kitchen instead of relying on highly processed grocery store versions. You'll find that not only are they more nourishing, but they taste far superior to their premade, packaged variant.

Four years of food blogging on *Simple Bites* has shown me how others are keenly interested in learning basic recipes and techniques for making pantry staples at home. Readers have passionately responded to my tutorials on canning, recipes for homemade pancake syrup and professional cooking tips for preserving summer produce. My most popular recipes are usually for a homemade version of a grocery-list staple, and a few of the recipes in this chapter are updated versions of those favorites.

SUMMER OF SIMMERING STOCK AND YOUNG LOVE

The first summer Danny and I were married, our situation wasn't exactly ideal for two starry-eyed newlyweds starting out in life together. I finished work late at night at a popular fine-dining establishment where I worked as a line cook, and Danny rose early to attend his university classes. One of us was always tired when we greeted each other, and one of us frequently smelled of soup, but I'm not saying who.

Fed up with seeing my new husband only from midnight till dawn, I petitioned my boss for a day position as a prep cook. I may have stammered, blushing, through my reasoning, but he only twinkled his eyes at me and agreed that, just for the summer, I could work days, and he would find someone to cook the fish and the foie in my place at night.

Stepping down the ladder in a competitive kitchen hierarchy was not a move that gained me respect among my co-workers, but I always have (and continue to) put family first over ambition. A "normal" nine-to-five job in fine dining is almost unheard of, and these new hours suited me to a T. That first night, in our tiny apartment, I went to sleep and woke up in Danny's arms. We went out for coffee and fresh croissants before parting ways, with lingering kisses, at the street corner.

Making stock was always the first order of my day at the restaurant, for it required long hours of simmering at an unhurried pace. I cranked the ovens to 400 and set to roasting bones for duck stock, veal stock, venison stock and roasted guinea fowl stock. I attacked a tray of carrots, onions and celery for my mirepoix, those flavoring vegetables essential for every stock, and gathered fresh parsley, bay leaves and peppercorns. By ten in the morning, the massive, sturdy pots would be set over burners, filled with roasted bones, mirepoix and cold water. Only then would I assess my prep list, left for me by the cooks from the night before, and organize my day.

My favorite place to cook, however, was at home in our honeymoon kitchen, with its high ceilings and next to no counter space. Always a planner, I would bring home a small container of dark stock from the restaurant (carefully recorded in the ledger under "staff purchases," of course) and turn it into a sauce that never failed to elevate our simple bowls of pasta and vegetables, eaten side by side on the rickety fire escape overlooking the leafy back alley.

Eventually, those days came to an end and I returned to working late into the evening while Danny pored over textbooks. But much like how bones are simmered long and low to infuse a good stock, we lived the summer to its fullest, recognizing the magic those early days held, and extracting the essence of each moment.

HOMESTEADING

7 Principles for Making Stock

As often as I make stock, which is about every two months in great big batches, I think back to my restaurant days and the methods we used to achieve the best results. A great dish is only as good as its sauce, and the base for most sauces is a perfect stock. Here are seven guidelines to help you achieve it.

1. Start the stock in cold water.

2. Simmer the stock gently, never letting it boil.

3. Skim the stock frequently.

4. Strain the stock carefully so you don't stir it up too much.

5. Cool the stock quickly.

6. Store the stock properly.

7. Degrease the stock.

That's about as technical as we're going to get; I don't want you to get scared off by a list of rules when really, making stock is perfectly simple.

DARK CHICKEN STOCK

An irreplaceable staple, homemade stock occupies much of my freezer space. I dip into my stash for all sorts of dishes, from Chicken Leek Shepherd's Pie (page 201) to soups and sauces all year long. It looks like a lot of steps, but once you make your first batch, you'll have learned a new life skill.

Roasting the bones for stock intensifies the flavor and gives it a beautiful rich color. You can make stock with chicken, veal, beef, duck or wild game bones. In this recipe, I use whole raw chicken carcasses that I ask my butcher to reserve for me. You can also freeze the carcasses from roast chickens until you have six or so.

MAKES 16 CUPS (3.8 L)

6 raw chicken carcasses
   (bones only)
1 large onion, peeled
2 ribs celery
1 large carrot, peeled
2 teaspoons (10 mL) olive oil
1 bay leaf
4 garlic cloves (unpeeled)
Handful of fresh parsley
2 sprigs fresh thyme
½ teaspoon (2 mL) black
   peppercorns

STORAGE
This stock will keep in the refrigerator for up to 1 week or in the freezer for up to 4 months. Freeze in mason jars, leaving 1 inch (2.5 cm) of headspace, or in sturdy reusable containers. Thaw overnight in the refrigerator before using.

VARIATION
For a nearly clear, light chicken stock, follow the same method but do not roast the bones.

1. Position oven racks in the top and lower third of oven and preheat oven to 375°F (190°C).

2. Do not rinse the bones. Spread them in a large oiled roasting pan. Roast bones, turning once with tongs, until they caramelize, about 1 hour. Do not let them burn or your stock will be bitter.

3. Meanwhile, prepare your mirepoix: coarsely chop the onion, celery and carrot and toss them with the olive oil. Spread them in a separate roasting pan or on a rimmed baking sheet and roast at the same time as the bones until lightly caramelized, about 25 minutes. Give them a shake every once in a while to avoid burning.

4. Transfer bones to a large stock pot, along with any fat that has pooled in the pan. Set the roasting pan over medium-high heat and add a few cups of water to deglaze it. Use a solid spatula to lift off any remaining browned bits on the bottom of the pan. Add this liquid to the stock pot.

5. Add the roasted mirepoix, bay leaf, garlic, parsley, thyme and peppercorns to the pot of bones. Add enough cold water to just barely cover the ingredients. Bring to a boil over high heat, then reduce heat immediately. Simmer gently for 6 hours, uncovered, occasionally skimming excess oil or scum off the top. Don't be tempted to stir the stock—it will result in cloudy rather than clear stock. You don't need to babysit it much; just make sure the stock is at a temperature where it will simmer but not boil.

6. When the bulk of the stock has cooked down and the bones are falling apart at the joints, the stock is finished. Using a sturdy spider or skimmer, fish out the larger bones. Allow them to drain a bit and then toss them in the garbage. (I usually haul my garbage bin right over to the stove, to make things easier.) When you have fished out all the large ingredients, strain the broth through a fine sieve into another pot. Cool to room temperature.

7. Divide the stock among clean containers for storage. Don't worry if a thin layer of fat forms at the top of your containers. This helps preserve the stock and can easily be removed with a spoon before using.

ROASTED TOMATO PIZZA SAUCE

As a wide-eyed teen backpacking through Italy in the late '90s, I learned a lot of lessons, in particular lessons about good pizza. Precisely? The secret is in the sauce. Since those days I have never been able to open a can of generic pizza sauce for my pies; instead, I roast bushels of plump paste tomatoes for homemade sauce.

My friend and canning mentor Jennifer Murch introduced me to this method for a smoky and robust pizza sauce, thanks to whole roasted and slightly charred tomatoes. Roasted garlic—and plenty of it—gives the sauce a slightly sweet taste, and fresh garden herbs further enhance the flavor.

This recipe has become an autumnal staple, and I always can a dozen or so half-pints for winter as well, so we can enjoy the flavors outside of their growing season. The sauce also freezes well, if that is easier for you. Stick with bottled lemon juice, never fresh, for this recipe, as it has a consistent and dependable acid level to it, an important factor for canning tomatoes.

MAKES 8 CUPS (2 L)

1 small head garlic

About ¼ cup (60 mL) olive oil, divided

6 pounds (2.7 kg) paste tomatoes, such as Roma or San Marzano

1 teaspoon (5 mL) salt

½ teaspoon (2 mL) black pepper

1 medium onion

1 tablespoon (15 mL) finely chopped fresh basil

2 teaspoons (10 mL) finely chopped fresh oregano

½ teaspoon (2 mL) finely chopped fresh rosemary

2 tablespoons (30 mL) raw cane sugar

1 tablespoon (15 mL) red wine vinegar

¼ cup (60 mL) bottled lemon juice (or 2 teaspoons/10 mL citric acid)

1. Preheat oven to 400°F (200°C).

2. Cut the top off the head of garlic so that the tip of each clove is exposed. Set the head of garlic on a piece of foil, drizzle the top with a teaspoon (5 mL) of the olive oil, and wrap it up tightly in the foil. Wash, core and halve the tomatoes lengthwise. Toss them with 2 tablespoons (30 mL) of the olive oil, the salt and pepper. Divide tomatoes between two rimmed baking sheets, cut side down. Nestle the foil-wrapped garlic on one of the trays.

3. Roast for about 1 hour, rotating the trays once halfway through roasting time. Some of the tomato skins will blister a bit and turn black—this is normal and will add a more caramelized flavor to the sauce.

4. While the tomatoes are roasting, coarsely chop the onion and finely chop the herbs. When the tomatoes are ready, in a large, heavy pot, heat 1 tablespoon (15 mL) of the olive oil over medium-high heat. Add the onion and sauté until tender and translucent. Add chopped herbs and sauté another minute.

5. Scrape the tomatoes into the pot. Unwrap the garlic and squeeze the soft roasted middle of each clove into the pot. Using a handheld blender, purée the mixture until smooth. Alternatively, process the pizza sauce in batches using a blender or a food processor.

continued ...

6. Return purée to the pot and stir in sugar and red wine vinegar. Simmer over low heat for 45 to 60 minutes, depending on how thick you like your pizza sauce (cooking it longer will make it thicker). Taste and add more salt or sugar if needed.

7. Review canning basics on page 146 and prepare a hot water bath with four 1-pint (500 mL) or eight half-pint (250 mL) jars and lids according to step 2 on page 147.

8. Working with one jar at a time, remove jar from hot water and place a wide-mouth funnel into the top. Ladle the sauce into the jar. If using 1-pint (500 mL) jars, add 2 teaspoons (10 mL) bottled lemon juice (or ½ teaspoon/2 mL citric acid) to each jar. If using half-pint (250 mL) jars, add 1 teaspoon (5 mL) lemon juice (or ¼ teaspoon/1 mL citric acid) to each jar. Stir gently (tomatoes need to be acidified when canned because botulism cannot grow in a high-acid environment). Wipe rim with a damp cloth and seal the jar. Repeat with remaining jars.

9. Process for 20 minutes in a hot water bath according to steps 4 and 5 on page 147.

STORAGE

This sauce will keep on pantry shelves for up to 1 year. Remove rings and label jars with the date. Alternatively, freeze in clean jars, leaving 1 inch (2.5 cm) of headspace, or in sturdy reusable containers. Thaw overnight in the refrigerator before using.

HONEY WHOLE WHEAT PIZZA DOUGH

Be prepared to fall in love with this oh-so-soft pizza dough that I adapted from an old culinary school recipe. It never fails to rise beautifully and has a delightful nutty flavor thanks to the whole wheat flour.

   The day I discovered you could freeze pizza dough was a happy one. Now my chest freezer is rarely without a couple of misshapen lumps of dough rolling around in it, that, when thawed, rolled out and coated with pesto, tomatoes and cheese, make for a mighty fine summer supper.

MAKES 4 (16-INCH/40 CM) OR 16 INDIVIDUAL PIZZA CRUSTS

½ cup (125 mL) warm water (about 110 to 120°F/43 to 50°C)

2 tablespoons (30 mL) active dry yeast

3 cups (750 mL) whole wheat bread flour, freshly ground if possible

2 cups (500 mL) all-purpose flour

1½ cups (375 mL) cool water

¼ cup (60 mL) olive oil

2 tablespoons (30 mL) honey

2 teaspoons (10 mL) salt

1. In the bowl of a stand mixer fitted with the dough hook, stir the yeast into the warm water until dissolved. Let stand for 5 minutes or until foamy.

2. Add whole wheat flour, all-purpose flour, cool water, olive oil, honey and salt. Knead with the dough hook on medium speed for 5 minutes, until dough is smooth and elastic. Alternatively, knead on a lightly floured counter for 7 minutes.

3. Place dough in a large oiled bowl and cover with a clean tea towel. Allow to rise until doubled, about 45 minutes.

4. Punch down dough and divide into 4 portions (for 16-inch/40 cm pizzas) or 16 portions (for individual pizzas). If not using soon, wrap portions in plastic wrap, place in resealable plastic bags and freeze.

STORAGE

This pizza dough will keep in the freezer for up to 3 months. Remove from freezer 8 to 12 hours before using and thaw in the refrigerator. Let rise until doubled in size, then punch down and roll out.

BASIC ALL-BUTTER PIE CRUST

An egg yolk makes this dough rich and golden, and also helps it to hold up better during shaping without getting overly tough. It is similar to the traditional French method for pie dough, called *pâte brisée*. In this recipe, lemon juice helps break down the gluten and results in a more tender dough. You can also substitute white vinegar, but I prefer the bright flavor that the lemon imparts to the baked crust.

Try to make your pie dough the day before you need to use it. Not only will it save you some time on Pie Day, but it will give the dough a chance to rest in the refrigerator, which results in a tender and flaky dough. This recipe yields enough for two pie crusts, but should you only need one, freeze the second disk. Store it tightly wrapped in plastic for up to three months.

MAKES 2 (9-INCH/23 CM) SINGLE PIE CRUSTS

To make in a food processor

1. Pour water into a measuring cup and drop in the egg yolk. Add lemon juice and beat with a fork. Drop in an ice cube to chill the liquid while you prep your flour and butter.

2. In a food processor, pulse together flour, sugar and salt to combine. Add butter cubes and pulse about 5 times to cut the butter into the flour. Butter should be in pea-sized pieces.

3. Drizzle the ice-water mixture through the feed tube and pulse about 10 times until the liquid is incorporated. Remove lid and squeeze a little dough between your fingers; it should form a ball. If it doesn't, drizzle in another tablespoon or two of cold water.

4. Empty the contents of the mixer onto the counter and divide into two piles. Press the damp crumbs together to form two disks of dough 6 inches (15 cm) across. Wrap tightly with plastic wrap and chill. Chill the dough for at least 2 hours or up to 2 days.

To make in a stand mixer

Follow method above, using a stand mixer fitted with the paddle attachment. Beat dry ingredients and butter together for about 30 seconds, until they are partially smeared together. With the mixer on its lowest speed, slowly drizzle in the ice-water mixture. Mix on lowest speed for another 30 seconds or until the dough just starts to come together. Stop the mixer and continue with step 4 above.

6 tablespoons (90 mL) ice-cold water

1 egg yolk

1 tablespoon (15 mL) lemon juice

3 cups (750 mL) all-purpose flour, sifted

1 tablespoon (15 mL) raw cane sugar

1 teaspoon (5 mL) salt

1 cup (250 mL; 2 sticks) cold unsalted butter, cut into ½-inch (1 cm) cubes

STORAGE

This pie dough will keep in the freezer, wrapped tightly in plastic wrap, for up to 3 months. Remove from freezer 6 to 8 hours before using. Thaw in the refrigerator before rolling.

SOFT WHEAT FLOUR TORTILLAS

A trip to New Mexico way back before we had kids was a gateway for Danny and me into a lifelong love of Southwestern flavors. I fell hard for their version of a flour tortilla, thicker and softer than any I had ever encountered, including in Mexico. Before we left, I begged our host, Jenny, for the recipe and brought it home, along with a suitcase full of canned green chilies, dried red chilies and pine nuts.

Flour tortillas may not be everyone's idea of a basic food, but these are, hands down, one of my children's favorite foods. We consume them as quesadillas, burritos (page 100) and wraps, or just straight off the griddle with a smear of nut butter. Once you sample homemade tortillas, the store-bought version tastes rather like cardboard. We'll pass, thanks.

They are a bit of work to make, but my boys and I have carved out a good rhythm: I mix up the dough while they are at school, then they team up on the rolling and I stand at the stove and flip the tortillas, then wrap them in a towel to keep them soft. Later around the table, we spoon Everyday Mexican Beans (page 274) in the center and top them with queso fresco, minced onion, cilantro and salsa.

MAKES 16 (6-INCH/15 CM) TORTILLAS

2 cups (500 mL) whole wheat flour

2 cups (500 mL) all-purpose flour

2 teaspoons (10 mL) baking powder

1½ teaspoons (7 mL) salt

1 teaspoon (5 mL) raw cane sugar

3 tablespoons (45 mL) cold unsalted butter

1 tablespoon (15 mL) bacon grease or lard

1½ cups + 2 tablespoons (400 mL) warm water

STORAGE
Once tortillas are cold, seal the bag and store in the refrigerator for up to 3 days or in the freezer for up to 3 months.

1. In a large bowl, combine whole wheat flour, all-purpose flour, baking powder, salt and sugar. Whisk to combine. Grate in the butter and add the bacon grease. Rub the fat into the flour with your fingers until it is evenly distributed. Pour in the water and mix with your hands until the dough comes together.

2. Turn dough out onto a floured counter and knead for 30 seconds. It should be pliable but not sticky. With a sharp knife, divide dough into 16 pieces. Roll each piece into a ball, then cover them with a clean tea towel and let rest for 15 minutes. This will help the dough absorb the whole wheat flour.

3. Using a rolling pin, on a lightly floured counter roll each ball of dough until it is very thin and about 6 inches (15 cm) in diameter. Dust the counter with a little all-purpose flour if the dough is too sticky. Don't worry if tortillas are not perfectly round; this is all part of their charm. If you are good at multitasking, begin frying the tortillas about halfway through the rolling.

4. Preheat a cast-iron pan or a griddle over medium heat and cook the flour tortillas for about 30 seconds per side. They will puff up and blister slightly. Reduce heat to medium if the pan begins to smoke.

5. If you will be using the tortillas right away, wrap them in a clean tea towel to keep warm until you are ready to use them. If you are storing or freezing for later, let them cool slightly on a towel, then transfer them while they are still warm to a resealable plastic bag. Leave the bag slightly open. The tortillas will sweat a little, which helps soften them further.

EVERYDAY SANDWICH BREAD

I've been making a classic sandwich loaf since as far back as I can remember. When I was around nine or ten, I baked four loaves at a time for our family, everything mixed and kneaded by hand. It was a fundamental staple in our diet, served up toasted with jam for breakfast and alongside soup for lunch. The satisfaction of turning out a hot golden loaf from the pan is every bit as gratifying today as it ever was. This recipe is my go-to versatile bread dough that sees numerous variations other than loaves. It's easily turned into cinnamon rolls, hot dog buns or hamburger buns, as the following recipe demonstrates. While you're shaping your bread, be sure to pinch off a small ball for the kids to shape and bake. That's how my own love of bread-making was birthed.

This soft oat bread is an ideal lunch box loaf, not too dense, nor too sweet. It is best enjoyed on the same day, so I suggest you wrap the second loaf in plastic and freeze for a later date.

MAKES 2 LOAVES

1½ cups (375 mL) warm water (about 110 to 120°F/43 to 50°C)

1 tablespoon (15 mL) active dry yeast

1 cup (250 mL) buttermilk

¼ cup (60 mL) unsalted butter

¼ cup (60 mL) liquid honey

1 cup (250 mL) old-fashioned rolled oats

2 cups (500 mL) whole wheat bread flour

2 teaspoons (10 mL) salt

3 cups (750 mL) all-purpose flour, plus a little more for shaping

VARIATION

If mixing by hand, follow the same directions, only use a sturdy wooden spoon to beat the dough in a bowl, followed by your hands to knead the dough on the counter. The dough will relax after 8 to 10 minutes of kneading and will feel elastic in your hands.

STORAGE

Well wrapped in plastic, this bread will keep for up to 24 hours or in the freezer for up to 3 months.

1. Pour warm water into the bowl of a stand mixer. Sprinkle with yeast and stir with the paddle attachment. Let sit for about 5 minutes, until foamy.

2. Gently heat buttermilk, butter and honey in a small pot over low heat. Stir just until butter is melted. Make sure the liquid does not get too hot or it will kill the yeast. Wrist warm is good (see "5 Tips for Great Homemade Bread," page 297).

3. Add buttermilk mixture, oats and whole wheat flour to yeast mixture. Beat on low speed for about a minute. Let this "sponge" sit for 30 minutes so the whole grains will absorb the liquid.

4. Replace the paddle attachment with the dough hook. Add salt. Add all-purpose flour ½ cup (125 mL) at a time, beating on low speed until all the flour is incorporated and a ball of dough forms. Knead the dough on low speed for 6 minutes. Dough will feel smooth and will pull away from the sides of the bowl. Transfer dough to a large, oiled bowl, cover with a tea towel and let rise in a warm place until doubled in size, about 1 hour.

5. Oil two loaf pans. Turn dough onto a floured surface and cut in half. Roll each half into a ball, then roll into an oblong shape and place in a loaf pan. Let loaves rise, covered with a clean tea towel, just until doubled in size, about 45 minutes. It's important not to rise past double or the loaf can be crumbly.

6. Meanwhile, preheat oven to 375°F (190°C).

7. Bake loaves for about 40 minutes, until dark golden and loaves sounds hollow when thumped (see "5 Tips for Great Homemade Bread," page 297). Turn out onto racks and cool completely.

HOMESTEADING

5 Tips for Great Homemade Bread

If you are a bread-baking beginner, these tips will help you get a feel for the process.

1. When you can, use freshly ground grain. It not only enhances the flavor but also makes the bread healthier. A wide range of home grinders are available; my preference is an attachment for my stand mixer that is easy to use. Spelt is a perfect grain for bread-making because it is lighter than whole wheat but offers the same health benefits.

2. How warm is the warm water in a recipe? The temperature of a baby's bath, or "wrist warm" as my mother used to say. If you use a thermometer, it is between 110 and 120°F (43 and 50°C).

3. Don't scoop your flour when measuring. Instead, spoon it into your dry measuring cups and then level off with a knife. Remember to gauge how much flour you actually need by how the dough feels. The dough should always be a little moist and slightly sticky.

4. Rising times are only guidelines. Keep an eye on the dough and make sure it has actually doubled in size before moving on to the next step. A warm place, free of drafts, is best.

5. The more you bake, the more you will learn how to tell when a loaf is finished baking. Because oven temperatures vary, the baking time in a recipe is only a safe guess. Armed with oven mitts or tea towels, turn the loaf upside down, remove the pan and inspect the bottom of the bread. It should be golden brown, and when you thump it with two fingers, it should sound hollow.

Remember, homemade bread doesn't have preservatives, so it is important to store it properly. Keep it airtight, and if you won't be using the loaf within 2 days, store it in the fridge or freezer. Slightly stale bread can be freshened by reheating it in a 350°F (180°C) oven for 10 to 15 minutes.

BUTTERMILK OAT HAMBURGER BUNS

My friend Tim (and this cookbook's photographer) says that the bun is the most underestimated component of a good burger. I have to agree. There are raging debates about "special" sauces, cuts of meats, cheese varieties and whether or not to add a fried egg. But how about a flavorful bun?

This one is soft on the interior but still holds up well to the toppings without getting soggy. It boasts a crunchy bottom and a perky sesame-studded top, in classic fluffy hamburger bun form. The recipe is a versatile one, and someday you'll want to shape the buns slightly smaller, brush the tops with butter and bake them into delightful dinner rolls.

MAKES 16 LARGE BUNS

1½ cups (375 mL) warm water (about 110 to 120°F/43 to 50°C)

1 tablespoon (15 mL) active dry yeast

1 cup (250 mL) buttermilk

¼ cup (60 mL) liquid honey

¼ cup (60 mL) unsalted butter

1 cup (250 mL) old-fashioned rolled oats

2 cups (500 mL) whole wheat bread flour

2 teaspoons (10 mL) sea salt

3 cups (750 mL) all-purpose flour, plus more for shaping

2 tablespoons (30 mL) cornmeal

1 egg

1 tablespoon (15 mL) 2% milk

3 tablespoons (45 mL) sesame seeds (optional)

STORAGE
These buns will keep in an airtight container for up to 24 hours or in the freezer for up to 3 months.

1. Pour warm water into the bowl of a stand mixer. Sprinkle with yeast and stir with the paddle attachment. Let sit for about 5 minutes, until foamy.

2. Gently heat buttermilk, honey and butter in a small pot over low heat. Stir just until butter is melted. Make sure the liquid does not get too hot or it will kill the yeast. Wrist warm is good (see "5 Tips for Great Homemade Bread," page 297).

3. Add buttermilk mixture, oats and whole wheat flour to yeast mixture. Beat on low speed for about a minute. Let this "sponge" sit for 30 minutes so the whole grains will absorb the liquid.

4. Replace the paddle attachment with the dough hook. Add salt. Add all-purpose flour ½ cup (125 mL) at a time, beating on low speed until all the flour is incorporated and a ball of dough forms. Knead the dough on low speed for 6 minutes. Dough will feel smooth and will pull away from the sides of the bowl. Transfer dough to a large, oiled bowl, cover with a tea towel and let rise in a warm place until doubled in size, about 1 hour.

5. Lightly brush two rimmed baking sheets with olive oil and sprinkle them with a little cornmeal. Turn dough out onto a floured surface and cut in half. Cut each half into 8 pieces. Shape each piece into a ball by folding the edges into the center, then turning it over on the counter and rolling it into a ball under your loosely cupped hand. Arrange 8 balls on each baking sheet. Flatten them slightly with the palm of your hand. Let shaped buns rise, covered with a clean tea towel, until doubled in size, about 45 minutes.

6. Meanwhile, preheat oven to 375°F (190°C).

7. In a small bowl, whisk together egg and milk. Brush tops of buns with egg wash and sprinkle lightly with sesame seeds, if using. Bake buns for 22 to 25 minutes or until they are dark golden on the bottoms and the tops have browned. Cool completely on racks.

HOMESTEAD HOMEMADE YOGURT

Gadgets and gizmos for making yogurt at home abound, but really all you need is a pot and a few jars. We always had homemade yogurt around when I was young, and I can remember marveling at how the milk set up each time. Now, years later, this little science experiment still gives me a thrill.

I've listed two perfected methods for incubating the yogurt, the first used by me, and the second by my elder sister, Haidi. Both use everyday items from the home. You will discover the best way to keep your jars warm.

MAKES 8 CUPS (2 L)

1. In a large pot, slowly heat the milk to exactly 180°F (85°C), stirring occasionally. Turn off heat and allow milk to cool to exactly 110°F (43°C). As the milk is cooling, measure the yogurt into a bowl to allow it to warm up a little; this is known as your "starter." Wash two 1-quart (1 L) mason jars and lids and fill with hot tap water.

2. Prepare your method of incubation. You can use a camping cooler or a laundry basket to hold the jars. Try a heating pad set to low and tucked in and around the jars. Alternatively, a quilt or a warm blanket and several quarts of hot water (120°F/50°C) set around the jars of yogurt will help maintain the heat during the incubation process.

3. Gently stir a ladleful of cooled milk into the yogurt starter. Now pour the starter into the pot of milk and gently stir again. Empty the jars of hot water, fit a wide-mouth funnel into the top of one and ladle the milk into the jar.

4. Wipe the rims of the jars clean, screw on the lids and place jars in your incubator. Keep warm for 6 hours using one of the methods suggested in step 2.

5. After 6 hours, check the yogurt by tilting the jar slightly to the side. It should be set and thick. If it still seems thin when you tilt the jars, leave for a couple more hours. The cooler the temperature of the incubator, the longer the yogurt will take to set, which will also produce a tarter flavor. When ready, refrigerate jars.

8 cups (2 L) organic 2% milk
½ cup (125 mL) good-quality plain full-fat organic yogurt

KITCHEN TIP

To make a thicker, Greek-style yogurt, tip the finished yogurt into a colander lined with cheesecloth. Place in the refrigerator and strain for a few hours. Use the whey (the liquid you have strained off) to replace buttermilk in recipes such as Buttermilk Buckwheat Pancakes (page 9).

STORAGE

This yogurt will keep in the refrigerator for up to 1 week.

WITH GRATITUDE

This cookbook is the result of a long and rewarding journey, and there are many people who made it possible. I would like to thank the following for their support and encouragement along the way.

Andrea Magyar, my editor at Penguin Canada, for reaching out to this food blogger and taking a chance on a first-time author. Thank you for your vision for this book and for being open and warmly receptive to my ideas as well.

Stacey Glick, my literary agent at Dystel & Goderich Literary Management, for your friendship, expertise, patience and professionalism.

Dianne Jacob, for letting me pick your brain at that initial FBC conference, and for everything ever since.

My entire team at Penguin Random House, on both sides of the border. You've all been a tremendous support.

My power team of recipe testers: Andrea, Laura W, Josh, Haidi, Melissa, Miranda, Zoe, Daria, Melanie, Kevin, Barbara, Jamie, Nicole, Arianne, Katheryne, Katie, Breanne, Terrie, Lynn, Christina, Cheri, Jenna, Dorothy, Laura C, Cecelia and Kelly. With honorable mentions to April Calo, Janice Lawandi and Lyra Telles (age ten—my youngest tester!), for going above and beyond the call. Thanks to Yvonne Tremblay for testing all my canning recipes and perfecting each one. Thank you all for your invaluable feedback, for making a special trip to the market, for dirtying dishes and staying up late on my behalf.

Christelle, for helping out on a few of the initial photo shoots until I picked up steam. *J'ai hâte de voir ton livre bientôt!*

Melanie Saad, for your creative input on events here and there for the book. You, *mon amie*, are seriously talented. Now send me that invoice already!

Tsh Oxenreider, for lending an ear and expert advice when I reached near-panic mode. Thank you for your friendship and mentorship. You are an inspiration on many levels.

Liz and Olivier, for being the best neighbors and friends anyone could ask for. You cooked, you cleaned, you trusted me with your gorgeous collection of kitchen items—thank you.

Katheryne Morrissette, for befriending my small brood and babysitting until all hours.

Mom Terrie, for your keen eyes and love of the written word.

My readers of *Simple Bites*, for being a receptive and gracious community and for supporting this project. Every day that I wrote, I had you in mind and that helped me tremendously.

My longsuffering friends, who attended events for this book and pretended it wasn't awkward at all. You baked beautiful cookies, jarred jams and put up with my unusual requests. Thank you for standing by when this book has taken up so much of my social time. Life is better with each one of you in it.

My parents, John and Zoe Wimbush, for giving me a homestead upbringing and for creating a family food culture that has endured and thrived and which I now pass on to my children.

Dad, I'm so thrilled you put pencil to paper for the illustrations; thank you for your creative contribution that brought a decidedly Wimbush touch to the book. Drawing from life is surely the test of the artist's eye as well as of the imagination, and you fully embraced the task with a passion that matched my own for this cookbook. Thank you from the bottom of my heart.

My siblings, Joshua, Haidi and Miranda, for keeping in touch and encouraging me when I was up to my ears in this book. You three inspire me as cooks and homesteaders; keep it up.

Tim and Angela, for embracing this project with open arms despite its magnitude. Thank you for *bringing it* to every shoot. It's been an honor to partner with you creatively. We started this project as good friends; now you are family. I love you both and those sweet boys too.

My children, Noah, Mateo and Clara, you encouraged me more than you will ever know. Thank you for taking part in this adventure with me, and looking so adorable along the way.

Danny, my love. You believed in this cookbook before I had a blog, an agent or even a properly functioning oven. Thank you for your unwavering faith in my capabilities and your steadfast support to see them come to fruition. What an adventure this project was! You've had my heart since I was seventeen, and because I put a portion of it into this project, this book is yours, too.

My God, for His unending love and grace and for planting and watering this little life of mine.

ABOUT THE PHOTOGRAPHERS

Tim and Angela Chin began their successful careers photographing portraits and weddings. Inspired by the authentic life, they have won multiple international awards for their images rooted in an editorial and documentary approach. While they certainly enjoy eating good food, it wasn't until they started swapping family photoshoots for gourmet meals with me that they began exploring the gastronomic side of photography. In addition to bringing their spoons and forks to the table, Tim and Angela also bring their philosophy of incorporating the lives and stories around the meals being prepared and eaten into the images they capture. Their continuing adventure of feeding their rambunctious boys can be found on their website, *The Chin Family Eats* (www.tchintchineats.com).

INDEX

A

apples
    cinnamon applesauce, 155
    cinnamon layer cake, 179
    and endive and almond
        salad, 169
    fall fruit chutney, 150
    hot spiced cider, 182
arugula and smoked salmon
    gougères, 55
asparagus
    gingery pickled, 51
    and niçoise salad, 33
    roasted, eggs and bacon, 30

B

bacon
    and mushroom broccoli rabe
        pizza, 198
    and roasted asparagus
        and eggs, 30
bars. *See* cookies, bars, and
    squares
beans
    baked, maple cider, 12
    cheesy, and gingered beef
        burritos, 100
    everyday Mexican, 274
    maple pumpkin chili, 262
beef
    Bolognaise sauce, 267
    cheeseburgers, 85
    gingered, and cheesy bean
        burritos, 100
    maple pumpkin chili, 262
    meatballs, 273
beets
    and chocolate cake, 204
    marinated golden, 120

beverages
    cold-brewed iced
        coffee, 108
    cold-brewed iced tea, 109
    cucumber honeydew
        agua fresca, 90
    eggnog, 236
    grapefruit and pomegranate
        spritzer, 244
    hot spiced apple cider, 182
    Mexican hot cocoa, 207
    stone fruit sangria, 133
    strawberry lemonade, 57
    toasted oat and cocoa
        smoothies, 254
blueberries
    and cardamom butter, 159
    and peach mascarpone
        trifle, 129–30
    sticky maple pudding, 20
bread. *See also* sandwiches
    buttermilk oat hamburger
        buns, 298
    cumin olive oil crostini, 47
    sandwich, 296
    zucchini cornbread, 163
broccoli rabe, mushroom
    and bacon pizza, 198
Brussels sprouts, 250
buckwheat buttermilk
    pancakes, 9
burgers: cheeseburgers with
    smoky onions, 85
burritos: gingered beef and
    cheesy bean, 100
buttermilk buckwheat
    pancakes, 9
butternut squash, cheesy
    penne, 265

butters
    basil brown, 124
    blueberry cardamom, 159
    radish chive, 48

C

cabbage, carrot and cashew
    slaw, 15
cakes
    apple cinnamon layer, 179
    chocolate beet, 204
    citrus cheesecake, 252–53
candy
    ice cider caramel
        popcorn, 230
    maple marshmallows, 104
    maple taffy, 23
carrots
    cabbage and cashew slaw, 15
    pickled gingered baby, 95
    roasted, and parsnip and
        thyme soup, 268
    spice oatmeal muffins, 195
cauliflower: sweet mustard
    pickles, 149
celery and fennel salad, 245
cherries, roasted, molasses
    cookies, 107
chia pudding with strawberries
    and pistachio crumbs, 61
chicken
    and leek shepherd's pie, 201
    roast, lemon oregano, 126
    stock, 286
    wings, Asian fusion, 82
chocolate
    beet cake, 204
    chunk cookies, 226
    cocoa date bites, 62

croissant bread pudding, 28
ganache, 229
Mexican hot cocoa, 207
oat and cocoa smoothies, 254
and orange oat bars, 103
chutney: fall fruit, 150
clam chowder, 194
coconut cream baked
    oatmeal, 27
cookies, bars, and squares
    cinnamon shortbread, 229
    cocoa date bites, 62
    currant scones, 160
    orange and chocolate
        oat bars, 103
    roasted cherry molasses
        cookies, 107
    rolled spiced
        gingerbread, 232
    whole wheat chocolate
        chunk cookies, 226
cornmeal
    pancakes, 193
    pecan streusel, 180
    zucchini cornbread, 163
corn on the cob, 124
cranberries and clementine
    relish, 224
crostini, cumin olive oil, 47
cucumber
    and bell pepper relish, 86
    and honeydew agua fresca, 90
    sweet mustard pickles, 149

D

dates and cocoa bites, 62
desserts
    blueberry-peach mascarpone
        trifle, 129–30
    chia pudding, strawberries,
        and pistachio crumbs, 61
    chocolate croissant bread
        pudding, 28
    grilled stone fruit salad, 88

maple blueberry pudding, 20
    rhubarb Eton Mess, 40
dressings
    apple almond, 169
    creamy ranch, 56
    maple soy vinaigrette, 15
    mayonnaise, 35
    for niçoise salad, 33
    vinaigrette, 216

E

eggs
    chocolate croissant bread
        pudding, 28
    coconut cream baked
        oatmeal, 27
    and roasted asparagus and
        bacon, 30
    and shrimp fried rice, 38
endive, apple and almond
    salad, 169

F

fennel and celery salad, 245
frostings
    chocolate ganache, 229
    cream cheese, 179

G

glaze, cider vinegar and
    maple syrup, 17
granola, maple walnut, 11
green beans, grilled, and
    portobello salad, 76

H

haddock: seafood chowder, 242
ham
    everyday Mexican beans, 274
    slow cooker, 247
honey and orange syrup, 193

J

jam: strawberry-honey, 152

K

kale, pomegranate and
    pine nut salad, 216

L

leeks and chicken
    shepherd's pie, 201
lemons: strawberry
    lemonade, 57
lettuce cups, and shrimp
    and spring peas, 52

M

maple syrup
    and blueberry pudding, 20
    cider baked beans, 12
    marshmallows, 104
    and pecan butter tarts, 18
    pepper glazed pork chops, 17
    and pumpkin chili, 262
    and soy dressing, 15
    taffy, 23
    and vinegar glaze, 17
    walnut granola, 11
mayonnaise, 35
melons: honeydew and
    cucumber agua fresca, 90
mincemeat, 176
muffins: one-bowl carrot-spice
    oatmeal, 195
mushrooms
    and bacon and broccoli rabe
        pizza, 198
    portobello and grilled green
        bean salad, 76

O

oatmeal
  buttermilk oat hamburger
    buns, 298
  carrot-spice muffins, 195
  coconut cream baked, 27
  and orange and chocolate
    bars, 103
  toasted, and cocoa
    smoothies, 254
onion soup, French, 266
oranges
  chocolate oat bars, 103
  and honey syrup, 193

P

pancakes
  buttermilk buckwheat, 9
  cornmeal, 193
parsnip and carrot,
  roasted, soup, 268
pasta
  butternut squash penne, 265
  spinach and ricotta
    pappardelle, 36
  sugar snap pea, tomato
    and orzo salad, 97
peach(es)
  and blueberry mascarpone
    trifle, 129–30
  preserved in honey syrup, 156
  roasted barbecue sauce, 81
pears
  fall fruit chutney, 150
  sour cream pie, 180
peas, sugar snap, and tomato
  and orzo salad, 97
pickles. See also chutney
  gingered baby carrots, 95
  gingery asparagus, 51
  marinated golden beets, 120
  sweet mustard, 149

pies
  all-butter crust, 293
  Quebec tourtière, 219
  sour cream pear, 180
pizza
  honey whole wheat
    dough, 292
  mushroom, bacon and
    broccoli rabe, 198
  roasted tomato sauce, 288–90
pomegranates
  juice and grapefruit
    spritzer, 244
  and kale and pine nut
    salad, 216
popcorn, ice cider caramel, 230
pork
  maple pepper glazed chops, 17
  meatballs, 273
  Quebec tourtière, 219
  slow cooker cider ham, 247
potatoes
  rosemary roast, 249
  tartiflette with Oka, 195
prunes, orange and chocolate
  oat bars, 103
pumpkin
  cream of, soup, 170
  and maple chili, 262
  maple-Sriracha toasted
    seeds, 172

R

radish and chive butter, 48
red peppers and cucumber
  relish, 86
relish
  cranberry clementine, 224
  cucumber and bell pepper, 86
rhubarb: Eton Mess, 40
rice, fried, shrimp and egg, 38
rolled oats. See oatmeal

S

salads
  cabbage, carrot and
    cashew slaw, 15
  Caprese, 123
  endive, apple and almond, 169
  fennel and celery, 245
  fruit, grilled, 88
  grilled green bean and
    portobello mushrooms, 76
  kale, pomegranate and
    pine nut, 216
  niçoise with asparagus, 33
  sugar snap pea, tomato
    and orzo, 97
salmon
  peach-glazed and grilled, 78
  seafood chowder, 242
sandwiches. See also bread
  banh mi, 98
  bread, 296
  smoked salmon and arugula
    gougères, 55
sauces
  for Asian fusion chicken
    wings, 82
  mild marinara, 270
  roasted peach barbecue, 81
  roasted tomato pizza, 288–90
scallops, balsamic-glazed
  with chard, 175
scones, currant, 160
shrimp
  and egg fried rice, 38
  seafood chowder, 242
  and spring pea lettuce
    cups, 52
smoked salmon and arugula
  gougères, 55
soups
  clam chowder, 194
  cream of pumpkin, 170
  French onion, 266

roasted carrot, parsnip
    and thyme, 268
seafood chowder, 242
spinach and ricotta
    pappardelle, 36
squares. *See* cookies, bars,
    and squares
stock, chicken, 286
strawberries
    and honey jam, 152
    lemonade, 57
    roasted, and chia pudding
        with pistachio crumbs, 61
sweet potatoes: honey ginger
    purée, 225
Swiss chard and balsamic-
    glazed scallops, 175
syrup, honey-orange, 193

T

tartiflette with Oka, 195
tarts
    maple pecan butter, 18
    mincemeat filling, 176
    summer squash and
        Parmesan galette, 119
tomatoes
    Bolognaise sauce, 267
    Caprese salad, 123
    mild marinara sauce, 270
    roasted, pizza sauce, 288–90
    and sugar snap pea and
        orzo salad, 97
tortillas, 294
tourtière, 219
turkey
    butter roasted, 220–21
    leftovers, 222

V

veal meatballs, 273

Y

yogurt, 301

Z

zucchini
    cornbread, 163
    summer squash and
        Parmesan galette, 119